MORALITY and IMAGINATION

Yi-Fu Tuan

MORALITY *and* IMAGINATION

PARADOXES OF PROGRESS

The University of Wisconsin Press

The University of Wisconsin Press
114 North Murray Street
Madison, Wisconsin 53715

The University of Wisconsin Press, Ltd.
1 Gower Street
London WC1E 6HA, England

Printed in the United States of America

Library of Congress Cataloging-in-Publication Data
Tuan, Yi-fu, 1930–
  Morality and imagination.
  Includes bibliographical references and index.
  1. Ethics.   2. Social ethics.   3. Imagination—Moral
and ethical aspects.   4. Human ecology—Moral and
ethical aspects.   I. Title.
BJ1031.T77   1989   170   88-40445
ISBN 0-299-12060-0
ISBN 0-299-12064-3 (pbk.)

Contents

Preface

When prospective readers see a book with the title "Morality and Imagination," their first response may well be "it is an important topic," but this response is quickly followed by the urgent need to classify: surely it is moral philosophy, history of ideas, literary criticism, or even current affairs. Yes, the book has a bearing on all these fields, it draws examples and ideas from them, but it is in fact written by a geographer, which may seem strange until we remember what the discipline, in the broadest sense, is about: it is about how human beings have created "homes" or "worlds" out of nature. Geography strives to describe and explain the visible material changes. But this is only one of its tasks. As the words "home" (at all scales) and "world" suggest, geography is also a humane study committed to interpret the meaning of human attachments and aspirations.

Anyone who looks at the earth can see that it has been differentially altered—in some places carelessly, in other places with imagination, and in still other places with an excess of imagination; that is, in irresponsible fantasy. Already I have used words that imply moral judgment. As we study the human use of the earth, moral issues emerge at every point if only because, to make any change at all, force must be used and the use of force raises questions of right and wrong, good and bad in the actors as well as in those who, like geographers, mostly observe and comment on the action. Human beings do not impose alterations on nature merely to survive. They aspire beyond mere survival to the good—good human relations and a good place in which to live. To achieve the good, certain precepts must be followed. Here again we see how the moral lies at the core of human reality. Whether we are conscious of the fact or not, mores (custom) and morals are a principal motif for all students—fictional writers as well as scholars—of the human scene.

Every scholarly discipline raises questions that emerge out of its own unique tradition. The result is a sustained thrust of inquiry, built on successes already achieved, that leads to knowledge of an increasing depth and subtlety. The cost, however, is in having to deal with a rather narrow range of questions; or if new ones are posed they tend to be posed in a familiar disciplinary context. May not "morality and imagination," approached from the angle of a field that does not normally address it, introduce an eddy of fresh air into the discourse of philosophers and other mainline humanists? I hope so. For them, I hope that this book will introduce a range of moral-ethical concerns, common to all people who have to struggle to make a living and to create cultural worlds, beyond that normally treated in standard philosophical texts. As for geographers and other students of the physical environment, I hope that this book will serve to link their traditional interest in transformed nature—in the built environment, the material edifice—with the moral-ethical systems that human beings have also constructed. A question close to students of the physical environment, namely, its relationship to human well-being, can never be adequately answered, it seems to me, unless we bring into focus a parallel relationship—that which holds between a people's moral edifice and their sense of well-being.

Since this essay does have a philosophical-literary tenor, I see a duty to acknowledge the philosophers and schools of thought that have influenced me. By "philosophy," I have in mind the old meaning of wisdom or an outlook on life and world. My greatest debt is to Iris Murdoch, Simone Weil, and Ludwig Wittgenstein, as much for their lives as for what they have written. They have all tried to live their philosophy: they are in this sense true moral philosophers. As for school of thought, existentionalism-phenomenology may well be the single strongest influence, but more for its concrete descriptive psychology than for its high ontological flights. And in this bias toward the concrete—toward the specific cultural instance—I no doubt reveal my own background of learning and thinking in anthropogeography.

Also a reflection of my background and of my limitation as a student are the way I approach my theme and the particular examples I select to illustrate it. The heart of the book is the theme. The examples are used to clarify and enrich it, as well as for their power to suggest new lines of development. "'For example' is not proof" (Yiddish proverb). Needless to say, the ones offered here are not intended to serve any such purpose. Perhaps the best way to describe my approach is the model of the ideal conversation. In such a conversation, one person offers a theme—a point of view—which he clarifies with an example or two. Usually not more, because more would not serve any purpose other than bore his listener. The listener then responds with a case of his own, to show that he has understood, or to show that the theme is capable of further development, or to show that it is problematical—that its application, for example, is less general than its proponent believes. Even in the world of science (at least, medical science), this conversational method of extending knowledge is still being used. A physician, interested in the general course of a disease, may well say to his colleagues, "Well, let's take case B in my file. She is fifty years old . . ."

But I should not have to lean on the prestige of science. Conversation itself is a high human calling. The distinction between oral and written methods of communication is not—and I would say—should not be as sharp as it can seem. Just as conversation may move from staccato exchange to sustained discourse by first one participant, then another, so scholarly writing should make room for not only the architectonic monograph but also the exploratory essay which has the flavor of the beginnings of a dialogue, more sustained than any oral presentation can possibly be and yet with no pretension to being—a ridiculous expression— "the last word." I see this book as my part of a dialogue. The ideal reader I have in mind will say, "yes, but . . ." and write her own book. In time, someone will move out of the exploratory, conversational genre altogether and produce the monographic treatise. But I doubt that the time will be the day after tomorrow. Meanwhile, allow me to make a start.

I now come to the pleasurable part of thanking the Graduate School and the Vilas Trust Fund of the University of Wisconsin–Madison for financial support and release of time. (Release of time— isn't this the quintessential gift of the gods?) I also wish to thank the American Geographical Society for its encouragement. The Cullum Medal, first given to the Polar explorer Robert Peary, winds its way eventually to someone who, following John K. Wright's advice, has explored quite another kind of world. My indebtedness to institutions is fairly specific and hence easily acknowledged. As for individuals, I am at a loss both in naming them (for any list can easily be expanded) and in how to express my thanks. Nevertheless I would like to record here my deep appreciation to the following individuals for their moral as well as intellectual support: R. P. Beckinsale, Martin Cadwallader,

Jack Kirshbaum, Gordon Lester-Massman, David Lowenthal, Douglas R. McManis, J. A. May, Joyce Melville, Emiko Ohnuki-Tierney, James J. Parsons, P. W. Porter, Miles Richardson, Joshua H. Sack, Michael Steiner, Hilgard O'Reilly Sternberg, George Thompson, Tai-Fu Tuan, David Ward, and the philosopher at Austin who reviewed anonymously the first draft of the manuscript. From them I hear the encouraging words, "Yes, but . . ."

MORALITY and IMAGINATION

Introduction
Human Dilemmas and Promise

1

I shall attempt in this book to explore the relationship between morality and imagination, which is an issue of far more than academic interest, for we live in a society that claims to be both moral and imaginative. Moreover, as individuals, we ourselves would like to be both. Yet these two words and the ideas they represent lie uneasily side by side. Morality calls to mind set rules of behavior and a certain rigidity of outlook. Imagination, by contrast, has an appealing ring because it challenges such rules; at the same time it evokes something negative as well, namely, a tendency to indulge in fantasy and to be irresponsible.

The word *moral* means much more than *mores*—custom and tradition. Indeed, under certain circumstances it is immoral to go along with the customary, to follow whatever happen to be the rules and injunctions of the tribe. A moral being, we can argue, is a thinking and reflective individual, alive to the paradoxes and dilemmas of life, critical of the crude generality of behavioral codes; and hence someone who, while he or she recognizes the need to attend to the difficulties of each case, also wrestles with the formulation of superior moral principles which can cope with problems of equity and justice for society at large. A moral person, in this increasingly ideal sense, is someone irresistibly drawn by the good. The energy provided by the good is translated into action, which may mean helping a neighbor, trying hard to resolve moral dilemmas, or devising five-year plans. The good itself must be left undefined if it is not to deteriorate into just another set of moral codes or the blueprint for a static utopia—if it is to continue to serve as a luminous horizon for aspiring society and individuals.

By extending the meaning of moral we have moved closer to the semantic field of imagination. No longer is it necessary to contrast a moral but dour person with an imaginative but flamboyant and irresponsible one. These are caricatures that lie at the defective extremities of morality and imagination. We may feel that it should not be difficult to envision individuals who lie somewhere in the middle range and embody the best of both worlds. But in fact this is not easy. The contradictions inherent in the meanings of morality and imagination are not easily resolved.

Nevertheless we can try to resolve them, and we begin to do so by envisaging another pair of archetypal figures: someone imaginative as well as wise, and someone simple but pleasing, not dour. Consider the first figure—an imaginative person who is also wise, which means that his knowledge is gained not through rote learning but through the steady application of an attentive and plastic mind on that which exists. The question of truth now comes to the fore. When the word imaginative or creative is encountered, one wonders: Is it a euphemism for daydreaming, or is it the rare virtue of perceiving reality as accurately as possible, doing justice to its complex processes and protean forms, its color and opacity? An indifference to truth is incompatible with morality. And yet certain kinds of truth are incompatible with that moral excellence known as charity. For instance, it is thought wrong to bring to light the private foibles and failings of our friends: should we be aware of them we are obliged by charity to relegate them to oblivion. More generally, knowledge of evil not only in its repellent darkness but also in its subtly attractive shadings seems contaminating. Perhaps for this reason it is easier to envisage a saintly artisan, or a saintly landscape artist, than a saintly novelist. A novelist, after all, is attuned to human imperfection: to do his work well he must be fully aware of the vanity, cruelty, delusions, and foibles of human beings.[1]

Someone who is both imaginative and wise is a problematical figure because, as I have just suggested, certain kinds of knowledge may be incompatible with charity. What, we may now ask, of the second archetype—a man or woman of natural simplicity and virtue, pleasing, not dour? This second figure is thoroughly familiar in the Western world. Best known are the first couple in Eden. There are others as well. In Republican Rome, Varro and Cato speak of the unsophisticated yet virtuous farmer with genuine respect, and in the works of Augustan poets he becomes an idyllic figure in a pastoral scene of dark woods and bright pastures. The eighteenth century, which recognizes land as the basic resource and agriculture as the fundamental generator of wealth, transforms the farmer into a glamorously independent and honest individual. To the one side stands the virtuous farmer, to the other the sinful city man—a caricature that has been remarkably successful in resisting the erosion of time and confrontations with experience.

In addition to the farmer, the eighteenth century has discovered the child and has made him, too, into a figure of charm and innocence. A barely furnished mind becomes a precondition for direct access to truth and a sort of natural wisdom. A growing sentimentality makes it possible to exploit two Biblical images: the wise child who can teach the doctors at the temple, and the innocent child who, by the nineteenth century, is the cynosure of adoration during Christmas.

Predating the child is the fool. Ignorance of the world enables him to see truth behind the meretricious façades of culture. In a fool, as in a child, moral force derives from this unspoilt perception. And what the fool sees he may announce. Bluntness is a token of truthfulness. More often, the fool is silent; or he tries to speak and is frustrated. A certain inarticulateness is a sign of moral weight and authenticity. In modern times, both fictional and real-life good persons are inarticulate as, for example, Billy Budd, Prince Myushkin, the peasant heroes of Tolstoy, and the peasant soldiers in the accounts of the Spanish War told by George Orwell and Simone Weil. Copious and decorated speech is suspect. It clashes with our image of the truly good person. A saint does not live in a palace, nor does he wrap himself in a towering fabrication of words. Both the palace of marble and the palace of words signify superfluity, willfulness, and the presence of a powerful but wayward imagination.

More common, however, than this bright picture of the child, fool, and peasant, is the dark picture of the child as an animal that needs to be whipped into shape, the fool as only marginally human, and the peasant as primitive and cruel. Take the example of the peasant. In the early Middle Ages, he was held in utter contempt. The bond peasant could not receive holy orders, but even if he were free he lacked the culture and the opportunity to enter the Church. In both early and late medieval literature, the peasant is depicted as a sort of monster that haunts the dark and wild forest. To youths and knights lost in the forest, the peasant-lumberjack looms out of the shadows as a loathsome beast with eyes fixed in a nonhuman stare.[2] In the eighteenth century, alongside the idealization of the rustic, is the image of a civilized island of Parisians surrounded by dark woods and their uncouth, often violent denizens—the peasants. Perhaps nowhere has the idealization of the countryman gone further than in the United States. Yet such terms as hick, yokel, country bumpkin, clod, and hillbilly are loud in contempt. Furthermore, the sense that backwoods people are violent and are themselves victims of violence (so many of them seem to limp when they walk or are short of a finger) continue to cast a shadow on contemporary American consciousness: witness, James Dickey's depiction of life in the backwoods of Georgia in his novel *Deliverance*.

Civilization is an achievement that transforms raw nature into orderly worlds and crude humanity into civil, moral, and enlightened beings. Almost all would concur with this proposition; only a few disgruntled individuals seriously plan to return to a primitive state, imagined as free from social conflict and the ambivalent rewards of material abundance and reflective awareness. However, if human achievement is to be measured by the quality of human relationship—by the depth of the affectional and intellectual exchanges between persons—one may well wonder how much of the material and institutional wealth of civilization is really necessary. Ever since the emergence of cities, people have wondered and we still do. Of course, the definition of what constitutes luxury and excess has changed with time and varies with individuals and cultures. Nevertheless, historically, thoughtful people have believed that an excess of the kinds of amenities that a rich society offers is harmful to one's moral strength and sensitivity. Here we return in another form to the issue addressed directly earlier, namely, the degree of congruence between morality and imagination: the one implies restraint and the other is naturally inclined toward excess.

Moral issues are closely linked to power—its use and abuse. Power governs all human relationships and, externally, relationships between human beings and nature. When people cooperate efficiently they gain a large degree of control over their environment, making it yield goods that sustain human life well above that of bare survival. But another kind of power thrives alongside the physical: the power of imagination. A mental world is created that parallels and interweaves with the physical one, and of both we may ask: How does it affect the quality of a people's moral life? Different types of mental and physical worlds exist. The type of mental world that affects how people see and behave toward each other is called moral or religious-ethical, and is itself an outstanding achievement of the imagination. With an articulated religious-moral system in place, customs and rules of behavior in ordinary life are given a spacious, meaning-laden context that enables them to resonate—to hint at an import well beyond themselves.

Does this mean that people without such a system lead stunted moral lives? Are we to think that people thus deprived are somehow less kindly and caring, less courageous when courage is called for? Surely not. At least, we resist this conclusion even though it has the ring of common sense. We know that some of the kindliest and gentlest human beings in the world lack the support of an elaborated religious-ethical structure. By contrast, cold, narrow, and devious personalities are a commonplace of cultures that have built the most intricate and exalted moral edifices.

Of those people who, despite the lack of a moral edifice, are kind and gentle, we may say, yes, but perhaps the kindness and the gentleness have not been tested. It may be that these virtues are fragile and will break under duress. As for people who remain morally obtuse despite the splendor of their moral edifice, the deficiency in connection has at least two causes. First, for many individuals, only a very small part of the total moral world is visible—only a few precepts and doctrines are understood and embraced which, taken out of context, can lead to bigotry rather than enlightenment. Second, the system or edifice itself may be largely vainglorious. A few genuine moral insights exist but these are buried in embroideries and encrustations of a superstitious and magical nature. It can also happen that the moral system has reached such a height of refined elevation that it loses touch with common human reality; it becomes irrelevant and untruthful. Imagination, detached from the realities of human existence, turns into fantasy. In the next two chapters, I will explore the relationship between moral edifice and conduct by taking a look, first, at the relatively simple world of forager-hunters, and then at the more complex worlds that have agriculture and cities as well as highly developed religious-ethical systems. By the expediency of referring to specific human groups and cultures, we will be able to see the dilemmas of morality and imagination more concretely—both dilemmas recognized by the people themselves and those that only outsiders are likely to discern.

Together with the mental-moral world, human beings construct a tangible physical reality of houses and gardens, farms and cities. Our next question, then, is: What is the relationship between this physical world and the moral sensitivity and imagination of the people who live in it? Whereas we may find it reasonable to wonder about the link between, on the one hand, a people's religious beliefs and moral values, and on the other, their behavior and spiritual well-being, it may seem inappropriate or wayward to ask this question of the physical world. Yet I hope to show that this is not so—that, in fact, the questions we have raised concerning these two worlds exhibit close parallels as well as, naturally, differences.

Here are a few parallels. A moral-religious system carries authority if it is not perceived as an arbitrary and fanciful human creation. Now, the architectural world of houses and temples is undoubtedly of human manufacture, and yet its authority too rests on the belief that it is not merely a product of willful imagination—that it somehow conforms to the fundamental principles of nature, that it is a suitable dwelling for the gods and their human servants, or that it stands for something honest and authentic.[3] Given such belief, the presumption of a close relationship between architectural milieu and human well-being is reasonable, and we can understand why the presumption not only exists but is quite commonly held. "Is this a good house?" does not translate simply into, "Does it keep out the rain?" and "Is this a good city?" cannot merely mean, "Is it an efficient city—that is, do the sewers work and do the buses run on time?" Two further parallels. Just as the mental-moral world may be an elevated, fanciful excrescence of the imagination that denies the sexual and excremental reality of human lives, so likewise the city, which as a beautiful dream of planners seeks to segregate and hide the ugly facts of poverty, sickness, and death that have been and are an ineradicable part of the human condition. And just as a person may not benefit from the grandeur of a moral edifice by focusing only on a few isolated precepts, so a person living in a great house may fail to be inspired by its greatness when his attention is confined only to the few, more eye-catching excellences.

There are differences between the two worlds as well, and perhaps the most obvious is this. One can think, contemplate, write a poem or a philosophical treatise without making any, or with making only the minimal, demands on nature and society. But before one can construct a material world one must first apply force to clear the grounds, and one must be destructive of nature before its elements can be extracted and processed for human use. Moreover, until modern times the necessary force is supplied by human beings and animals working under conditions of hardship and danger. So, unlike the propounding of a moral philosophy or religion, and unlike the making of poems and paintings, the construction of a material world must confront the issue of the damage that the use of force inflicts on nature, on laborers, and on the people who must be evicted to make way for the new.

We are thus brought to human relations which lie at the heart of morality. In this book, I shall consider the moral implications of reciprocity or exchange—the kinds of exchange that hold people together and that lie at the basis of their power, including power over nature. Exchange of regard or disesteem often occurs unconsciously, as, for instance, in the way people look at each other or in the tone of a voice, but it can also be highly calculating, as, for instance, in the reciprocation of gifts. Exchange may be between two individuals; by contrast, the circle of giving may be so large that the donor cannot know most of its members and has no assurance that her own expression of good will and generosity will eventually repay her in some form. What does generosity mean? What types of economy and society are capable of supporting acts of giving that appear not to be motivated by quick material reward or the garnering of prestige? Generosity may be a personal impulse tied to vitality or a sense of well-being—a natural endowment. But it is not merely a personal bent that some have and others don't. A large and open economy encourages the generous impulse, as do certain myths—that is, idealized stories of what reciprocation can and should mean. What are these myths? And if they are merely myths, what is their moral standing? Are they to be judged romantic fantasies that delude? How are we to view acts of selflessness motivated by imaginative constructions that, to a critical outsider, have no hold on truth?

Having reviewed these points, it may then be possible to examine, with a firmer sense of empirical grounding, the qualities that constitute a good person and how "good" and "moral" are ambivalently wedded to the imaginative aspirations of the mind. We need not be confined to the polarized images of the "moral but dour" and the "imaginative but frivolous," or of the simpleton-saint and the philosopher-king. Perhaps what is most seriously defective in these images is that they are static. It may be that the tension between morality and imagination exists only if morality is conceived as proper conduct that one learns once and for all or as a gift of nature—golden rules engraved in the heart; and if imagination is conceived either as license or as the method for attaining a permanent state of wisdom. But what if morality is an ideal toward which individuals and society must endlessly strive? What if the effort to imagine the moral and the good, boldly and yet responsibly, is itself an endless moral undertaking?

One *becomes* more moral, society becomes more moral, with the help of an imagination disciplined by respect for the real. This stress on "becoming" forces us to entertain the possibility of genuine progress, which can be exhilarating. Progress, however, introduces new dilemmas and paradoxes for aspiring moral individuals, particularly those who, rather than withdraw, wish to live fully in the complex interlocked society of modern times. Every step forward in moral sensitivity and in the awareness of the possible consequences of action places a new burden on human beings. Every step forward is, moreover, only a time-bound gain, for like any delicate architectural achievement, additions to the moral edifice are subject to erosion unless they are vigilantly conserved. Moral life, without the presumed stability and certainties of the past, is therefore a severe challenge in our modern secular age. It demands courage, imagination, and a high degree of tolerance for ambivalence. If the challenge is nevertheless taken up by conscientious people, as I believe it is, one possible reason (perhaps unacknowledged by the people themselves) is the irresistible lure of the good.

Moral Edifice and Life
Simple Societies

2

Moralists suspect imagination for its tendency to excess. In both the West and the East, they have criticized civilization which, almost by definition, is excess. A superfluity of material goods is a bane to moral life. Moralists may oppose the luxury of high culture with the image of a natural unspoilt Eden, itself a conjuration of high culture. Many literary accounts of Eden exist, but are there real places on earth that at all correspond to the vision? Westerners, even more than Orientals, have searched for this ideal place on remote islands and in isolated valleys. Because the desire is great, the likelihood of self-delusion is also great. What appears at first sight Edenic, on second view shows nearly all the faults of a real place and a real people; and it can never be entirely clear as to which view is more true. The first may be too dewy-eyed, but the second may be too jaundiced; and with each revision—built on or in reaction against the previous one—we become less rather than more sure that we are moving closer to the truth.

Amoral Edens?

Every ethnographic account is unavoidably partial and biased. A student of human culture, on revisiting his field area after a lapse of years, may significantly revise his opinion. Even more telling, the student may change his interpretation of his field notes even without additional data because the mood of his own society and of his own discipline has changed. A degree of scholarly skepticism is therefore in order, although it should not go so far as to deter us from making use of the more detailed and responsible reports of "Eden," among which are those on the Mbuti Pygmies, hunter-gatherers of the African equatorial forest.[1]

The life of the Mbuti appeals to the visitor from modern society for a number of reasons. We may start with rootedness itself. The Mbuti have lived in the forest for so long that they are biologically as well as culturally adapted to it. Their small stature is adaptive to a hot dense-textured environment, as also is their skin color—yellowish brown to deep chocolate red—which provides them with camouflage but which makes them prone to sunstroke when they venture out of the forest.[2] Food is ample and close at hand. The animals they hunt, for example, roam within small compass. This accommodating environment has encouraged the formation of a community that is egalitarian and cooperative. The people appear relaxed and happy; they lack even the word for evil in the sense of interpersonal malevolence. A morning of hunting and food gathering will have given the Mbuti band enough food to last a day or two. Such mild chores as repairing the huts and the hunting nets take little time, after which the adults are free to play with the children, educate them in the ways of the forest, sing, and dance. To a visitor, the most vivid impression of a Pygmy camp is its "sheer exuberance and joy of living."[3]

The Mbuti Pygmies have the most intimate contacts with nature. Infants are bathed in water mixed with the juice of forest vine, the forest being viewed as their protector and life-giver. At the puberty ceremony, girls renew their tie to the forest by making symbolic contact with its vines and leaves. Lovemaking generally takes place in the forest, near a stream, in a splash of sunlight or moonlight. When the anthropologist Colin Turnbull asked one Mbuti why he was dancing alone, he replied that he was not alone: he was dancing with the forest and with the moon.[4] Occasionally, the hunt is not successful and, moreover, the Mbuti suffer the usual human sorrows of sickness and death. When a crisis or a disaster occurs, the Mbuti try to attract the attention of the benevolent forest spirit, who will see their plight and come to their rescue. The adult men will sing, "The forest is kind," "the forest is good." Their object is to "rejoice" the forest, to "awaken" it. But there is no cure for death. When death occurs, the Mbuti may say that "Darkness is all around us . . . but if Darkness *is* [if the forest allows it], then Darkness is good."[5]

In literary accounts of Edenic life, how food is obtained and prepared, which cannot avoid violence altogether, is left rather vague. The food is just there, ready to eat. Thus, the heroes on the Isles of the Blessed thrive on nature's own harvest, an ideal reaffirmed by Gonzalo on whose island Eden "nature should bring forth, of its own kind, all foison, all abundance, to feed my innocent people" (*The Tempest*, act 2, scene 1). In a Taoist paradise, when the people feel hungry or tired, they simply drink the water in the rivers, and they immediately find their vitality restored; no destruction of any kind, not even the harvesting of crops, occurs.[6] In a poetic conception of an unspoilt world, written during the T'ang dynasty, the people are described as having a childlike exuberance. "They swarm to the tops of the trees, and run to the water to catch bream and trout." They live, presumably, on fish.[7] From the ethnographic literature, which unlike legends and poetry presents (one assumes) factual reports, the Semang of the tropical forests of Malaya come through as showing an exceptional sensitivity toward the animals they capture. Killing, in their view, should be done quickly and without pain; mistreating captured animals, or even to laugh at them, is an offense punishable by serious illness.[8]

Now, when we turn to the Mbuti Pygmies, we do not find this degree of sensitivity. Their world is stained with animal blood, as indeed almost all human worlds are, a fact which imagined Edens artfully skirt. The Mbuti show a great gusto for life, especially after a successful hunt, which ensures them abundant food for a number of days. Occasionally, a hunter equipped only with a spear brings down an animal much larger than he—an elephant. Without doubt this is an uncommon feat of courage and skill. The hunter climbs up the belly of the beast in triumph and dances on top of it. Cutting up the carcass is a riotous occasion in which many participate. After the foul-smelling liquid and gas have escaped explosively through a puncture in the swollen stomach, the Pygmies swarm over the body in an orgy of butchering. Within a couple of days, the scene of slaughter is a blood-spattered field of skin, bone, and intestines. Celebration may continue for weeks. People eat overmuch, the singing becomes lusty, and the dancing overtly erotic.[9]

The Mbuti kill animals for food without any sense of guilt because they regard the game as a gift from the all-providing forest. There is, however, a Mbuti legend which suggests that killing can be wrong under certain circumstances. The legend tells of a boy who hears a bird sing with extraordinary beauty. His admiration for the song persuades the bird to fly down and perch on his shoulder. Together they go to the boy's home. The boy's father also admires the song and asks his son to feed the bird, after which it is returned to the forest. A few days later, the boy brings the bird back home again, and then for the third time. On the third occasion, the father becomes angry. He kills the bird and thereby the beautiful song. The man himself dies soon after.[10]

The Mbuti do not hold animals in special esteem. The bird with the beautiful song is the outstanding exception. According to Colin Turnbull, this legend is the only one among the two hundred or so collected that suggests the existence of the supernatural. Many legends feature talking animals and animals that can turn into people, but to the Mbuti these phenomena remain a part of the natural world. The bird and its beautiful song point to another level of being. They symbolize the spirit of the forest and hint at a life beyond death. Also important to the Mbuti is the distinction between killing for food and snuffing out a life out of annoyance—particularly the life of a bird that can sing, for singing well is admired and adds greatly to the joy of the forest.

Moral customs and rules are justified by their promotion of good relationships, especially those between people. What is the quality of human relationships among the Mbuti? This is an important question, for the test of Eden and Utopia is ultimately the way human beings treat each other. If they do not treat each other especially well, then all the natural beauty of Eden and all the planned beauty and order of Utopia become mockery. When we consider the Mbuti we shall find that the emotional texture and style of their mutual regard is fairly typical of those in small, egalitarian, nonliterate communities. On the positive side is human warmth, a feature that makes a vivid impression on Western observers who are charmed by the open gestures of affection. Impressive too are such qualities as selflessness, considerateness, and courtesy.[11] These attributes are necessary to effective cooperation and survival, but no functional explanation can detract from their inherent appeal. For the outsider, there exists also a debit side—disturbing characteristics that would seem to be a consequence of the sociopsychological stress of living in close proximity to each other and of the lack of any clear articulation of moral values and ideals—a lack that can lead to inconsistent attitudes and cruel behavior.

Working and living close to each other over long periods of time generates tension, which finds outlets in barbed humor, malicious gossip, insulting jokes, open quarrels, and violence. It may be that the bulk of humankind share these traits, but they differ in frequency and virulence, and tend to be more common in small tight-knit communities than in those that are large and open, where the problem is more likely to be one of impersonality and indifference. In a Pygmy camp, during rainy days when hunting is impossible and people are cooped inside their tiny huts, even the smallest gesture, considered inappropriate or insulting, can flare into a heated quarrel and the use of physical force. A fight between two individuals almost always draws in kinsfolk and soon the whole camp is in an uproar. But the fight does not last long. The entire drama from initial tiff to battling tooth and nail passes with the swiftness of a tropical storm. Who are in the right and who in the wrong? At the start of a fight these questions may have some urgency, but they are soon forgotten and people take sides on other grounds, including who are the better fighters and who are likely to win. Fights and quarrels quickly abate because the Mbuti need to cooperate with each other. Peace is considered of such overriding value that blame may be laid on the loudly complaining victim rather than on the aggressor.[12]

Deviations from accepted social practices are reprehensible, and this is especially true of incest and stealing. Sexual concourse between cousins is considered incest and a major offense. Yet at times it can seem that the real offense is the stupidity of being caught. Pygmies value cleverness highly: they think of themselves as small, agile, and clever, in contrast to large animals such as the elephant and the pig and to the larger Bantu-Sudanese villagers, whom they regard as clumsy and stupid. The Mbuti appear to believe that the clever have the right to take advantage of the stupid. As for stealing, it is wrong when practiced among the forest hunters themselves, but not wrong when the victims are the villagers who, in Mbuti taxonomies, fall into the category of animals rather than human beings. Here we are reminded again of the forest hunters' indifference to the fate of animals. Some animals are cleverer than others and some are clever enough to talk: they receive respect. On the other hand, a dumb Pygmy receives little sympathy and no respect. Take the example of a young man, a deaf mute, who is the camp clown and mercilessly teased for his stuttering speech, which fellow campers call animal noises. The teasing may perhaps be excused as natural Pygmy exuberance, but the unkindness can go well beyond it. On one occasion, the deaf-mute youth climbed up a tree with a companion to collect honey. The task has its risks, which are considered worth taking because honey is for the Mbuti the forest's single most desirable gift. Back on the ground, the youth rattled his rusted tin cup and with gestures and noises indicated that he wanted his share. He was roundly ignored.[13]

Like all human beings, the Mbuti have customs and rules of appropriate behavior. They are moral in the first sense. The rules do not, however, weigh heavily on them; no one cares to assume a mantle of righteousness. The Mbuti are thus blessedly free from temptations of moral hypocrisy and rigidity. They are spontaneously generous and are quickly forgetful of the wrongs done them. But the reverse side of spontaneity is arbitrariness and a disinclination to examine consistently failings in human relationship. A moral edifice is unlikely to rise on a foundation of such virtues and defects. Moreover, what motivation is there for critical reflection, which is the first step in the making of a moral edifice? One possible motivation is a strong sense of the good. The Mbuti seem to possess such a sense. It appears in their images of the benign forest and of the bird with the beautiful song. These idealizations, which stand high above day-to-day practices and beliefs, enhance life for the Pygmies by making it more secure as well as more beautiful; they may even add a note of exaltation, but they have not served as a lure for criticism and change.

Great Hunters and Guilt

Tropical forests are a rich environment. The hunter-gatherers who live there do not have to struggle hard to make a living.

Meat is a valued item in their diet, but it is not absolutely essential: forest dwellers depend more on plant foods than on game for the bulk of their nutritional needs. Plants, moreover, provide the material for shelter and clothing. Blood does not stain deeply the hands of foragers, nor haunt their dreams and imagination. By contrast, consider the harsh Arctic environment and the Eskimos, who have successfully adapted to it. Eskimos are great hunters, far more skilled and better equipped than are the tropical forest dwellers. Indeed they have to be greatly skilled to survive. But is survival the right word? From a certain angle, this word—with its suggestion of barely hanging on—is singularly inappropriate. Early explorers have often commented on the vigor of the Arctic people, who take delight in work and play as well as in their country, which they regard as the most desirable and beautiful in the world. This joy in living is not just survival. On the other hand, from a different angle, the word is accurate enough. Given both the harshness and the unpredictability of the environment, the Eskimos, for all their skill and courage, can seem at times to be barely coping.

To Eskimos, nature is full of spirits that are not so much evil as unconscionably severe. Sila, which manifests itself as wind, snow, and blizzard, is such a spirit. It is feared and propitiated. Yet in a relaxed mood, the Eskimo can weave a fantastic tale about Sila that mixes half-believe with teasing entertaining fun. Peter Freuchen provides the following version of the tale. "It happened once that people found a giant baby lying abandoned on the ground. His mother had lost him while she was collecting grass. Merrily, the people gathered around the baby. The women showed how its penis was so big that four of them could sit side by side on it; yet they fell down when he had the slightest convulsion. As the people now continued their wickedness, the giant baby was suddenly lifted up into the sky, and there he became Sila, the weather. When he loosens the caribou skin that is his diaper, he lets loose wind and the rain."[14]

We can easily imagine how such a story, told with embellishments, can entertain. It makes jovial sense on those occasions when it is told, and the question of truth and falsehood would have seemed pedantic and does not arise. The blatant exaggeration of the size of the male member is a commonplace of Eskimo social discourse. Sexual jokes are related openly, with gusto. The erotic surge of life is thrown against the sweep of death—of Sila as wind and blizzard.

Some stories are deeply serious. Best known among them

is the one which shows why the relationship between Eskimos and sea mammals is fraught with a sense of crime and guilt. Different versions exist. Their essential features are given in the following account. "As game became scarce, the villagers decided to move to another hunting area. However, too many people got on the raft and it started to sink in the open waters. An orphaned girl was thrown overboard to lighten the load. She clung to the edge of the raft, hoping to be allowed to climb back. To prevent this from happening, a man picked up a knife and cut off her fingers. She slipped to the bottom of the sea; her fingers turned into sea mammals and rose to the surface; and the girl herself became the Spirit of the Sea and the Mother of its animals."[15]

This story combines fantasy with psychological realism. It shows a willingness on the part of the Eskimos to confront the severity of life. To an outsider coming upon the story for the first time, the most striking impression is likely to be one of unbearable harshness. In real life, orphaned children and the enfeebled old do receive care from their kinsfolk. But in times of desperate need, they are abandoned, blocked up in snow houses, or (in the case of adults) ceremonially killed. To assuage feelings of guilt, tales of the miraculous rescue of the sufferers and of punishment for those who acted against them are invented. Other ways to soothe the conscience also exist. Thus, it is the victim who initiates the act that ends in abandonment or killing: he or she pleads for death when life is too burdensome. The transition from life to death for victim as well as society is further eased by wrapping it in festive ceremony. Killing and death take place in the midst of a party, among kinsfolk and friends. Suppose an old man wants to die. A shaman dances around him to chase out evil spirits. A special rope of walrus skin is put around his neck. Victim and executioner rub noses. When the time comes to do the actual hanging it is done in the consoling belief that the victim will go to the Happy Hunting Ground.[16] Yet there is no real peace. People are unable to delude themselves so easily. Perhaps there is no happy thereafter, which means that the spirits of the dead, especially the spirits of those who have been abandoned or killed, cannot rest in peace. Full of envy of the living, they will seek revenge.

The story of the orphaned girl whose fingers turned into walruses and seals illustrates the painfully difficult, haunted nature of the relationship between human beings and animals.

Animals can be killed but they do not necessarily die. As Aua puts it, "All the creatures that we have to kill and eat, all those that we have to strike down and destroy to make clothes for ourselves, have souls, like we have, souls that do not perish with the body, and which must therefore be propitiated lest they should revenge themselves on us for taking away their bodies."[17]

Here then is a dilemma, which the Eskimo imagination deals in a variety of ways. One way is to draw attention to another problem—the hardships in the hunter's life. Perhaps they can be understood as a form of justice. The story concerning the origin of sea mammals makes it predictable that the Sea Spirit would resent human beings, would make life as difficult for them as she can, and give up her own children only grudgingly. Death in fact dogs the footsteps of the hunter. Any time he may die of an accident or be killed by an animal; and in old age he may even seek death at the hand of a relative rather than suffer sickness and uselessness. Violent forms of death are believed to have a purgatorial effect. Their victims go straight to the Land of Day where the benign Moon Spirit lives, and where human souls can hunt to their hearts' content. However, if the hunter were killed by his prey he would not go straight to heaven but rather descend to the bottom of the sea and there do penance. In this case, violent death is viewed as not totally unjust; hence it does not by itself purify, and some additional form of penance is necessary before the human soul is fit for heaven. The severity of the Sea Spirit makes life difficult for the Eskimos, but they can count on the Moon Spirit to mitigate the severity, for the Moon Spirit is not only kindly disposed toward human beings but it alone has the power to affect the Sea Spirit and the Mother of Beasts—a belief that rests on the observed impact of the moon on the tidal oscillations of the sea.[18]

Respect and propitiation are another way to ease the conscience of a people who, in order to live themselves, have to take so many animal lives. Thus the Netsilik Eskimos believe that a freshly killed seal should never be laid on a dirty floor; moreover, the seal, though dead, can still be thirsty, hence some water should be poured into its mouth. Such gestures of respect and consideration encourage the soul of the animal to reincarnate out of gratitude and allow itself to be killed again by the same hunter. The soul of the caribou needs special care. While caribou hunting proceeds, the scraping, stretching and sewing of skins to make clothes are strictly forbidden. Scraping in particular can wound the animal soul, and if a grazing caribou catches sight of it, it will not allow itself to be caught.[19] The idea that the hunted animal agrees to be caught and slaughtered is common among hunting tribes all over the world. It is a convenient belief, one that assuages guilt, but it is also a part of a deep-seated notion of reciprocity—the virtue of exchange that governs all aspects of nature.[20]

There are days in the Eskimo world when the sun shines, animals are abundant, and happiness covers the earth. More often, life is uncertain and hard. Under the circumstance, to live more or less contentedly calls for an ability to inhabit the present and ignore what the future may bring. Dealing with problems as they arise, requesting a spirit's help when appropriate, and doing whatever is necessary to maintain the harmony of the present are ways that the Eskimos have found practical in surviving the severities of the Arctic. Right and wrong, truth and falsehood tend to be situationally defined. Consistency in thought and behavior would prove dysfunctional in a world where permanence is an illusion and nature itself is notably inconsistent. Action, including speech, has of course consequence, but Eskimos prefer not to trace them into the future, for looking into the future presumes a stability—an orderliness in the processes of nature—that is not normal human experience in the Arctic. "Is it possible to travel to the end of the peninsula?" a stranger asks. The Eskimo's answer may be "yes" because the affirmative reply creates a genial mood for now. That the trip may be dangerous and have a fatal consequence for the traveler lies too far into the future for the Eskimo to feel responsible.[21]

Knud Rasmussen, the Danish explorer, wants to plumb the intellectual life the Iglulik Eskimos—how they make sense of nature and of life. He bombards his hosts with questions and receives answers that seem to him piece-meal and disappointing. Then, it is Aua the Eskimo's turn to attack. He asks Rasmussen: "Why does death overtake one hunter rather than another?" "In order to hunt well and live happily, man must have calm weather. Why this constant succession of blizzards and all this needless hardship for men seeking food for themselves and those they care for? Why? Why? Here is this old sister of mine; as far as anyone can see, she has done no evil; she has lived through a long life and given birth to healthy children, and now she must suffer before her days end. Why? Why?" At the end of the bombardment, Aua says to the Dane: "You see. You are equally unable to give any reason when we ask you why life is as it is. And so it must be."[22]

Questions concerning truth and justice, the meaning of life, and the whyness of unmerited suffering do not have a direct bearing on the practical concerns of life. They are philosophical in nature and are likely to emerge when people have leisure and a certain freedom from pressing material needs. As a more or less routine event, philosophical dialogue occurs only in specialized communities within advanced civilizations. Nevertheless, in all societies, a few individuals probably exist who take upon themselves to raise these broad issues from time to time and attempt to resolve them in the form of stories and, more implicitly, in ritual performances. The Eskimos are a case in point. Their story of the Sea Spirit, especially if it is combined with that of the Moon Spirit and placed in a cosmic frame, is an intellectual-moral construction (edifice) that gives life meaning. Such stories are an undoubted achievement. Eskimos, however, are ambivalent about large achievements, whether mental or material. Complex and extended stories are no part of an Arctic hunter's ambition, no more than it is his ambition to build large huts and camps.

In addition to stories, certain performances serve to integrate nature and life. At the center of a performance is the shaman. Through words and gestures enacted in a state of trance he calls forth and presents as a dramatic whole, on the one hand, natural forces and the world of spirits and, on the other, the needs of society and of individuals. The superiority of a shaman's performance over storytelling alone is that it more effectively engages the audience's emotions; moreover, it is able to address the current problems of society as well as those of an individual—for example, a man's prolonged illness or persistent failure in hunting. The promise of a cure gives the shaman's performance its special power and appeal. Yet, just as Eskimos may enjoy stories and philosophical saws without wholeheartedly believing in them, so they may attend a ritual or a shaman's enactment and even participate in it while at the same time entertaining doubt as to its relevance and effectiveness. If the inconsistency is pointed out to them, they may say, "Well, what else can one do?"[23]

Cultivators: Their Moral Universe

Foragers of the simplest material culture take what nature has to offer. Destroying and killing little, they have no cause to feel guilt. More advanced hunter-gatherers such as the Mbuti kill for food, but since animals are regarded as a gift of the benign forest they too feel little or no guilt. The Eskimos, by contrast, are great hunters and we have seen that they do feel guilt and fear. We now ask: What about agriculturists? They certainly have power over nature. In high civilizations, however, virtue rather than power comes to mind when one speaks of the farmer's way of life. Guilt and immorality are attached to smoke-begrimed or glittering cities, not to the "smiling landscapes" of the countryside. Yet it is in the countryside that people most directly and frequently face violence and death—the feeding of animals for slaughter and the slaughtering itself.

To modern city dwellers, the word farm is likely to evoke an image of fields of waving corn that signify abundance and well-being; death hardly enters the picture. Plants and plant life have not always been viewed so simply. According to one school of anthropological thought, headed by Adolf Jensen, plants can take on a far more emotion-laden and even rather ominous meaning if we go back far enough into the past—into the archaic planting communities of tropical latitudes. Embedded in the myths of tropical root-crop cultures is a story of the origin of plants and of human beings.[24] A composite sketch, based primarily but not exclusively on Southeast Asian case studies, goes like this. In the primal past, the earth was populated by the Dema, some of whom possessed human shape, others the shapes of animals and plants. Among the Dema were especially creative beings known as Dema-deities. One Dema-deity was killed by the Dema, an act that brought primal time to an end. The Dema became ordinary human mortals and propagated themselves as such. The killed Dema-deity introduced death into the world, an event that every human being would then have to undergo. Death itself, however, lost a little of its terror by reference to this sacral event. A further effect of the killing was that crop plants emerged from the body of the slain god. To eat a tuber, which could grow to the size of a man, was to eat a god. Human life and all living things depended on the commitment of a crime, so fortunate in its consequences, that it is commemorated in subsequent acts of ritual killing. Unlike the sentimental city dweller's view of farming, early cultivators might see even the harvesting of plants as killing—the destruction of one form of life to promote another. In Europe, a remnant of this belief appears in the powerful image of death as Reaper—a skeleton cutting off the heads of grains with a scythe.[25]

Tropical root-crop cultivators have gods who dwell under the earth, the grave of all things but also the progenitor of life. Where seed farming is the common practice, as in subtropical and mid-latitudes, sky gods emerge to complement those of the earth. Sky and earth, light and darkness, summer and winter at these extra-tropical regions are the dominant polarities of a multilayered cosmos. The cosmos thus conceived suits an agricultural people in their seasonal activities: it interprets reality for them, justifies to them the ways of nature and of man, and serves as a religious-ethical or moral edifice under which ordinary rules of social behavior reverberate to larger meanings. Many examples of this type of cosmos exist in both the Old and the New World.[26] Let us look at one example—at the cosmos and, in particular, the moral edifice of the Pueblo Indians of the American Southwest, a people whose social organization is relatively simple compared with those of the larger societies and political states of the Old World.[27]

Pueblo Indians believe in the existence of a harmonious universe made up of many components, among which are human beings, plants and animals, cosmic forces, and spirits. All of them are personalized, and each has the power to affect the other. Most components are both good and evil, although some have more good, some more evil, in them. Human beings, as an important part of this universe, have the power to upset or maintain its system of balances. Human power rests on knowing precisely what to do. Whether one of the eagle feathers of a mask has been taken from the shoulder or the breast of the bird makes a difference.[28] Attention to this level of detail implies a belief in causation that is impersonal and almost mechanistic.[29] On the other hand, a priest can only be effective if he is purified through ritual continence and entertains "good thoughts." When a priest, thus purified, addresses the spirits in appropriate formulary they have no choice but to bestow blessing. Automatism, then, operates even in the sacred realm, as it does in relationships between human individuals such that when a request is made of another in the prescribed manner the one so addressed is compelled to render help or tell the truth.[30]

Nature and society are so intimately interlocked that to the extent the Pueblo Indian sees harmony in nature he sees it in society. He believes that his society is good and peaceable. The Hopi, in particular, like to regard themselves as nonviolent human beings. Indeed, "Hopi" means peaceable. The Hopi expressly urge nonaggression. One should not be forward and argumentative, one should not complain even when treated unjustly, and one must not think of revenge. Above all, one should not deviate from the teachings of right and wrong handed down from long ago (*hiisat tataavo*).[31]

Such are the stated beliefs. Reality is predictably rather different. Social harmony, even when it holds, is tenuous. Bickering is commonplace and can explode into heated fights and quarrels. Gossip of a more or less malicious kind is rampant, especially among women. So-and-so is taking all the water at the irrigated gardens, or is too lazy to build a decent house for the family, or is unfaithful, or is a big liar, and so the talk goes on. One woman proudly says that when she quarrels with people she is "able to hit them in the right place." The Hopi are skilled at wounding with a word. A proverb says: "An angry word is like striking with a knife." Economic hardship engenders bad thoughts and gossip. The Hopi are aware that gossip tends to diminish after rain, with the promise of a good crop. When they feel more secure in their livelihood they are better able to heed the *hiisat tataavo*.[32]

Human relations among the Hopi, as among other Puebloans, do not seem very warm or deep. Even affection between parents and children lacks intensity. This is partly the result of living in large households in which the real mother is only one caring figure among several. Partly it is the result of the fairly common experience of abandonment. When food is short, children are given nothing to eat; in times of famine they are abandoned by their parents. The Hopi say: "You have to save your own life. Children's aren't worth it to you when starvation comes." They may also say that they cannot be burdened with children when they flee from the area in desperation, or that the children may as well die to escape the horrible suffering. Hopi children, predictably, do not go out of their way to care for their needy parents. "Most Hopi don't care for old people. Both men and women. . . . It was the same when I was a boy. Sometimes they'd put them out alone where nobody lives and wouldn't build a fire for them."[33]

Friendships seem cool and formal, and consist chiefly of

reciprocal rights to hospitality between individuals living in different villages. The men, at least, do not see friends as people they would wish to confide in. Relation with animals is also nonchalant. Richard Brandt writes: "The Hopi say that hurting animals is wrong. But their behavior raises some doubt about how strongly they disapprove. . . . Burros and dogs are sometimes executed at dances, apparently in a cruel way. It was reported that a certain Hopi allowed an animal, whose intestines came out as a result of faulty castration, to stand around in pain for some time before killing it. One Hopi, expressing unconcern for the fate of dogs, said: 'They can't talk; they can't say ouch.'" Once the usefulness of an animal is recognized it is treated more kindly. The Hopi, for instance, appreciate birds that kill worms and cats that catch mice which get into their flour; and once they have learned to use burros and horses in plowing these animals too receive better treatment.[34]

Social stress in Pueblo communities is glaringly manifest in the phenomenon of witchcraft. In view of the fact that Indians believe in a harmonious universe, one that moreover can be influenced by ritually purified and skilled human beings, how will they explain drought, other natural disasters, and epidemics? Can it be that the priest has been incontinent or has broken other taboos? A smallpox epidemic may produce witch hysteria. Someone must be responsible. Although ordinarily Pueblo Indians tend not to regard any being as inherently evil or good, when inexplicable disasters occur they feel the need to focus their fear and hatred on a single evil figure—the witch. Punishment for those accused of witchcraft is extremely severe. Take, as example, this incident from the Zuni record. Forest fire swept over the mountains. Under questioning the suspect confessed that he had not only set the fire but had also caused the prior drought. He said that he was jealous of people who had better crops than he, and claimed moreover that he and some others had the power to bring sickness to the tribe, and that indeed once they were the cause of a smallpox epidemic. Members of the War society clubbed the culprit to death; they then proceeded to his house and killed all seven members of his family who were thought to have helped him.[35]

Disaster may descend on a single individual rather than on the whole group. For some inexplicable reason, one man falls ill, has a serious accident, or suffers loss, while the others around him are unaffected. The sufferer of misfortune then suspects that the cause is the personal enmity of a witch, who may be his neighbor, a relative, or even his own father or mother. During World War II, certain Hopi witches believed that they are able to kill a relative by directing German bullets at him.[36] Stories of this kind show the intensity of resentment that can exist between kinship members. In a close-knit community, dislike turns readily into hatred, and under the additional pressure of misfortune can erupt in witchcraft accusation. The accused, rather than proclaim shocked innocence, may acknowledge and even boast about the deed, as though relieved to have a repressed jealousy and hatred brought out into the open.

Pueblo Indians believe in an ordered moral universe, one that responds to prayers if the petitioners are pure. In their ceremonies, particularly those that occur during the equinoxes, the ideal of moderation and balance is conspicuously on display. To the Hopi, the presence in the dance of the elaborately dressed ancestral deities (or katchina) are a reminder that if they participate scrupulously in the rites of supplication life will continue in abundance and harmony. To the Zuni, the presence of the Koko—rain and sky gods—is especially reassuring, for the Koko, who wear masks of intricate design representing the building blocks of the world, stand for an achieved order. Countering this emphasis on order and harmony in the Pueblo world view and ritual is the jarring intrusion of chaos and destructiveness. Thus, poised against the Koko are the Koyemici, who represent the earth and the raw primordial creatures of the earth. In sharp contrast to the elaborate attire of the Koko, the Koyemici appear in the dance semi-naked or in rags; they are, in a sense, lumps of clay that have yet to be molded by a skilled potter.[37]

The Zuni recognize a certain crudity in nature as well as in their own nature. Beyond that, they recognize the ineradicable presence of obscenity and destructiveness. What is felt and repressed or tentatively enacted in normal social life becomes, in the spatiotemporal frame of ritual, grotesquely exhibitionary. The Newekwe dancers of Zuni pueblo illustrate the extreme to which antisocial, uninhibited, and (as it were) precultural behavior can be enacted in public. They chew and try to swallow pieces of dirty rag, and they make it a point of honor to eat the excrements of men and dogs that have accumulated in the plaza. Unlike the Koyemici who represent the disorder of innocence and primordiality, the Newekwe are deliberately perverse.[38] In their extremity, the Newekwe may be considered specialists among clowns who, as irreverent jokers and conveyors of offensive sex, are a feature of all Pueblos. Among the Hopi, apprenticeship in clowning begins early: boys are appointed temporary clowns during which time they not only *may* be obscene but are taught to be so. Obscenity is coupled with destructiveness. Both oppose the ideal of ritual purity and harmonious order. Obscenity, mock, and real violence can all take place in the course of a ritual: for instance, during the initiation of a new member to the clown fraternity the clowns may, after a prior orgy of excrement eating, take up axes and destroy ovens and other properties that catch their attention.[39]

Excrement eating is regarded by some clowns, those of San Juan for example, as an act of humility. Crude behavior in general and all childish acts of destructiveness are mocking commentaries on the pretensions of self and of culture. They are deprecatory gestures made to counter the boast of purity and other human attainments. A hard note of realism infects the world view of the Pueblo Indians, who want reality to be benign and harmonious but can see that it often is not. Ceremonies are dignified texts interlarded with the jeering countertexts of the clowns. What effect does this moral-religious structure have on the moral aspirations of the Pueblo people? I would say, little. This is to be expected of realistic depictions of life, which mirror both the good and the bad part of existence. Virtues such as propriety, patience, discipline, and reverence all figure prominently in the ceremonies, as they do in ordinary life: the one confirms the other. Eroticism and destructiveness appear in the ceremonies, and of course they also exist outside their ceremonial contexts. Does the enactment of destructive impulses in such a context serve a useful social purpose? The answer is not clear. It has not, in any case, effectively contained hatred and violence in times of stress. As for the criticism of the clowns, which challenges the most sacred of the rites, whatever purpose it serves it is not an act of demolition that prepares the ground for people to build something better. The closed and closely integrated world of the Pueblo Indians does not allow for "better." The way things are can be adjusted or restored to an earlier, more harmonious state, but not significantly improved.

3 Moral Edifice and Life Complex Societies

A people whose material culture is simple may nevertheless have acquired complex rules of social behavior. Again, in distinction to the plainness of the material artifacts, such a people's oral tradition may contain tales of a richly wrought and highly imaginative kind. However, skill in language does not necessarily mean that it will be used to build a moral edifice—an integrated view of reality which attempts to understand the things that befall humankind as well as delineate in a fairly systematic way how people ought to behave. The Mbuti and the Semang do not see the need for reflections on moral issues; like many other nonliterate peoples they have not sought solace in an elaborated moral-ethical system. Eskimos are indeed sensitive to moral dilemmas that go beyond accepted rules and practice, but (as we have noted) they doubt the wisdom of seeking self-deluding answers in an intellectual edifice, as they also doubt the wisdom of creating a large material reality even if they have the means to do so. As to the Pueblo Indians, we find there both a sophisticated material culture—they have, after all, built the largest multistoried "apartment houses" in North America before the mid-nineteenth century—and a sophisticated world view that integrates nature and human beings into an interdependent whole. However, the term "world view" is misleading. What they have is less a view—a picture of how things are—than enactments and rituals that can themselves affect the cosmos; furthermore, in these ritual enactments the Pueblo Indians, for all the heightened drama and color they put into such occasions, hew close to the real as they know it through common experience.

In this chapter, we move from nonliterate groups to larger societies—to peoples of more advanced material culture (the Greeks, the Chinese, and the Indians) whose ways of seeing the world have been influenced in the course of time by the existence of a written record and literature. Of these peoples, chosen in part for their striking sociocultural differences, I will again ask: What is the tenor of their moral life? This question addresses the mores or customs of a group, but it will go beyond them to probe whether a people recognize moral dilemmas as they struggle to reconcile certain ethical ideals with the exigencies of livelihood. A further question is whether an articulated moral-ethical system—a moral edifice—has been built, and if so, what is its character? What kinds of value does it embody? In erecting such an edifice, to what extent has imagination been used to deepen the sense of reality, and to what extent has it (as fantasy) served to cast a delusory spell over it? For all the beauty and spaciousness of a moral edifice, what influence does it have on the capacity for good of the people who live in it?

Realism of Ancient Greeks

The Greeks, not only in archaic times but as late as the fourth century B.C., lived close to nature and were fully conscious of their need to propitiate it so that it would temper its violence and provide for human nourishment. Nature's forces were personified as gods, which made them seem accessible to moral appeal. Like many of their contemporaries, the Greeks practiced animal sacrifice, believing that the offering was pleasing to the gods and would compel them to respond with blessings and favors. Reciprocity was the fundamental moral law, as applicable to human beings as to nature and nature's presiding spirits. Knowing this gave the Greeks confidence. Moreover, in the act of making a blood sacrifice, contact with divinity could seem tangibly real. We can imagine the heightened emotion of priest and participants as the ax struck its death-dealing blow and blood gushed out of the victim and, later, when the acrid odor of burning flesh and bones rose in the air. All cities had altars for the ritual killing of animals. We fail to understand the culture of ancient Greece, G. S. Kirk says, if "we overlook the ubiquitous altars reeking with fresh blood, the constant throat-slitting of bulls, cows, sheep, goats, pigs, and occasionally dogs." Greek cities had no abattoirs. The slaughtering of animals was done mainly in front of temples. Priests were also butchers, hacking up corpses for the altar, selling parts of the carcass to the worshipers, and keeping back portions for themselves.[1]

This grisly picture may well repel modern sensibility. It throws into focus a characteristic common among archaic and preliterate cultures, namely, the juxtaposition of the sacred and the profane, life and death; the priest is also a butcher, and the temple a slaughterhouse. If we regard these sacrifices and juxtapositions as unbearably crude and ridden by superstitious fantasy, the ancients for their part might look upon our world of segregated realms, in which civilized living is quarantined from its blood-stained charnel foundations, as one of pathological self-deception. There is more than one way to lose touch with the real. Ours is through willful ignorance made possible by sociospatial segregation, theirs is the belief that the gods can be palmed off with pieces of burnt offering.

To the Greeks, animal sacrifice was sanctioned by ancient usage, the example of their non-Greek contemporaries, and the fact that it was part of a broader moral principle of reciprocity. Yet they did not feel entirely at ease. The feeling of guilt aroused by the slaughter of animals could not be altogether stilled. One way to assuage the feeling was to show respect for the victim. Decorated, its horns covered in gold, the animal was transformed into a sacred being that walked compliantly and even willingly to the altar. "Shake yourself!" When the animal moved in response to the command, the presiding priest interpreted the movement as consent to a death that was necessary to the renewal of life.[2] The guilt of slaughter found further relief in the idea that the sacrificed animal itself could regain life. The practice of gathering up the bones, of raising a skull or stretching a skin pointed in that direction. Another source of unease lay in the quality of the human relationship with the gods. The Greeks were sufficiently self-critical to see that the sacrificial rite might simply be an excuse for human feasting. Some meat had to be offered to the gods, but it was only a token. The gods had cause to feel that human beings failed in their duty and deserved punishment. When Zeus withdrew fire from men, it was as though he intended to say, "If you are not going to give us gods a fair share of the burnt meats, there shall be no burning at all. You will, like animals, eat the flesh raw."[3]

If human beings failed in their duties to the gods, the gods or powers of nature for their part often failed in their obligation to provide adequately for human needs. Their dispensations seemed arbitrary: sometimes they gave, other times they unaccountably did not. Were the gods playing with mortals? And didn't this divine proclivity for arbitrariness and trickery justify mere mortals, in their turn, to practice cunning? Prometheus, a minor god and a culture hero, offered an example for human behavior. In his quarrel with the supreme ruler Zeus, Prometheus unhesitatingly used deceit into which Zeus—himself described by Hesiod as one "of undying cunning"—could fall. However, so far as power over human lives was concerned Zeus demonstrated his superiority by tricking Epimetheus, brother of Prometheus, into accepting Pandora who opened a jar out of which poured such banes as disease, painful old age, poverty, and the need for unremitting toil.[4]

Myths such as the Promethean show that the Greeks were well aware that propitiary rites and sacrifices did not in themselves guarantee the desired results. To survive and prosper, human beings had to be disingenuous and ingenious—that is, skilled in the arts. Culture heroes of archaic Greece showed these traits. Prometheus himself was a cunning individual who stole fire from heaven and introduced the arts to mortals. Hercules, another culture hero, exhibited an even more discordant nature: crude, brutal, and obscene, he was also a founder of the Olympic games, of rituals and cities, of warm springs and shrines of healing. Most Greek heroes were likewise contradictory, perhaps because they could boast of both human and divine progenitors. Heroes were ordinary mortals writ large. In portraying them, the poets and storytellers were at the same time depicting realistically themselves, for mortals too can be both destructive and constructive; they can be lewd and anarchic, and yet on other occasions uphold propriety and order; in their own way they too are givers of life and death. To the modern eye, Greek myths may seem tales full of wonder and unlikely events, yet within them, lodged unobtrusively between such events, are realistic portrayals of human experience—of the true nature of ties among people as well as ties between people and the forces of the universe (the gods).

Myth (*mythos*) meant originally an oral utterance such as a command, a precept, a conversation, and importantly from the earliest times, a story. However, a story did not imply then, as it does now, something other than a true statement. The split between fact and fiction had not yet occurred. In modern society, a story is mere entertainment for private individuals. In the ancient world, its role in the community was far more central. As an oral performance accompanied by gesture and music, it could certainly entertain, but it was also a public occasion suited to the deliverance of moral lessons, including practical guidance on how one ought to conduct oneself in specific social contexts. The fantasy and exaggeration in a myth, as Eric Havelock and others have demonstrated, were not embellishments but rather features inherent to oral presentation. One of their functions was to implant the narrative in the listener's memory.[5] Thus the poet of the *Iliad* set his story in the misty and glamorous Mycenaean age rather than in the present; he used a somewhat artificial and archaic language to give an aura of authority and universality to what he had to say; he introduced deities as well as kings and heroes to provide a certain portentousness and permanence to human lives and projects; and he used exaggeration (e.g., Priam's fifty sons who required fifty bedrooms) to enhance the importance of his principal characters who therefore merited the listener's close attention.[6]

Homer was the revered teacher of the Greeks. Within the capacious edifice of his epical tale are accounts of ordinary human experience and detailed lessons on how to perform rites due to the gods, how to honor the dead, what to do when people disagree over property or spoils, how to behave appropriately and honorably in the presence of one's kinsfolk, friends, inferiors, and superiors, in war and in peace. Homer also taught the Greeks to face, with open eyes, intransigent facts in human nature, society, and the external world. Interwoven with the exaggerated magnificence and impossible feats of an epic are hard lessons in realism, one of which is the almost infinite variety and contradictoriness of attitudes and behavior notwithstanding the existence of norms. Homer taught the norms but he showed at the same time their inadequacy to the demands of the individual case and of particular situations. As for morality, people are not good or bad, but good and bad, proud and humble, courageous and cautious, aggressive and passive, contented and greedy, and they will be one rather than the other, depending on the ever-shifting impingements of circumstance.[7]

Another lesson in realism is the clear-eyed recognition of the severe limits to human freedom: people, no matter how elevated their social standing, live under constraint. This feeling of being under constraint and necessity pervades Greek thought and culture. Consider the famous words inscribed on Apollo's temple at Delphi: "Know thyself." It does not mean, as it would to a modern man or woman, the advantage of introspection—of knowing one's own psychological make-up. It means, rather, "know that you are human and nothing more."[8] The gods or the fates have control over human destiny. Inequality and the rule of force are the facts of nature, and it is useless—indeed irrational—to appeal for justice or mercy. Thus (in Hesiod) the hawk addresses the nightingale which it holds in its sharp talons:

> Silly thing,
> Why do you cry? Your master holds you fast,
> You'll go where I decide, although you have
> A minstrel's lovely voice, and if I choose,
> I'll have you for a meal, or let you go.[9]

In nature, as in society, force rules. When the Melians beseech their Athenian conquerors for mercy, Thucydides puts into the mouth of an Athenian the following candid words: "Of the gods we hold the belief, and of men we know, that by a necessity of their nature they always rule wherever they have the power."[10] Justice exists, but it operates only between equals. In the *Odyssey*, Menelaus can challenge Antilochus to an oath because they come from the same social stratum; he would not have done so with Thersites, his inferior. Again, Odysseus, to curb the panic that threatens the Greek forces, appeals gently to the captains but with the rank and file he issues a command and backs it up with the club.[11] More humbling than the constraints of external reality on high human aspirations is the way that even the strongest affections can be diverted or diluted by an ordinary mortal's psychological limitations and physiological needs. In the *Iliad*, Homer reminds his listeners that the dead

---

bodies of the warriors are dearer to the vultures than to their wives, and that Niobe, after weeping inconsolably for her slaughtered children, soon discovers that she wants to eat.[12]

Morals, at one level, refer to customs and tradition. In ancient Greece, they are *nomos*, which means traditional practice in the apportionment of land, and *ethos*, which means traditional behavior in place. Being moral has two higher levels of meaning: a conscious attempt to articulate principles of conduct and, above it and serving sometimes as its ultimate lure, a yearning for the ineffable good, the approach toward which requires that one periodically reexamine accepted morals.

Consider now these two higher levels. In the archaic period of Greek history, justice (*dike*) was retributive justice. Before the state could exercise firm authority, *dike* meant in practice revenge—blood feud when blood was shed, continued down the generations. Where injury did not end in death, families confronted one another with ritual formulas, oaths, co-swearing, and the bearing of witness in the presence of a judge who, however, had little real power and functioned primarily as a referee, proclaiming the victor in tests of familial strength. With the emergence of the polis toward the end of the seventh century, justice thus conceived and the method of dispensing it began to change, as Jean-Pierre Vernant has shown. Murder was no longer thought to be directed solely against the family, placing it under obligation to exact revenge, but rather against the polis. Therefore the responsibility for seeing that justice be done rested on the conscience and the will of the community, personified now by the powerful judge, and under the guidance of rules of conduct that were not merely custom but a consciously devised code—the written law. To win a combat, one no longer resorted to arms or depended on the number and prestige of co-swearers, or on sacred oaths convincingly sworn, but on facts that could be marshaled and evaluated in public. Facts and arguing from them rose in importance, along with the notion of objective truth. A new ideal grew in ascendancy, one that stressed the golden mean, moderation, proportion—*sophrosyne* as against *hybris*, those impulses toward excesses of pride or wealth characteristic of the nobles and the rich.[13]

Justice was elevated as a standard high above the contentions of proud individuals and great families. Promulgated by a sage, justice could also be evoked by him as a divine power that ensured true equilibrium among the citizens. In the absence of such an equilibrium—that is, without an equitable distribution of duties, honors, and powers—a harmoniously unified city could not exist. Secular ideals commanded a large measure of support by high classical times; nevertheless, the ancient cults and mysteries did not disappear. Authority must still be seen to come from an external source, and the law, though coded by mortals, was still of divine inspiration and, indeed, itself a divine power. Human reason must be applied to the just maintenance of the common good, but the Greeks could not forget those supernatural powers—Herodotus' Fate and Thucydides' Chance, for example—that defied human reason and yet must be taken into account in the organization of human affairs. Wisdom or philosophy was thus saddled with an unresolved ambivalence. On the one hand it favored public disputation based on evidence in the open democratic setting of the agora; on the other hand it favored and, in fact, it owed its origin and inspiration to initiation into the mysteries. Root in the mysteries gave philosophy the impetus and the vocation to search for transcendent truths, a search that could be conducted only in a secluded place, and the aspirant himself must undergo a discipline—an *askesis* of body and mind—away from the distractions of the world.[14]

Plato exemplified this ambivalence. He not only envisaged an ideal state but sought a role in government—that is, he sought to apply wisdom, in its guise as justice, to human affairs. But he also yearned for the transcendent good, for which he provided two powerful images. One is the sun that illuminates the world but cannot be looked at directly (*Republic* 514), and the other are the eternal forms, intangible and yet more real than anything one can apprehend with the senses. Here, in clearest expression, is morality in the third sense: being moral is a way of seeing and a way of being consequent upon a purified desire for the transcendent good. Seek first the good and the rest follows, which in Christian language becomes "love God and do what you will." Obedience to this injunction is the highest form of morality.

Several difficulties quickly come to mind, two of which are considered by Plato at length. One is the near certainty that human beings will be sadly deluded by what constitutes the good. Two sources of error, almost impossible to overcome, are the passions of the body and the dictates of society. To try to overcome these sources of error calls for the disciplining of body and mind. The body must be purged of its gross appetites and the mind weaned from the pablum and falsehoods of myths. Ascetic practice, by purifying body and mind, also enables the seeker to free himself from servitude to the false goods of society, which Plato calls the Great Beast. But whereas the temptations of the appetites and of worldly good are familiar experiences, what is there in the world that can direct people's attention away from them to the supernal good? This is the second difficulty, and Plato's answer is beauty or eros, which has the proven power to arouse in people the strongest desires, and perhaps some individuals will see that not all such desires can be satisfied by sensual indulgence and societal accolades. The good, of which physical beauty provides the barest intimation, lies elsewhere.[15]

In addition to these two difficulties, there is a third, which revolves around the relationship between the good and the real. The good that inspires must be real, and that raises the question of the nature of reality. Are there degrees of reality? Like Oriental mystics, Plato tends to regard tangible things as having a lower degree of reality than the transcendent truths, the eternal forms, or God. These thinkers insist, furthermore, that bodily appetites are the primary causes of illusion. The senses are not to be trusted, least of all when inflamed by passion. To secularists of the modern world, such ideas offend common sense. Of course material things are real; one can bump into them or fall over them. And appetites are certainly real—real enough to cause illusion and wayward behavior. What purpose is served by denying what is the case? Plato, in one of his more severe moods, casts a jaundiced eye on myths. Yet one reason why a modern man or woman can still admire the ancient Greek myths is that notwithstanding all the magic and fantasy, they confront unflinchingly the harsh facts of life: the great myths do not, out of a misguided yearning for some pure ideal, exclude from sight and mind the grossness of the body, the contradictoriness of human desires, and the often brutal mechanical operations of power.

Two worlds exist—the earthbound and the empyrean. When we speak of Greek philosophical ambivalence, which (as we have noted earlier) is an effect of philosophy's mixed genesis in the two worlds, it is natural to think of Plato. However, Plato, for all his brief flirtation with politics, is temperamentally drawn toward the empyrean: he is, foremost, a poet and a philosopher-mystic. What, we may now ask, about Aristotle? He, with his feet firmly planted on the ground, would seem to be a corrective to Plato. And he is. Compared with Plato's myths and his conception of the ineffable good, Aristotle's ethical discourse hews close to common sense. Aristotle is less inclined to polarize: he does not, for instance, elevate reason to the status of a ruler that controls the lowly and unruly feelings. For Aristotle, the feelings themselves may embody reason. His celebrated "doctrine of the mean," which argues that virtue consists in observing the mean between excess and deficiency, has an air of sweet reasonableness. Moderation is a virtue for Aristotle, although he also clearly recognizes that in certain circumstances real anger rather than a gentle shaking of the head is the reasonable and hence appropriate response. Aristotle eschews the laying down of abstract rules of behavior applicable to all occasions and times. He asks that one attend to the particular context. Moral knowledge is acquired not through the textbook but from practical experience and by habituation: one picks it up as a member of a civilized community. Moral, here, almost comes to mean mores or custom, except for Aristotle's emphasis on the role of rational feeling and reason. Aristotle's moral philosophy seems rooted in the realities of the sociopolitical world. Like the tragic poets, he recognizes the burden of choice, not so much between a greater and a lesser good as between two equally exigent though incompatible values. Goodness, for him, has a fragility that is the inevitable consequence of people's involvement with the confusions of life. Yet this is not all. Toward the end of his *Nicomachean Ethics*, he unexpectedly reintroduces the idea that the highest good or happiness is not to be found, after all, in living the rational emotional life in the midst of the world, but rather in contemplation apart from the world.[16]

We have been considering two broad types of imaginative construction. Under one are all the full-bodied myths of ancient peoples, including the Greeks, and under the other are the ineffable visions of the ascetics and mystics, among whom is (preeminently) Plato. Both types of construction or moral edifice provide lessons for how people are to see and act; and both, in their practical expressions, are compounded of fantasy and truth. They differ, however, in one important respect. Myths that are rich in drama, full of incidental details, and address the dilemmas that human beings recurrently face are fundamentally conservative. Despite the accounts in them of unorthodox and socially disruptive behavior their long-term effect is to enforce the mores of society. As for the ethics of Aristotle, to the degree that he emphasizes practical wisdom or knowledge in the conduct of personal and societal affairs, the effect is to preserve society's standing principles of moral order. To the degree that he lays stress on the sustained application of reason, his teaching may bring about change in both feeling and conduct.

There remain contemplation and the mystic vision. As otherworldly activities, they can have no impact on human beings other than on the practicing philosophers and visionaries themselves. And yet, paradoxically, the contemplative posture and the visions, by offering radical challenges to what is, can bring about disruptive and progressive change. The contemplative person himself may become an exemplary and charismatic figure, with a large and influential following. As for the visions, once they have been clearly articulated and presented to the public they can—under a favorable sociopolitical climate—acquire the power to beckon to the people, moving them to believe that their contentment is delusory and that where they stand morally is not necessarily where they ought to be.

Chinese Moral Imagination

Greek myths, compared with those of the Near East, lack supernatural protagonists and spectacular events. By the time the Greek gods have been installed on Olympus, they are human in form and almost human in behavior. This human cast of the gods has been offered as evidence of Greek rationality. If so, the Chinese have pushed rationality a step further. In their accounts of the origin of the world and of society, supernatural powers play only a shadowy role. Stories exist of the separation of heaven and earth, of the flood, and of a primordial paradise, but notwithstanding such supernatural elements they seem inhibited—they lack unbuttoned drama. Conspicuously absent, for example, are a frank concern with bodily processes and the sexual performances of the culture heroes and creators, a willingness to dwell on violence and death, and a raw rowdy humor that erupts unselfconsciously in the myths and legends of other peoples.[17]

Distinctive to Chinese culture is the antiquity and perdurance of its moral vision. The moral is deeply embedded in formulations of what nature and society are like and ought to be like. From the time of the first historical dynasty (the Shang of the eighteenth to twelfth century B.C.), the idea of the moral includes the twin components of order and reciprocity: order implies reciprocity and reciprocity order. Since this order is hierarchical, obligation takes a different form depending on one's social standing. Thus respect is due from inferior to superior, protection from superior to inferior. Included in both is natural affection. The affection is natural because the model for social bonding is the family. Thus a nation is a family, and by the early Chou period the ruler was already known as "the parent of the people." Indeed even the harmonious universe is a family. This early and persistent emphasis on order and reciprocity has had, in itself, the effect of curtailing colorful biographies, whether of gods or of culture heroes, and unique dramatic events, in favor of the more static pictures of roles and functions.[18]

Natural forces in China are not, of course, stable. The Chinese could hardly have ignored the floods, droughts, and earthquakes that have so often disrupted their lives. But in their conceptualizations of the natural realm they have pushed its instabilities into the background, choosing instead to focus on its grand periodicities, and to see even its moods—described by human analogy as anger, love, joy, and sorrow—as phenomena that manifest themselves at appropriate times and places in the seasonal cycle. Ancestors, too, have been shorn of temperament and individuality. They cannot disturb or surprise. Ancestors are defined not so much by their personal histories as by their statuses and assigned roles; they have been integrated into the world of the living for the functions they perform.[19]

Ancestors and the forces of nature are not sharply distinguished from one another. At a very early date, the forces of nature, like ancestors, were drawn into the social structure and life of human beings. In one of the earliest literary sources, the Book of Poetry, Ti or Heaven—the supreme power in the universe—is said to have given birth to the founders of both the Shang and Chou dynasties. In the same source Heaven is said to have "given birth to the multitudinous people." The idea that Heaven is parent to all human beings has two important consequences, one of which is to universalize reciprocal obligations, and the other is to implant the belief that not only the rulers but ordinary people should show in their behavior the propriety that is discernible in the suprahuman realm of Heaven. Besides the supreme power Heaven, numerous lesser powers and spirits exist; they are identified with various natural forces such as rivers, mountains, wind, rain, earth, and the stars. All of them are part of one great family, governed by the rules of kinship duties and obligations. Sometimes the order of the universe is presented as a well-run protobureaucracy rather than as a family—a reflection of the size of the social organizations that existed even in the Shang period. Oracle bones speak, for instance, of Heaven dispatching the winds as his emissaries and the rain and clouds as his ministers.[20] Nevertheless, despite the early appearance of the language of bureaucracy, the fundamental model of natural and social order is the family. As society increases in size and complexity, the need to formulate rules of conduct, to give reasons for appropriate behavior, becomes more pressing. Inevitably the question arises as to how morality can be formally specified, provided with a bureaucratic underpinning, and still seem to have the authority of nature. The Chinese, like other peoples who have become self-aware, waver between the authority of nature and the authority of culture or civilization. They wish to continue to believe in the naturalness of the family, and yet they have in time made the family, as the cornerstone of a vast moral edifice, the quintessential expression of culture.

A key term in the Chinese moral universe is *li*, which meant, originally, "sacrifice" and the rituals of sacrifice, but later the meaning was extended to cover almost every aspect of human social relations and behavior. This stress on *li* suggests that the Chinese, and especially the Confucians, have moved away from the need to ground morality in the natural. After all, it takes time to learn the rules of *li*. People who have to labor in the fields or otherwise work with their hands have neither the time nor the resources to master the intricate social and ritual skills. They may well be good people, and they are certainly necessary to society, but their position in it is a humble one. In contrast, their superiors (*chün-tzu*—ruler's son, and *shih*— gentleman or knight) have the wherewithal to learn the *li*; they know the roles and statuses of deities, ancestral spirits, and men, and how to behave seemingly in their presence.[21] A consequence of this stress on knowing the *li* is that people ignorant of it are regarded as crude and barbaric, and a further consequence is to dismiss as unworthy of notice the biological functions and passions as well as manual labor that together make up so much of human life.

Li is an attainment. All human beings are potentially capable of it. Confucians, and above all Confucius himself, believed in natural equality. "By nature, men are nearly alike; by practice, they become very different," was how Confucius put it.[22] Confucians expected miracles of education. They succeeded in introducing state-supported schools in the Han dynasty, and a major aim in their historical projects was to find moral exemplars from the past. But, as we have just noted, not everyone had the time and the resources to acquire an education. This might be seen as a defect of society which could ultimately be put right. However, Confucians appear to have also believed in natural *in*equality. Some people are simply better endowed with the synoptic powers of intuition. Confucius himself said: "Those who are born knowing the *tao* [which here is synonymous with *li*] are the highest. Those who know it through learning are next and those who toil painfully but cannot learn it make up [the bulk of] the people."[23]

We see here an example of how the Chinese have wavered between nature and culture as ideal. They have shown, historically, a deep-seated ambivalence toward civilization. On the one hand, there is pride in it and its finest attainment—the harmony of *li*. On the other hand, there exists the doubt, in Confucianism as well as (more obviously) in Taoism, that anything that is a mere product of human will and application can claim one's highest allegiance. One way to resolve the ambivalence is to say, with Confucius, that learning is, or ought to be, effortless; the idea of effortlessness is assimilated to that of natural. The heart finds delight in continuous study and in following the prescriptions of *li*. Just as studying is not hard because it is natural, so mourning for one's parent over a three-year period is not hard because it is a natural expression of human feeling.[24]

"Talking of *li*, talking of *li*—Does it mean no more than presents of silk and gems?" asked Confucius in exasperation. Outward gestures, however correct, are essentially empty and meaningless. To have meaning and effect they must be accompanied by genuine feeling. The inner state of the man, out of which public action emerges, is of great importance to Confucius and Confucians.[25] This idea of *li* as rooted in genuine feeling, and hence in nature, is enforced by two ancient beliefs. One, recorded in pre-Confucian texts, asserts that social norms and proprieties have their ultimate source in Heaven, who displays these virtues in his own dealings with spirits and men. The other belief contains the idea that the sage kings of antiquity promulgated the *li* in conformity with both human nature and external nature—that is, the cosmic principles. Yin and yang, the dyadic principle that underlies all cosmic phenomena, take on social and moral meaning when yang is characterized as high, yin as low, and when Heaven is described as yang and noble, and earth as yin and humble. The cosmos itself becomes a model for, and justifies, the social distance between father and son, prince and minister, magistrate and people.

In the late Chou period, the dyadic principle yin and yang was combined with other cosmic principles, including those of the five elements, the cardinal points, the five colors and animals; and to this cosmic frame were then attached human roles and institutions to make up a comprehensive system that linked, processually, the periodicities of nature with human cyclical activities.[26] This grand correlative cosmology exerted its most powerful influence on Chinese thought and life through the long span of the Han dynasty. Its hold suffered vicissitudes thereafter, but continued to exert a subdued and fragmented influence on both high ceremony and folk festivities until the end of the nineteenth century. The cosmology may be viewed as a vast moral edifice that provides lessons for proper conduct. In a Han text, we see how the *li* of human life are applied to the five cosmic elements themselves. "Each of the five elements circulates according to its sequence; each of them exercises its own capacities in the performance of its official duties. Thus wood occupies the eastern quarter, where it rules over the forces of spring; fire occupies the southern quarter where it rules over the forces of summer." Another text asserts that when the elements operate within their borders, all is well, but when they overstep them disasters ensue.[27] The worlds of human beings and of the cosmic elements are so linked that action in the one has a specific effect on the other. Intimate linkage to nature gives people a sense of power and of being in control but with it also the burden of acting responsibly and morally so as not to upset the cosmic equilibrium. Thus, during the Han dynasty, officials thought that death sentences should be carried out only during the "descendant" (yin) seasons of autumn and winter; and because the times of the solstice were especially delicate, governmental activities should be suspended to prevent unintended adverse interference.[28]

The moral universe of the Chinese rests on a profound attachment to the sense of order. We have already noted that they choose to focus on the great regular cycles of nature rather than on those aperiodic events that so frequently cause famine and death. But these events cannot be ignored. How have the Chinese tried to explain them? The oldest explanation (one already adumbrated in the Shang dynasty) as well as the most enduring is that disasters, both natural and those of human creation, are signs of displeasure from Heaven; they are a form of punishment and they can also mean that the ruler has failed to follow the *li* and that his mandate to rule has therefore been withdrawn.[29] This explanation, with its emphasis on the ruler, has been extended so that bureaucratic transgressions can also disturb the cosmic rhythms. Unfortunately, rulers and responsible officials can never be sure just precisely what they have done wrong. When an eclipse of the sun occurred in A.D. 31, the emperor knew that he must have done something wrong, but what? He was unable to think of a specific cause, so "he ordered all officials who could throw any light on the subject to write a confidential letter, saying frankly (and being careful not to address him as 'Holy Man') what they thought he had done wrong."[30]

Individual misfortune is equally perplexing. Why the untimely death of a friend? How can tragedies of an individual and personal nature be understood? We have seen the perplexity of the Eskimo in the face of personal disaster. Thoughtful Eskimos have learned not to seek answers in a moral edifice; they seem to believe that the edifice itself is vainglorious and possibly an offense. The Chinese, by contrast, have gone ahead to build such an edifice. They have their imposing correlative cosmology. But appeals to such an abstract system of values and beliefs do nothing to assuage hurt and a deep sense of wrong when tragedy strikes a friend or a family member, or when the waywardness of a single person can do great harm to society. Confucius could not be reconciled to the death of his disciple Yen Yuan: "Alas, Heaven is destroying me! Heaven is destroying me!" Mencius was human enough to blame Heaven itself for the failure of the prince of Lu to put his correct social policies into practice.[31]

Another source of perplexity to the ancient Chinese, shared by any reflective people, is knowing how to act morally, righteously, in an ambiguous situation. Confucians have always preferred *li* to formulated law, for they readily see that the *li* cover far more types of behavior than can possibly be embraced by law. Since laws deal only in general types, dispute is always still possible. To Confucians, their very existence encourages contentiousness. In contrast, a person brought up to know the *li* through example and practice is seldom at a loss as to how to act. But there are the exceptions. Even the *li* cannot possibly cover all the infinitely varied situations in real life. Perplexity remains. It may be that if a person possesses *i* (righteousness or appropriateness) he will always know how to act. Confucius greatly values *i*, but he says of himself that he is unable to attain the ideal of being "wise without perplexity." In his own eyes he falls short of being a truly wise and noble person. What makes Confucius an appealing figure to us now is this honest acknowledgment of doubt. His own moral stature, for us, increases when he is able to admit bewilderment.

Confucianism has dominated the Chinese conceptions of society and life. The Chinese moral edifice is essentially of Confucian design, but it has been stretched and enriched by rival doctrines. Thanks to their contributions, the Chinese moral edifice is not by any means a monolith. If it were, it would have been a fanciful creation with little influence on the way people—outside of their ceremonial functions—live or can aspire to live. The Confucians have been challenged by the Mohists and the Legalists. As challengers and critics they point to the lack of realism in Confucian doctrine, but as creators they introduce doctrines of their own which may in turn be faulted for their imaginative excesses—their loss of touch with common experience.

Consider, first, the challenge of Mo-tzu (ca. 480–390 B.C.). He attacks the central Confucian teaching that the family provides a model for society. To Mo-tzu, family bonds and other local attachments, far from having the qualification to serve as a natural and inspirational model for the larger society, represent a degeneration of universal love which prevailed during the time of the sage kings. Local attachments are fragments of a once greater whole. These fragments may be admired for the strength of their internal bonds and yet their existence is a source of friction and conflict. Mo-tzu notes that even robbers love their own families. "They steal from other families in order to benefit their own."[32] While Mo-tzu's criticism rings true, his positive doctrine—that of universal love under the rule of sage kings—is vulnerable to attack by Confucians as without foundation in human nature and, moreover, immoral. To Confucians, Mohist doctrine is unrealistic because it ignores the natural hierarchies and immoral because it fails to distinguish filial piety and kinship obligations from the general love for humankind.

Legalism, a school of thought which powerfully challenged Confucianism, arose during the Ch'in dynasty, when China was consolidated into a large empire for the first time. Legalists criticize Confucian doctrine for its unrealistic application of ideas and values that can work, if at all, only in small societies. In a complex empire of continental size such as the Ch'in, submission to unwritten customs and codes of behavior—the practice of *li*—will end in injustice and chaos. Necessary to the effective rule of empire are written laws that apply to everyone. Laws are necessary because, contrary to Confucian belief, human beings are not essentially good. They have a natural tendency to favor their own kind, which in practice often means taking unfair advantage of those who lie outside the fold. Mohists and Legalists are thus in agreement in having a somewhat skeptical view of the family, which for them is more an expression of human limitation than an inspirational ideal.

Another important difference between Legalists and Confucians is this. Given the Legalists' desire to make the rules of behavior explicit, they have more opportunity than Confucians to become aware of society's contradictions. Society does not run smoothly, for all the guidance that tradition and the *li* provide. Han Fei-tzu (280?–233 B.C.), who is the last and greatest of the theorists of the Legalist school, insists on the value of recognizing the contradictions, for once recognized they can be removed through the enactment of rational and uniform laws. He opined, "What are mutually incompatible should not exist. To reward those who kill the enemy, yet at the same time praise acts of mercy and benevolence; to honor those who capture cities, yet at the same time believe in the doctrine of universal love; to improve arms and armies as preparation against emergency, yet at the same time admire the flourishes of the officials at court; to depend on agriculture to enrich the nation, yet at the same time encourage men of letters; . . . strong government will not thus be gained."[33] The criticisms of the Legalists can be admirable in trenchancy and insight, but the positive program they offer—the enactment of rational and uniform laws and their imposition on a large and heterogeneous population by a strong and highly centralized government—is itself a fantasy if the Legalists really think that by such simplifying draconian measures a harmonious and just society can be created.

Besides philosophers and social reformers, historians have contributed significantly to the elaboration of the Chinese moral edifice. They owe their impact to the volume of their output, its semi-official standing, and to the traditional esteem for literary works, especially those that describe the past. Chinese historiography has been strongly influenced by a book called the "Spring and Autumn Chronicles," believed to have been edited by Confucius himself, which purportedly documents the events of the State of Lu in the period from 722 to 481 B.C. Confucius' principal reason for editing the documents of his own state is to draw moral lessons from them; and the principal moral lesson he draws is that virtuous people are rewarded and wrong-doers bring calamity down on their own heads, if not immediately then in the long run. Under the influence of the Chronicles, Chinese historians have tended to treat history as a morality play. Facts have been distorted, even by Confucius, to provide suitable lessons.[34] However, the Chinese understanding of the past has another major source of inspiration, namely, the *Shi Chi* (Historical Records) written by China's greatest historian, Ssu-ma Ch'ien (ca. 145–90 B.C.). Although the *Shi Chi* too is heavy with moralism, it makes an effort to respect the facts, including those that are disturbing. Of Ssu-ma Ch'ien as a historian, Pan Ku (the annalist of the Former Han dynasty who died in A.D. 92) wrote: "His writing is direct and his facts are sound. He does not falsify what is beautiful nor does he conceal what is evil. Therefore his may be termed a 'true record.'"[35] Ssu-ma Ch'ien reveals his own distaste for imaginative excess when he criticizes the Taoist Chuang-tzu's works as for the most part allegorical; "they are empty tales without basis in fact."[36] Respect for fact means that Ssu-ma Ch'ien's portraits of important people include warts; it means recognizing the world as a fickle place in which virtue must be its own reward. His respect for accuracy in depicting the socioeconomic scene enables him to acknowledge the important contribution of industry and trade to the wealth of a nation. For this achievement in accuracy, he earned the disapprobation of later historians who sought to maintain, at least publicly, the superiority of the life of farmers lest they abandoned their vital occupation.[37]

How will the *Shi Chi* fare from the standpoint of our modern conception of realism? It will be seen to have certain weaknesses. One is Ssu-ma Ch'ien's reluctance to depict heroes as complex personalities with both good and bad traits. A hero is shown full of virtue in the chapter devoted to him; true, the blemishes are also revealed but they are revealed elsewhere in a chapter devoted to another individual. This practice makes historical figures sufficiently one-dimensional to serve as props for moral lessons. Another weakness is Ssu-ma Ch'ien's disinterest in the common people. The grand historian himself says that he will study only extraordinary men, both good and bad, for there is little likelihood that insight and inspiration can come from dwelling on the commonplace. Whatever the merits of this view, it is not devotion to knowing how human beings, high and low, live—to a rounded, realistic understanding of society.[38]

If historical writing can overlook large areas of ordinary human experience, works of a more abstract and philosophical nature are even more disposed to do so. Confucianism and its rivals, Mohism and Legalism, can all be faulted for being too abstract, too remote from basic human needs and passions. Within Confucian thought itself, critics have urged a return to the relative simplicity of the original thinkers—above all, Confucius and Mencius. But, whether fanciful and sophisticated or simple and sincere, almost all the major conceptions of people and society in China suffer from an unwillingness to confront an unruly or indifferent nature and the biological facts of the body. The outstanding exception is Taoism. Under the name of Taoism is a wide range of ideas and practices. Religious Taoism is concerned almost exclusively with the search for immortality. It devotes more words to discipline and technique than to world view. In contrast is the philosophical Taoism of the *Chuang-tzu* and the *Lao-tze*. Here we find views on nature and life that, unlike those of Confucianism, are rarely comforting, perhaps because they are for the most part amoral.[39] In the *Lao-tzu*, for instance, the *tao* is shown as indifferent to the welfare of living things. "Heaven and earth are not benevolent. They treat the ten thousand things as straw dogs."[40] At times it seems as though a blind fortune rules over the human world in total disregard for its values. As the Taoist work, the *Huai-nan-tzu*, puts it: "The city of Li-yang in one night sank beneath the waves and was turned into a lake, and the brave and strong, the sage and wise suffered the same fate as the weak, the cowardly, and the unworthy. When fire breaks out and the wind sweeps it across Wu Mountain, the tall poplars and purple iris together with the lowly sagebrush perish in the flames."[41] The *Chuang-tzu* espouses a total moral relativism in human affairs. "Right" and "wrong" are just words. "For each individual there is a different 'true' and a different 'false.'" Indeed, from the perspective of philosophical Taoism, the advocacy of such Confucian virtues as benevolence and righteousness is not only foolish but likely to do harm, for the advocate is deluded: in urging such postures he betrays an unwarranted, hence dangerous, confidence.[42]

Among Taoism's most daring departures from the norm of religious-ethical discourse is its willingness to contemplate the lowly facts, including the waste products and weaknesses of the body. The Taoists are able to introduce an earthy element into their picture of reality that is refreshingly different from the unremittingly elevated moral tone of the Confucians. Consider this exchange on the *tao* in the *Chuang-tzu*.

> Tung-kuo Tzu asked Chuang-tzu, "Where is that which you call *tao*? Chuang-tzu said, "Everywhere." Tung-kuo Tzu said, "You must be more specific." Chuang-tzu said, "It is in this ant." "In what lower?" "In this grass." "In anything lower still?" "It is in tiles." "Is it in anything lower still?" Chuang-tzu said, "It is in ordure and urine." Tung-kuo Tzu had nothing more to say.[43]

Deformity and crippling disease, which are rarely considered a suitable topic for Confucian discourse, make an appearance in the *Chuang-tzu*. "Master Yu fell ill. Master Ssu went to see how he was. 'Amazing,' said Master Yu. 'The Creator is making me all cramped up like this. My back sticks up like a hunchback's and my vital organs are on top of me. My chin is hidden in my navel. . . . It must be some dislocation in my yin and yang *ch'i*.' Yet his heart was calm and unconcerned."[44] We soon realize, however, that the topic here is not really the grim experience of deformity and disease. Taoism is not much more willing to confront affliction in all its gross physicality, tragic contingency, and social isolation, than does Confucianism. The reported event is really meant to illustrate the triumph of the disciplined and lofty mind over the body, left as it were by the side to undergo the playful transformations of the *tao*. Moreover, Benjamin Schwartz makes the perceptive comment that, compared with Job, Master Yu's misfortune is devoid of subjectivity. "We are nowhere told anything about the agonizing subjective pains which must accompany the progress of the disease. In Job, we are fully aware of the maddening itches which accompany his skin disease."[45]

Earlier I have noted that one of the human predicaments is the need to kill animals for food and clothing. Somebody else's blood must be shed so that human beings can survive and prosper. Wherever moral ideas are conscientiously developed, this need to kill has presented a dilemma that allows no easy solution. It is a curious fact that native Chinese philosophies take little or no account of this problem. Unlike ancient Greece, Rome, and India, China did not produce thinkers who pondered on the suffering of animals. The vast majority of the people in China were poor, and the poor in China, like those in other civilizations, never had much opportunity to slaughter animals and eat meat. The well-to-do, including Confucius and the Confucians, certainly ate meat but they all seemed to have done so with an easy conscience. If certain foods were proscribed, as in religious Taoism, it was done as a hygienic measure and as a technique for attaining immortality. No doubt all civilized Chinese abhorred violence and bloodshed—the profession of butcher was, after all, held in disesteem. Nevertheless, Chinese culture—Chinese moral sensibility—was able to flower in neglect of an entire world of pain.

For two millennia, Confucianism and Taoism have, to a large measure, successfully catered to the Chinese need for control and consolation, knowledge and a vision of the good. But the success has not been total. In the native systems, certain basic human experiences are not addressed, or are only lightly touched upon, and certain basic human needs are not fully met. Understandably, when Buddhism found its way into China, it soon won acceptance by both the populace and the elite: the populace for its compassion and supernatural consolations, and the elite for its depth of insight into the nature of suffering and for its understanding of those complex mental states—envy, jealousy, hatred, love, melancholy, and joy—over which institutional society has little influence.

Buddhist Originality

Compared with the Buddhist world view, Confucian cosmology even at the height of its elaboration is modest in scope. The disparity is most clearly manifest in the size of their respective universes. The Chinese cosmos, like that of the Pueblo Indians (chapter 2), is stretched along a coordinate of cardinal points. No doubt a great distance separates east and west, north and south, zenith and nadir, but the Chinese have not tried to imagine the vastness of space. On those ritual occasions when cosmic harmony is affirmed, the coordinates of space must be presented symbolically and therefore at a scale accessible to feeling as well as to mind. Each ceremony has the effect of reducing the cosmos to a familiar human scale. It is easy to understand why people refrain from trying to conceive an order of size that diminishes their own selves to utter insignificance. The grandeur of Indian thought (both Hindu and Buddhist) lies in its willingness to imagine the vastness. The Indian space of many suns and moons, which in dimension compares with the one known to modern astronomy, is an outstanding example of how the mind can leap beyond ascertainable facts to intuit a more or less true picture of physical reality. However, the Indian imagination (both Hindu and Buddhist) has not stopped at an abstract picture. It goes on to populate space with multiple levels of heaven and hell, using not only the resources of poetic language but the authority and the quasi-magical appeal of numbers. Thus Buddhists speak of the thirty-one abodes of existence, twenty-seven of them desirable, of which twenty-six are abodes of the gods and the remaining one is for human beings; in addition, animals, demons, ghosts, and those consigned to hell inhabit the four "planes of woe," and hell itself has seven subdivisions.[46]

The gods live longer and better than do human beings, yet in Buddhist thought it is more blessed to be born human. The reason is that the gods are still subject to the law of "desire or action and inevitable consequence"—that is, the law of karma: they will fall back to a lower state of existence once their meritorious karma have been exhausted. Human beings, by contrast, have a chance to move out of the cycles of rebirth altogether and attain Buddhahood. Although it is better to be born a man, it is also extremely difficult to do so. How difficult? Here the Buddhist answer, though it takes the form of an anecdote, demonstrates an ability to conceive immensity and formulate an order of probability (or improbability) that transcend anything premodern peoples have dreamed of. "Imagine a limitless expanse of the ocean, on which a tile is floating, with a hole in it just large enough for a turtle's head to go through. Now imagine also a turtle which comes up to the surface of the ocean just at the right time and the right place to put his head into the hole in the tile floating aimlessly about." Well, the Buddhists would say, it is more likely for a turtle to do just that than for a being to be born a man.[47]

Vast space is frightening, but even more so—more a threat to self-esteem—is the idea of endless time, which reduces the most enduring human accomplishments to passing shadows. In the Western world, medieval thinkers took immense space in stride, but their conception of secular time lacked comparable reach. The world was created some 6,000 years ago, a notion that was retained, half-seriously, into the eighteenth century. It took the cumulative evidence of the new geological science to shatter Western man's temporal innocence.[48] In India, by contrast, Buddhists (following Hindu thought) conceived of immense duration (*kalpa*), reckoned either by number or by simile. The numbers compare with those of modern astronomy. One estimate of a *kalpa* is 1,280,000,000 years. But the similes are even more powerfully evocative of the awesome reach of time because they are better able to force people to "experience" immensity. One example: "Suppose there is a mountain, of a very hard rock, much bigger than the Himalayas; and suppose that a man, with a piece of the very finest cloth of Benares once every century should touch that mountain ever so lightly—then the time which it would take for him to wear away the entire mountain would be about the time of a *kalpa*."[49]

Imagination directed at the cosmos has given Buddhists an austere truth: its vast compass puts it beyond accommodation with the ordinary needs and passions of mortals. Buddhists have also applied their minds to the individual human person, with a willingness to confront unwelcome facts far beyond the pale of the Confucians. A monk is exhorted to look at the body as "just like an old bag with orifices at top and bottom, and stuffed full of groceries, encased with skin and full of impure matter from the soles of the feet to the crown of the head." Furthermore, he is asked to meditate on the corpse, "deposited at a place for the dead, that is one or two or three days dead, bloated, purple, and decomposed," and then say, "this body of mine is the same potentially as that body, and will one day resemble that body: it cannot escape mortality."[50]

A number of religions and philosophies have considered the body to be of little account, even contemptible. What matters is the soul. In the Upanishadic tradition of Hinduism, for instance, the soul (*atman*) is viewed as identical with the essence of the universe (*brahma*). Both are everlasting. Enlightenment is the intellectual comprehension that all is one, that in the depth of one's own life the unchanging unity of the universe can be experienced. Buddhism's uniqueness lies in its radical denial of the permanence of the soul. No permanent self exists. Indeed the Buddha taught that belief in such an entity is among the most powerful of human delusions. He searched everywhere for the permanent self, but all he could find were the five aggregates of material body, feeling, perception, predisposition, and consciousness. At any moment, the self is a combination of these aggregates, and just as each aggregate is subject to change, so is their conjoint existence. This rejection of a core enduring identity is perhaps the hardest Buddhist teaching for self-important human beings to accept. It undermines the common belief in a personal fame that can be savored after death. Fame or honor is the spur for good conduct and bravery in many societies, including old Europe and China: Homeric warriors, agora politicians, medieval European knights, Chinese scholar-officials all recognize its authority. Placed against the stern teaching of the Buddha, these figures, as they stride across the historical stage, show the pathos of boastful children.[51]

In high literate cultures, moralists tend to consider not only observable behavior but intention in judging a person's moral worth. Right action alone is insufficient. Confucius thinks little of men who merely go through the gestures of a ceremony without the appropriate feelings. As to the Greeks, their emphasis on sight—on seeing truly, on vision, without which action is blind—again predisposes an individual to recognize the importance of an inner state. Nevertheless, it is possible to argue that the Buddhists, more than people of other faiths, have probed the inner state, urging on seekers after truth the need to purge it of desires and passions that give rise to more or less virulent forms of delusion. Outward behavior may earn a man the name of virtue when in fact he is filled with envy or hatred. A true disciple of the Buddha is aware of this discrepancy, and will admit to the falsehood of the publicly presented self. Telling truth is a high and difficult virtue. To Buddhists, moreover, it is a virtue that emanates power, as the following story from Burma illustrates:

> A young boy, after being bitten by a cobra, was taken by his parents to a monk to be cured. The monk said that

no medicine could cure the boy, but that he would attempt a cure by an act of truth. Poison started to drain out when the monk admitted that in his fifty years in the robes he had been happy only during the first seven years of his ordination. More poison drained out when first the father said that he did not like to give to charity, although he had been doing it all his life, and then the mother said that she had not been happy with her husband during their entire married life.[52]

Some Buddhists consider telling the truth the principal virtue. Others consider it to be loving kindness (*mettā*), which (let us note) is far more inclusive than the *jen* of Confucius or even of Mo-tzu, for *mettā* covers not only people but all living things, even insects. Hinduism, it is true, also preaches against the killing of animals, but more out of regard for the principle of nonviolence and for the doctrine of reincarnation—the pig one kills may be one's grandmother—than from loving kindness. In addition to *mettā*, Buddhists preach compassion or *karuna* for the afflicted and empathetic joy or *mudita* for the fortunate. They urge, in other words, not only doing good works but doing them feelingly, in empathy with the suffering or joy of all living things.

Buddha has laid the foundations of a large and austere moral edifice. People who live in it can benefit from its insights and wisdom to reach a level of moral excellence that, without such assistance, is beyond their conception and grasp. An example of outstanding moral achievement, under Buddha's inspiration, is Asoka, who acceded to the throne of the Mauryan dynasty in 273 B.C.[53] Asoka was at first a rather typical potentate in that he wished to extend his power, acquire more territory, whenever it was possible to do so. In the ninth year of his reign he sought to round off his dominions by taking over the Kingdom of the Three Kalingas located on the coast of the Bay of Bengal. His armies were successful and the Kalingas became a part of his empire. However, victory was achieved at the cost of 100,000 lives and the taking into captivity of 150,000 prisoners. Most potentates would have disregarded the horrors to concentrate on the sweetness of victory, but for some reason not explained by the historical records Asoka was overcome by remorse. He converted to Buddhism and a few years later took holy orders. His life was transformed; likewise, under his vigorous guidance, was the moral tenor of society in much of his empire.

Asoka proclaimed noninjury to living things, obedience to parents and elders, reverence to teachers, and liberality toward friends and acquaintances, which included tolerance for their creeds should these differ from one's own. But the most original and ambitious of Asoka's enterprises was to introduce some kind of welfare system for all his subjects, including animals. He began by restricting the slaughter of living creatures in his kitchen. The number killed fell from the incredible "many hundred thousands to make curries" to two peacocks and one antelope the day after his conversion (Rock Edict I).[54] He prohibited animal sacrifice at the capital and abolished the royal hunt for pleasure. He denounced extravagant ceremonies and luxurious excursions and substituted in their place edifying spectacles and pious conferences. He tried to provide care and comfort for all. "He made curative arrangements of two kinds—one for men and another for beasts. Medicinal herbs also, wholesome for men and wholesome for beasts, wherever they were lacking, everywhere have been both imported and planted. And along the roads, he caused wells to be dug and trees planted for the enjoyment of man and beast" (Rock Edict II, Pillar Edict VII).[55]

Buddhism presents an austere view of reality and the human condition. "Know that the way of the tranquil sage is a hard way: hard to find and hard to follow," says the Buddha (Nālaka Sutta).[56] No one is surprised that in practice adepts fall short of Buddha's high ideals. Where his followers have earnestly tried to pursue a disciplined life they may achieve, ironically, worldly success. In both the Orient and Europe, monasticism that begins with self-denial and dedication to hard work ends in wealth—collective if not private. Institutions dedicated to poverty and spirituality may acquire in time art treasures, productive farms, and beautiful gardens. In the process of this unplanned accumulation of worldly goods, the purity of their original vision is lost. This is a familiar story. Rather than recount it, I prefer another approach, which is to show how Buddhist belief and practice have softened as they adapt to ineradicable human weaknesses, in particular, to the human desire for comfort and consolation of both a material and a fantasy-ridden kind. I shall take my illustrations from two countries, China and Burma, that have acquired Buddhism from India.

To prepare the ground, we need to review certain key events in the life of Siddharta Gautama, who later became the Buddha. The son of a petty king, Siddharta as a child lived in extreme luxury. The Buddha himself recalled: "Monks, I was delicately nurtured, exceedingly delicately nurtured. For instance, in my father's house, lotus pools were made thus, one of blue lotuses, one of red, and another of white lotuses, just for my benefit. . . . By night and day a white canopy was held over me, lest cold or heat, dust or chaff or dew, should touch me. Moreover, I had three palaces; one for winter, one for summer, and one for the rainy season. In the four months of rain I was waited upon by minstrels, women all of them."[57] But Siddharta discovered that he was still subject to the Wheel of Existence—to old age, disease, and death. He left the palace to practice the great austerities which, however, failed to bring him enlightenment. So Siddharta resumed eating and drinking as a normal person. The turning point of his life came when he went to Bodhgava and sat under a tree. There at night, through successive stages, Siddharta finally gained knowledge of the four holy truths and the eight-fold path. He learned how to destroy the cankers of desire for existence and sensual satisfactions and the cankers of ignorance and false views that together or separately blocked deliverance.

But what is the state of deliverance? What is it like to be rid of personal existence, freed from sensual desires, and able to see reality plain? Terms used to describe Nirvana—the abode of the enlightened—are usually negative: in Nirvana, greed, lust, hatred, and ignorance do not exist. As for the positive ascriptions of purity and eternal beatitude they fail to call up any specific image, which is what one should expect because Nirvana is beyond phenomenal experience. After enlightenment the Buddha returned to the phenomenal world in order to free people from the chain of desire. Significantly he refrained from practicing the severities so common among Indian anchorites, but rather lived as a tolerant and wise individual who cured people of their passions and delusions with medicine, strong or gentle, in accordance with their capabilities and needs. Of one thing we can be certain: the Buddha never again wanted to return to the palace of his childhood and youth, or to their supernatural equivalent—paradise—for quite apart from the stern steps necessary to achieve enlightenment, mere morality (in the Buddha's view) calls for abstention from the use of large and lofty beds, from accepting silver or gold, and eating more than one meal a day.[58] Yet in Mahāyāna Buddhism, the Buddha Amitābha (Infinite Light) is believed to preside over Western Paradise, envisaged as fertile, comfortable, adorned with fragrant trees and flowers, and decorated with the most beautiful jewels and gems. Western Paradise appears to be just a more extravagant model of Siddharta's childhood playground, with the difference that in paradise one can hear the Buddha's compassionate words everywhere. In such a place, sensual as well as spiritual fulfillment is obtainable. Western Paradise, obviously, is not Nirvana. Yet the Amitābha cult in China and Japan has been strong enough to encourage the widespread belief that once a sentient being is reborn there he has attained salvation and is no longer subject to rebirth.[59]

Outside of India, Buddhism has taken on the coloration of its host culture. In China, for example, it is influenced by the Chinese people's strong desire for prosperity and numerous offspring, and by their perception of filial piety as the paramount virtue. The desire for worldly well-being and even supreme devotion to parents are not really compatible with the Buddha's doctrine. "Son, wife, father, mother, wealth, chattels, relations—all that is prized in worldly life—leave, once and for all, and roam, like the unicorn, alone!" (Sutta Nipāta).[60] Such an injunction goes directly against the traditional Chinese conception of the good and moral life, which assigns a central position to the family. Confucian scholar-officials, jealous of the success and power of the new religion, have periodically attacked it. The success of Buddhism in China, we have noted earlier, is evidence of a need for personal consolation and for certain kinds of spiritual food that the native religions and philosophies have failed to provide. However, only a very small minority could embrace the Buddha's "hard way." Accepted by large numbers were the fantasized and humanized versions of Buddhism—a Western Paradise that promises ceaseless bliss, for example, and the material rewards of the Maitreya (laughing Buddha) cult.

Maitreya was already a well-known deity in China in the fourth and fifth centuries, but it was only in the thirteenth century, when he took on the shape of a legendary Chinese monk of wrinkled forehead and bulging stomach that he gained a fond and permanent place in the Chinese imagination. The fat belly of the Buddha denotes prosperity. In some images of Maitreya, children are shown climbing all over him, and the children signify of course the paramount value of large family.[61] Popular Buddhism in China has departed far indeed from the stern teachings of the original Buddha. To the Chinese, as well as to people almost everywhere, the good life necessarily includes prosperity and numerous offspring. In the light of common day, healthy men and women nominally Buddhist must feel that not the world but the ascetic disciplines and Nirvana are illusory—overwrought creations of minds that have lost touch with the common joys of life.

Filial piety is the linchpin of Chinese morality. From this center, duty and affection extend to other human beings, though not to animals. By contrast, the Buddha exhorts an impartial loving kindness to all sentient beings, animals included. Chinese Buddhists, to gain converts, predictably emphasize those parts of Buddhist teaching that address filial piety. A *Jātaka* story from the Pali collection, translated into Chinese in the Western Chin dynasty (265–317), is among the best known. In this story, "a bodhisattva scanned the world and saw a blind couple without children who wanted to retire into the forest and live as recluses. Recognizing the dangers of such a life in the wilds the Bodhisattva chose to be reborn as the son of the blind couple so as to serve them. He was named Shan-tzu (Sāma in Pali), and when he grew up he devoted himself to helping his parents in every way. As he fetched food and drew water for his parents he became such a familiar figure in the forest that all the animals accepted him as one of them. He for his part disturbed the wild life as little as possible, to the extent of donning a covering of deerskin so as not to frighten the deer who came to drink at the watering place. One day the king of the land went hunting and shot Shan-tzu when he was in the disguise of a deer. Whereupon, suddenly, a storm arose and the birds and animals cried out in grief."

The *Jātaka* story focuses as much on a man's caring relationship with animals as with his duty to parents. To the Chinese, however, the story is important and stays in the mind because it is considered a touching illustration of filial piety. By the Sung dynasty, popular literature has accepted the Shan-tzu story as one of the twenty-four standard models of service to parents. In the later Chinese versions, the acts of sympathy to animals have been toned down or removed. In one of them, Shan-tzu (now called Yen-tzu and pushed back in time to the venerable Chou dynasty) donned a deerskin and under this disguise he was able to move among a herd of deer to obtain the milk which his aged parents needed. But in this fully Sinicized version, the wearing of the skin was merely a clever hunter's trick and not a consideration for the peace and well-being of the animals drinking by the pond.[62]

Buddhism in China is Mahāyāna or Great Vehicle, which differs from Buddhism of the Hinayāna (Lesser Vehicle) school in its expansion of spatiotemporal scale and elaboration of detail—in the way, for example, it introduces many incarnations of the Buddha, pantheons of deities, interdigitations with Chinese cosmology, and supernatural formulas and techniques for the overcoming of natural limits. Mahāyāna Buddhism is, in other words, a large and exceedingly complex cosmic-moral edifice. Few people who live in it can hope to grasp it in all its richness of legend, doctrine, and practice. One becomes familiar with a small part and derives from it what uplift and consolation one can. By comparison, Hinayāna Buddhism is simpler, but simpler does not mean easier to follow. Indeed it may mean quite the opposite, for it implies a doctrine that is more austere, less subject to casuistical interpretations, and without the alternative byways—choices for different vocations and temperaments—that a more elaborated doctrine allows.

The religion of Burma is Hinayāna or Theravāda Buddhism. (Theravāda means "the elders"). It interdicts the killing of all beings—a hard teaching which the Burmese have tried to follow. "Almost all slaughterers in Burma are Muslims," Melford Spiro reports, and "it is rare to find a Buddhist cattle-raiser," for to a Buddhist even raising animals for the slaughter is a tainted occupation. Even fishermen are viewed with distaste, and few Buddhist parents would want their daughters to marry them. "If flies, mosquitoes, or other insects alight on a Burman, he brushes them off. Similarly, if a poisonous snake is discovered in the house, it is caught and later released in a safe place."[63] By living in the Theravāda house, the Burman rises to a level of awareness and to a moral stature that he would not otherwise have. On the other hand, many revered doctrines must simply be set aside as too difficult for lay Buddhists to follow. Foremost among them is detachment. Although all the major world religions preach detachment from the "things of this world," it lies at the heart of Buddhist inspiration. Being attached is the source of all suffering. This lesson has taken hold to the degree that even Burmese villagers insist that "everything, even picking up a cup of tea, is suffering." Nevertheless the belief has little effect on practice, for like Westerners and human beings generally, Burmese villagers are strongly attached to the world's goods and pleasures—to food and sex, wives and children, fine homes and expensive clothes.

The impermanence of all things is a major Buddhist doctrine. Since the burning down of a house and the loss of political office belong to the ever-changing nature of reality, one should learn to be indifferent to them. Understandably, Buddhists have found this precept difficult to follow. Impermanence is easier to accept when it is applied to feelings and human relationships. People who want to hold on to their wealth and social status may find it convenient to regard responsibility and obligation as temporary. Why take human ties and promises as binding if it is agreed that all things, including mutual feelings, are subject to change? "He is my friend today," the Burmans say, "but he may be my enemy tomorrow."[64]

An ideal that is too demanding can be transformed into something easier to follow, but in the process the intent of the original ideal may be distorted or even turned into its opposite. Buddhism exhorts charity. Important is not the amount given but the "pure intention" of giving, for what makes a gift valuable is the spiritual quality of the donor. Most lay Burmans cannot comply with this ideal. Instead, they act as though the gift is meritorious in proportion to its amount and to the spiritual quality of the recipient. Attention is thus directed to tangible things such as food and money rather than to an inner state, and to the spiritual standing of the other rather than of self. Burmese villagers consider it good to give to orphans and widows, good to contribute money to the building of a school, but better to support the erection of a religious edifice, better still to give to monks, and best of all to give to those monks who are famous for their piety.[65]

What about the monks themselves? As people who devote their lives to an exalted and austere vocation, are they notably superior spiritually to lay Buddhists or to non-Buddhists, followers of less demanding creeds? The answer is unclear. To one practiced observer, Spiro, Burmese monks indeed show gentleness, patience, courtesy, and kindness. These traits make a powerful first impression on the visitor. As one enters a monastery and sits in the presence of a monk—with the world outside a distant noise—one does feel a certain serenity. Yet this is not the whole picture. The monks, Spiro believes, are detached, but not because they have overcome the ego and its unruly affections; rather they are detached from fear of affection, from a certain emotional timidity. The ego itself is very much alive. In interviews with monks, Spiro notes that they often indulge in self-praise and repeatedly make invidious comparisons between themselves and other monks. Their compulsive criticism of others amounts to a barely repressed hostility.[66] It is sad to think that with so much sacrifice of ordinary human happiness, these spiritual athletes have not been able to defeat even the most childish forms of vanity. The otherworldliness and serenity of a monk's life would seem to be largely an illusion. How ironic to know that a moral edifice as austere and truth-seeking as Buddhism should, for many people, turn into a haven for deceptive dreams.

Built Worlds I

4

We are born into culture. There never is a time when we are free of its guiding hand, which touches us so lightly that we are seldom aware of it. Culture is our second nature. What we do and see others close to us do seem as natural and right as breathing. This attitude of almost total unreflexive acceptance applies primarily to how we feel, think, and behave in daily life, but it applies also to artifacts. The humanly made things in our environment—clothes, tools, and shelter, for example—do not normally obtrude on our consciousness as willfully constructed. They are simply there, no more artificial than gestures and speech, and hardly more so than air and water, vegetation and earth that quietly support our being.

But at times people do become aware of culture—that is, they are sensitive to its human origin, and therefore its willed and possibly arbitrary character. A pot stands out egregiously from other pots; it is somehow not the right size and shape. A gesture or a phrase can seem affected, not suitable to the occasion. In folk or nonliterate communities, the perpetrator of the unusual is also the perpetrator of the unnatural: he or she is suspect and may be regarded as a witch. Culture itself is not in question; group values themselves are not challenged. Indeed, the shocked recognition of departures from the norm pays homage to the norm.

What, however, if doubt is directed not only at the eye-catching behavior or works of marginal individuals, who can be readily chastised and dismissed, but at the highest achievements of society as a whole, including its moral codes, its great public works and ambitious architecture?

The authority of religious and moral codes lies in the belief that they have their source in a transcendent realm and were revealed to the people by the gods and culture heroes at the beginning of time, or suddenly and dramatically to a great teacher. Commands and laws come to human beings as voices out of heaven—that is, through language. The privileged recipients of the divine message convey it in turn to their people by means of language, which is all the more effective if it has the support of ritual gestures and an appropriate setting. Language, gesture, and setting together compose a cultural world which can in time become more and more encrusted with ornamentations. A society able to create such an embellished world is likely to have at least a few critical thinkers for whom this world, because it is perceived to be humanly constructed, is uncertain in its moral sway. Such individuals may show deep ambivalence toward human creativity, proud of what it can do and yet uneasy with its larger achievements. For them, high civilization is suspect, as is, more generally, culture and even language itself. While they may accept the idea that refined artworks can enlarge human understanding, they also feel strongly that works of human ingenuity can lead people morally and intellectually astray. In this chapter, we shall explore doubt concerning the moral standing of language and culture when these are seen as excessively embellished or developed. In the next chapter, we shall turn our attention to the constructed material environment, for which a similar ambivalence exists.

Linguistic Worlds

Language is creative. A people, poor in material tools and power, can nevertheless use speech to call worlds of a tropical luxuriance into being. The Yạnomamö of the Amazon are a case in point. Their impact on the natural environment is small, but they are able to assert themselves in other ways, one of which is storytelling. Yanomamö culture is rich in stories of all kinds, prominent among which are those on the nature of the soul, the types of infernal punishment, and the physical character of the cosmos. Such stories are not sacrosanct. Individuals feel free to embellish them. In general, the Yąnomamö take pride in their ability to speak forcefully and fluently.[1]

Pride in speech is common throughout the world. Speech is widely regarded as the trait that uniquely distinguishes human beings from those who fall short of that stature. From this it follows that the more effortlessly and abundantly one is able to speak the more fully human one appears to be. Thus foreigners, because of their incomprehensible tongue, are viewed as less than fully human, and within one's own speech world stutterers are subhuman and figures of fun. In Western society, rhetoric is taught in the schools to develop force and fluency. From classical antiquity to modern times, a common perception of the orator is that he has "an abundance of things to say and of ways to say them, copia in Latin rhetoric, 'flow,' 'abundance,' such as Erasmus sought to provide in De duplici copia verborum ac rerum."[2] In our time politicians and preachers are among the professionals who are still expected to exhibit copia and fluency. Truth is not their overriding concern. It is not that they intend to deceive; what happens rather is that as they speak they feel the welling up of a rhetorical power and are swept up by the torrent of their own words.

A certain indifference to factual accuracy characterizes oral presentation. We have already noted that in an oral culture exaggeration serves to add drama and prestige to a story, making it and its useful lessons easier to remember. Furthermore, an orator is tempted to exaggerate and be factually careless because he faces a live audience that expects his words to flow. In his need to hold its attention he cannot risk frequent pauses. By contrast, a writer in the privacy of his study is not under such constraint. He can always pause and self-critically ask, "Do I really want to say this?" A written document lends itself to revision and, consequently, to economy and truth.

On the other hand, the opposite may happen. The written page is a mnemonic device that enables the writer to build up a sprawling plot and introduce a multitude of characters whose lives intricately mesh. Such a story can become a turreted castle in the air that has little to do with the social realities and psychological truth. The written page which makes critical reflection practicable obviously does not compel it. Nothing in the writing process itself curbs the inclination to distort for effect. Moreover, literary traditions differ greatly in the degree that they encourage factual accuracy. Chinese chronicles, for instance, are histories in the modern sense; they are an attempt to record historical events and personages truthfully. By contrast, Indian chronicles are a type of epic poetry that makes little demand on conformity to the facts. Indian chronicles try to beautify the past. A modern scholar notes: "They ignore precise figures, exact sequences of events, and other details of time and place. Far from exerting themselves to give exact sizes of armies, say, or expenditures, they exaggerate astronomically with magnificent and brilliant hyperbole."[3] Yet an uninhibited imagination can net a truth. For example, although premodern armies did not number in the millions, figures of this dimension happen to be appropriate when applied to the cosmos.

People's pride in their language is periodically shadowed by doubt. What stirs unease is not the ordinary daily use of language, or the lore and proverbs that have been handed down from the past, but speech that has a theatrical, "builded" character. Linguistic creations, like other manmade objects, are open to challenge, all the more so if they are conspicuous by virtue of scale or elaborateness and if they are clearly the works of familiar individuals. Nonliterate peoples are heavily dependent on the authority of speech to maintain a sense of continuity and tradition, yet among them thoughtful persons may occasionally question the genuineness of their linguistic artifacts. What the wise man says may not really be true. Perhaps stories are told and perpetuated for the consolation they provide—benign fabrications that give their listeners the mere illusion of security. Doubt of this kind may lie at the back of the Navaho's mind when he explains why he tells the coyote tale to his family. He tells it not so much because he believes in it as because "we need to have ways of thinking, of keeping things stable, healthy and beautiful. We try for a long life, but lots of things can happen to us. So we keep our thinking and our lives in order with these stories. We have to relate our lives to the stars and the sun, the animals and all of nature, or else we will go crazy or get sick."[4]

Truth dwells, if anywhere, in simple speech. Christ said: "Plain 'Yes' or 'No' is all you need to say; anything beyond that comes from the devil" (Matthew 5:37). Great teachers of the past tend to speak in aphorisms and parables, or in simple statements that command assent. They may also raise questions that invite answers and hence initiate dialogue, but they refrain from extended arguments and expositions. Large edifices of thought are likely to be the works of their talented disciples in later times, and although these can be both esteemed and influential they also invite the suspicion of being human rather than divine. Plato believed that truth, if it occurs anywhere, occurs in the sparks of exchange between individuals in earnest dialogue: truth, in any case, cannot be netted in artful speech. Confucius, a very different type of thinker from another world, also distrusted wordiness, if not words themselves. As a person who earnestly sought to influence the rulers of his time he had to use reasoned and persuasive speech. He did so knowing that in an ideally harmonious universe speech would not be necessary. "I would prefer not to speak," Confucius said. "Does heaven speak? The four seasons pursue their course; all things are produced by it, but does Heaven speak?"[5]

The appearance of a complexly argued moral-religious doctrine almost demands the countervailing emergence of its opposite in the form of simple precepts or mystical sayings. Thus a Confucian doctrine that swelled with yin-yang cosmological interlardations prepared the ground for the belief that one must return to the original teachings of the master—to the core idea of benevolence (*jen*) between persons. In Buddhism, too, the elaboration of doctrines and proliferation of deities had the effect of ushering in a school of thinking (Ch'an or Zen Buddhism) that made a virtue of pithy and apparently nonsensical speech. In Europe, the development of a theological scholarship that culminated in a *Summa Theologica* was balanced by the cult of simplicity in mysticism and in devotional works such as *The Imitation of Christ*. The newest blow against fulsome and eloquent speech was dealt by the ideological arm of science. The scientist observes nature; he classifies his findings, and in presenting them he resorts unavoidably to words, but he does not indulge in verbose egotistical discourse. The Royal Society of London championed this view and Jonathan Swift (1667–1745) made fun of it when he suggested that in the learned academy words can be dispensed with altogether. "Since words are only names for things, it would be more convenient for all men to carry about them such things as were necessary to express the particular business they are to discourse on. . . . The room where company meet who practice this art, is full of all things ready at hand, requisite to furnish matter for this kind of artificial converse."[6]

People who suspect elaborate speech may yet believe that

direct unpretentious statements and the individual words themselves contain both truth and moral lessons, and that language is to be used with the utmost respect and care. This attitude, of common occurrence in literate as well as nonliterate societies, has one root in magic—specifically, magical incantations, which in turn rest on the conviction that names capture the essence of things and words are living powers, capable of real effect. Of course, not all words have such power, nor are all names true names. Barbaric tongues, like animal noises, are without effect. Moreover, potent words in human speech can lose their potency through misuse. Confucius, in his effort to reform rulers and their governments, called for a "rectification of names" (*cheng ming*). Donald Munro explains: "The original intent [of *cheng ming*] was ethical, based on the belief that once names have firm meanings they will almost magically serve as effective standards of conduct."[7] In the West, the story of Babel—a major myth that is firmly rooted in Western consciousness—signifies a longing for an original linguistic paradise in which things have *proper* names given by God or prelapsarian Adam.

How can the original holy language be recovered? Longing for it has led to a deep and recurrent interest in magical and ritual formularies, in Cabalism and the whole esoteric tradition. Nevertheless, since classical antiquity, the reverential view of language has had its critics—thinkers who sought to strip words of their supernatural halo by arguing for their conventional nature. The most influential critic in the early modern period was John Locke. His linguistic relativism lent support to the rationalist iconoclastic posture of eighteenth-century intellectuals and social philosophers. The nineteenth century, however, witnessed a rebirth of faith in language as a fount of permanent knowledge and wisdom. What made this revitalization possible? Certain changes in the intellectual climate had helped. One was the political conservatism that followed the French Revolution, but as important was the growing prestige of comparative philology, a new systematic field of study that had about it an aura of objective science, and the rise of etymology, which gave credence once more to the type of esoteric learning that took delight in tracing word meanings to their distant, presumably purer origins. It became respectable again to see the multiplicity of tongues as, possibly, degeneration. When Sir William Jones suggested, in 1786, that an affinity existed between Sanskrit and Persian on the one hand and Greek and Latin on the other, he encouraged such belief. Etymology further promoted the idea of a holy language. Copious discourse may be little better than fabulation and even sentences can distort truth, but etymology directs its focus on individual words, which unknown to their users, carry the buried wisdom of humankind. There emerged in the Victorian era what Hans Aarsleff calls "prophets of words"—sages of learning, with a European reputation and wide influence over the public. Richard Chenevix Trench was a prime example. He saw language as a "faithful record of the good and evil working the minds and hearts of men," and, much like a "moral barometer, it indicates and permanently marks the rise and fall of a nation's life." In common with the linguistic sages of his time and of ours, he attempted to derive moral lessons from the root meaning of certain key words. Take "education" and "instruction." Trench noted, with no doubt a sense of real enlightenment, that whereas the root meaning of instruction is the filling up of a mind with knowledge, that of education is "the opening up of its own fountains," for "education must educe, being from 'educare,' which is but another form of 'educere'; and that is 'to draw out,' not 'to put in.'"[8]

The intellectual vantage point of the linguistic sage discourages empirical observation. It also tends to undermine the idea that moral knowledge is cumulative and progressive. The sage believes that if the quest is for truth and the essence of things, one must turn to the study of aboriginal, uncorrupted language. In our own time, the philosopher Martin Heidegger seems to think that a careful and reverential study of the root meaning of certain Greek and German words can uncover for us the fundamental nature of human reality. Language reveals and illuminates provided we do not presume to be its master. When we presume to speak, we speak falsely. It is speech that speaks (*Die Sprache spricht*); and speech does not merely give form and make public our understanding of being, "it *is* the house of Being." Things and their names are born together; an intimate bond exists between them. Heidegger hints at this bond when he quotes the poet Stefan Georg's words, "Let no thing be where the word is missing."[9] G. E. Moore, an analytical philosopher of a very different tradition, nevertheless shares Heidegger's mystique of language. Moore seems to believe that fundamental moral questions can be elucidated through thinking intensely about the meaning of words, that an inherited vocabulary (English) is the ultimate oracle and the final guide to life.[10]

Sages, both Victorian and those closer to our time, did not examine impolite words or slang with comparable fervor for insights into the real. This ostensible lack of interest is in sharp contrast to nonliterate folks who show a fascination for words of a sexual and excretory nature, as well as for those that tell of killing, death, and decay. The acts and conditions to which the words refer are of course a common part of human experience everywhere. They are suppressed in high culture out of deference to good taste. We have seen how people, in rebellion against the elaborate verbal edifice, seek truth and moral insight in a simpler and more direct language. This move is populist insofar as it pays respectful attention to ordinary speech, scholarly insofar as it is linked to etymological and philological research, and ascetic insofar as it aspires to simplicity and purity. But in each case, cuss and foul words are neglected: a narrow moralism censors them from ordinary speech; a received notion of propriety makes a sustained interest in them seem improper for the scholar; and a still potent puritanism warns the model citizen to shun them as from temptation.

Culture and Civilization

In creating a humanized environment, language has temporal priority and primacy over physical manipulation. Nevertheless, when we think of making a world today we have the imposition of material changes in mind. Moreover, it seems natural to credit people everywhere with pride in material achievement. When cultivators clear the bush to create a landscape of fields and houses, they do so in answer to the needs of survival, but that cannot be all: the humanized world, existing visibly and tangibly before them, gives shape to their lives and serves at the same time as a flattering and reenforcing mirror of their humanity. To be driven out of this world by human enemies or natural disaster is a searing experience from which the victims do not easily recover.

Yet the ethnographic and historical literature suggests that what premodern people expressly value is not the large created world of houses and fields but rather the less tangible things— language, ceremony and ritual, moral codes, lineage, as well as small material objects such as figurines or pots that, in association with ritual performance, have come to be invested with the numinous power of ancestral and nature spirits. Paramount in value for many societies (literate and nonliterate) is lineage. Its prestige lies in its effectiveness in guaranteeing an individual's and a people's immortality. Lineage signifies permanence rather than fields that can be overrun by wilderness, houses that can rot, and cities that can be razed to the ground.[11] I have just said that a humanized landscape may serve as a flattering mirror to its creators, and this is true. But it need not be so and it has not always been so. Curiously, subsistence cultivators may not even see the landscape as their own handiwork. It simply exists for them; it has always been there. When they do pay it attention, they may be reminded of the constant and unpleasant labor needed to maintain it. Consider the Gimi of New Guinea and the Lele of Kasai (Africa). These villagers experience their humanized worlds as arenas of stress—physical stress in the struggle to keep the fields productive and sociopsychological stress in the unavoidable tensions of living close together in mutual dependence. City people, we know, periodically feel the need to escape from the harrowing demands of culture for the simple life in nature's midst. But even villagers can feel this need. The Gimi and the Lele have at times found life in cultural space too taxing and have yearned for the adjoining forest, which provides them with ample game and fruits as well as a cool shelter that needs no repair.[12]

Culture makes people truly human and distinguishes them from other animals. This is a widely held view. Common sense suggests that if this is true of culture, then *high* culture in complex societies enables people to explore the further reaches of human potential in both an intellectual and a moral-spiritual sense. Nevertheless, ambivalence toward culture and especially its larger works has always existed. The desire to build is shadowed by the fear that the gods or nature might take offense, by the dim awareness that ambitious constructions are perpetrated by the few often in arrogant disregard for the welfare of the many, and that they drain energy from the proper pursuits of civilization, such as the fine arts, literature, and philosophy. Finally, there is the opinion that not only monumental buildings and cities but even the most refined arts and philosophies are largely irrelevant to the highest human goal of all—moral excellence.

Ambivalence toward culture is expressed in a variety of

ways, but I think most clearly and concisely in attitudes toward progress. The basic question then is: Are people building a better world, and if so, in what sense is it better? Put bluntly thus, even in the West the idea of progress was embraced confidently for only a brief period lasting from the eighteenth to the end of the nineteenth century.[13] In our time, few individuals with intellectual pretensions would give it unqualified endorsement. Historically, people have seldom been able to feel totally at ease with their own achievement unless they perceive it as sanctioned by a transcendental power and as a step toward a more stable and perfect world. To illustrate this thesis, we will consider the Chinese and the Greeks in the early vigorous stages of their civilization when, objectively and retrospectively viewed, they would seem to have made impressive progress on all fronts.

Progress in Traditional China

The idea of progress presupposes a more primitive and less happy state from which a people have moved up by their own effort. It cannot exist if either an original Eden or a Golden Age is postulated. In China, the Taoists have postulated an original Eden. The *Huai-nan-tzu* speaks of an era of Great Purity during which men, genuine and simple, sparing of speech and spontaneous in conduct, were united in spirit to the yin and yang and enjoyed harmonious relationship with the four seasons. Then came hunting and fishing, the chopping down of trees to build houses, and the mining of mountains for minerals. As a cultural world emerged, the quality of life paradoxically declined, for nature itself turned less accommodating and people had to work harder to earn a livelihood. Another chapter of the same Taoist work presents an even more primitive Eden in which people could without fear tread on serpents and grasp the tails of tigers and entrust their young to be nurtured in birds' nests.[14] This happy state ended with the emergence of civilization, which was not only a new, materialist way of life but a new, analytical mode of consciousness that existed nowhere else in nature. This mode, according to the *Tao Teh Ching*, has the fatal power to isolate the parts so that they lose their proper places within the unity of the whole. In isolation, the parts become the irresistible allurements of sensual pleasure, wealth, honor, power, and even individual moral perfection. When people strive for these separate and often incompatible goals, they create all the artifacts and artifices (*ta wei*) of society.[15]

Civilization has the double meaning of refinement and power. It promotes gentleness in speech and manners as well as the cultivation of the fine arts and literature; at the same time, it seeks to establish sociopolitical institutions that enable people to control and transform nature. In both Europe and China, the primary sense of civilization has been refinement rather than power. In Europe, the word civilization itself appeared only in the middle of the eighteenth century as a synonym for civility. In China, the word *wen* meant originally an articulated pattern, thence a literary composition, a pattern of culture, and the refined attainments of an individual. First, there was the simple undifferentiated stuff (*chih*) or unsophisticated goodness; later came the differentiated *wen*. The idea of progress is clearly embraced by this ordering of events, but the new must not totally displace the old. Confucius said: "When simple goodness [*chih*] prevails over cultivation [*wen*] you get the boorishness of the rustic. When cultivation prevails over simple goodness, you get the [slick smoothness] of the clerk. Only when simple goodness and cultivation are duly blended do you get the noble man."[16] Confucius himself favored cultivation; he promoted ceremony and ritual which in his time were often accompanied by music and dance. He and his followers could see that the proper performance of the higher rites depended on a certain level of material support. They also knew that material culture and refinement (*wen*) could deteriorate into hollow shows, pursued for themselves, thus becoming hindrances to rather than supports for the practice of *li* and the human virtues.

In distinction to the Taoists, Confucius believed in a Golden Age in which people lived peacefully under wise princes—that is, he envisaged a cultivated society rather than a primitive Eden. Confucius was committed to civilization. What had appeal for him was an achieved, all-embracing, ethicopolitical order; and it was this order, rather than the recurrent natural processes, that best exemplified the Way or *tao*. Confucius discerned a Golden Age in antiquity, which included the Hsia and the Shang dynasties as well as the Early Chou. He even suggested that the Chou represented a higher realization of the

Way because it could benefit from the experience and accomplishments of its two predecessors. "Chou could survey the two preceding dynasties. How rich is the pattern of its culture. We follow Chou!"[17]

Civilization rests on an agricultural base. In traditional China, rulers and ministers recognized this dependence when they participated ceremonially in the rhythms of nature. Agricultural life was closely integrated with a cosmological world view and ritual. Knowledge of the world view and correct practice of ritual lay at the heart of what it meant to be civilized. Farmers enjoyed a well-defined, essential place in traditional society. The role of merchants was, however, more ambivalent. They were not tied to land, did not make things, tended to encourage a dependence on luxuries, and could not be fitted into any cosmological schema. Yet in the densely populated, prosperous states of ancient China, it must have been obvious to everyone that merchants played an important role in economic life. Mencius was sufficiently supportive of merchants to urge King Hsuan not to levy excessive taxes on them. Merchants generated wealth and ought to, as Mencius put it to King Hsuan, "enjoy the refuge of your marketplace."[18] Ssu-ma Ch'ien also spoke up for merchants and manufacturers. He agreed with other Confucian scholars that farming was the most honorable enterprise; on the other hand, he could see that trade and industry earned more profit and said so. Recognition of merchants by such influential figures as Mencius and Ssu-ma Ch'ien suggests that wealth-generating and change-inducing economic activities received a measure of official approval.

Although civilization is obviously power over nature, people in premodern times could not altogether rid themselves of the feeling that its exercise was impious. Only semidivine culture heroes could be doers on a grand scale without risk of impiety. In China, the supernatural element in myths has been toned down or removed. The heroes were depicted not as semidivine beings but as wise human rulers who labored on the people's behalf against nature's recurrent threats. Nonetheless, a certain ambiguity exists in the accounts. Consider the story of Yu, known to myth and history as the conqueror of flood and founder of the first hereditary dynasty, the Hsia. Yu and his father Kun are shown as human beings, although their original superhuman status is betrayed by their names, which contain animal radicals. In one version of the myth, flood waters rose and threatened widespread destruction. The people were miserable. Their groans were heard by the Supreme Lord who commanded Kun to control the flood. Kun attempted to dam up the waters and failed. Yu, his son, was asked to continue with the task. Rather than trying to dam up the waters, Yu dug channels to drain them off to the sea. He was successful and thereby made the land suitable for human habitation. Note that the hero Yu succeeded by following the grain of nature rather than by fighting against it, as his father had tried to do. In another version of the story, more laden with supernatural elements, Yu (whose name contains the radical for reptile) received the help of a dragon which showed him where the channels should be dug by trailing its tail on the ground. In myths concerning Yu, he was often presented as an extremely hard worker. Flood control called for sustained practical action rather than an appeal to the power of magical formula and ritual. Yu worked so hard that he wore the nails off his hands; on his travels, he was so busy supervising the waterworks that though he passed the door of his home several times he did not stop to visit.[19] Yu fought nature either by following its own grain or with supernatural help; and he did so to make it possible for his people to live. It was for this specifically human end, and not because he began the process of building a sophisticated cultural world, that the Chinese have consistently admired him and attributed to him the highest virtue.

Ambivalence toward civilization is evident not only in myths but also in the historical works of thinkers such as Mo-tzu and Mencius. Mo-tzu, like Confucius, believed that good order was an achievement rather than a natural state; but unlike Confucius, he thought that the good order achieved under the rule of the wise kings was not one of partial loyalties to family, kinsfolk, or one's own state, but one of love for the whole of humankind. Mo-tzu's view of the attainable depends very much on whether the moral or the material sphere is in question. On the one hand, he had so much confidence in human nature that he could believe that people at one time were capable of universal love and that such love was still possible; on the other hand, although Mo-tzu himself emerged out of the artisan class, he had no great faith in material culture: he did not envisage and would not have wished for a world of material abundance. He spoke of the sage kings of the past as having built houses just high enough to avoid the damp, sturdy enough to withstand the threats of nature, and with walls high enough to keep the sexes apart. Houses, in other words, were built out of necessity and to sustain a moral life, not for show. Mo-tzu believed that luxury could be pursued only at the expense of the people.[20]

Mencius held a similar view. He was, however, less a populist than Mo-tzu: his idea of the *chün-tzu* or superior man presupposed the availability of leisure to cultivate the mind; moreover, Mencius assumed that those who worked with the mind deserved greater esteem than those who worked with the body. This Confucian sage, who could find something good to say about the merchant class, no doubt also recognized that the rulers needed a certain level of material affluence to maintain the dignity of court rituals. Nevertheless, when the rulers of petty kingdoms asked Mencius whether they were entitled to their magnificent possessions, he referred them to King Wen of old who had a hunting park that was open to woodcutters and trappers; more important, King Wen saw fit to indulge in luxuries only after his people had reached a certain level of prosperity. Parks and gardens have always been an amenity of civilization. We tend to regard them as art and as productive of innocent wholesome pleasure. Yet moralists have periodically spoken out against them. When Mencius looked at the great parks and gardens of his time, he saw evidences of immorality. "After the death of the Emperors Yao and Shun," he observed, "the principles that mark sages fell into decay. Oppressive sovereigns, arising one after another, pulled down houses to make ponds and lakes so that the people knew not where they could rest in quiet, and threw fields out of cultivation to form gardens and parks so that the people could not get clothes and food."[21]

Finally, we may note that Chinese ambivalence toward world-building is revealed in the attitude of historians toward the two emperors, Wen and Wu, of the Former Han dynasty. Without question Wen has been the favorite among the traditionalists. He was an exemplary "refrain-from-action" (*wu wei*) ruler, who dressed his empress in homespun and lived himself in a modest palace. His reign happened to correspond to a period of peace during which the people were able to enjoy a state of relative well-being, and for these blessings Confucian scholars, preeminently Pan Ku (32–92 A.D.), gave him high praise. Emperor Wen was, however, simply fortunate; he did not face much less solve the mounting problems of the empire ranging from the external threat of the barbarians to the internal threat of private estates that had become arrogant with wealth and power. He left these problems for his successors to solve, in particular, Emperor Wu, an activist who made it his duty to demonstrate to the world the glory of Han rule. Emperor Wu constructed towers, palaces, and vast parks in the capital at Ch'ang-an, which dazzled both citizens and foreign envoys; he centralized his administration and thereby weakened the power of feudal lords and wealthy merchants; he extended the rule of law, thus adopting the governmental tool of the Legalists, yet promoted Confucianism over other schools of thought; he traveled and showed himself to his subjects throughout the empire, performing sacrifices to the gods and spirits on the way. The scale of his achievements stirred national pride and confidence. Another golden age would seem to have arrived. But Emperor Wu also had many critics from different layers of society. Local populations objected to carrying the heavy cost of imperial road construction. Confucian scholar-officials criticized him for his political and architectural excesses and abhorred his search for personal immortality in magic. To administer a sprawling populous empire, a large measure of centralized rule supported by standardized (bureaucratic) procedures and periodic ceremonial display was necessary. Emperor Wu began his reign well, but toward the end his lust to build, to dominate nature and extend territory, and to achieve personal immortality, showed the flaws of an imagination so inflated that it could no longer accept limits—it aspired to transcend the natural cycles of life and death.[22]

Progress in Greek Classical Antiquity

Like the Chinese, the Greeks envisaged a Golden Age in the distant past. Unlike them this age was not an achievement of human beings—a cultural world—but rather a gift of the Olympian gods. The Greek Golden Age boasted a naturally fertile land that "gave up her fruits unasked." People lived off it free from burdensome work and sorrow until they died in sleep, after which they continued their lives as the holy spirits of the earth. The age of gold was succeeded by those of baser metals. In later times, the land remained fertile, but people could not derive benefit from it because they had abandoned the sacred rites. In place of a life of ease they had to toil for a meager living.

Rather than enjoy the fruits of the earth freely as in the age of gold, by the bronze age they became meat-eaters. They had lost their innocence and learned how to kill. Their bodies, without their earlier powers of resilience, wasted away before ending in death. Hesiod's story speaks primarily to the theme of moral degeneration. Gold, silver, bronze, and iron carry moral overtones and serve to suggest stages of moral decline rather than of cultural and technological change. Such a story obviously denies any idea of progress.[23] Equally inimical are legends that attribute the arts and crafts to the tutelage and patronage of the gods and culture heroes. Arts and crafts, being coeval with the origin of the world, are as they have always been.

In contrast to and alongside these views are those that express a belief in human ingenuity—in the power of human beings to create a world with or without the help of the gods. Hesiod's version of the Promethean myth suggests that men, far from being given the arts and crafts, possess and practice them against the divine will. By drawing attention to human initiative and power, the myth raises the old and recurrent question of piety, for it can seem impious to steal fire from Zeus and take the path of culture. The idea of progress, already present in the seventh century, is much more clearly articulated and common in writings of the classical period. Ludwig Edelstein has collected the evidence, which I will now use for a sketch of the Greek attitude toward culture and the built world. The purpose behind this sketch is to see how the Greeks relate material achievement—a product of human ingenuity and imagination—with the good life, that is, the moral life.[24]

Among the pre-Socratic philosophers of the sixth century, Xenophanes stood out as one who most clearly expressed the idea of progress. He noted, for instance, that "the gods did not reveal all things from the beginning; rather men through their own search have found in the course of time that which is better." Progress was not inevitable, for as Xenophanes surveyed the past he could see retrogression. Nevertheless he believed that on the whole the human estate was improving and that, moreover, it would continue to improve. He was helped to reach this view, Edelstein says, by his skepticism concerning the gods traditionally credited with introducing human culture and, more important, by witnessing the almost revolutionary changes of economy and technology in his time. Outstanding among them were the use of coin money, the standardization of measurements and weights, and in the field of engineering the construction of the tunnel near Miletus and of the long bridge over the Hellespont. To judge from the memoranda of the architects who erected the great temple of Artemis at Ephesus, builders took pride in finding ingenious devices for the completion of their work.[25]

Xenophanes argued for new values. Rather than give laurels to warriors or their peace-time surrogates, the athletes, he thought that they should be bestowed on artisans, engineers, and thinkers who competed not only with each other but with the dead as well; that is, they attempted to improve upon the works of the dead, and by doing so they enabled people to find in time a better life. Xenophanes' was a minority view. His contemporaries generally held artisans and philosophers in low esteem. Although society by the sixth century had climbed from the rude living conditions of the heroic age to a markedly higher level of refinement, the ideology remained aristocratic, which meant that peak moments of existence were still thought to be those that gave immediate sensual satisfaction—games, festivals, and the great affairs of the city. Activities that led to cumulative achievement but lacked immediate sensory arousal in the presence of partisans and spectators were far less popular and prestigious.[26]

The idea of progress gained wider acceptance in the fifth century, although by no means all thinkers considered it worthy of attention. Among those who did were Anaxagoras and Democritus and Sophists such as Protagoras and Hippias. In distinction to Xenophanes, these later believers in progress were concerned with the broad issue of the stages in the rise of civilization. How could human beings acquire culture and rise above mere animal life? One answer was that, unlike the brutes, they had hands, which enabled them to develop skills. Human superiority thus had a biological basis. The upward path was, however, uncertain. As Protagoras saw it, despite the natural advantages human beings possessed, their existence was for some time precarious because they could not get along with each other. They tried to live at first separately but were unable to cope with predation by wild animals; they sought refuge in the cities but found they could not live together in peace and so had to disperse again. Protagoras concluded, then, that people must first recognize reverence, justice, and the need for reconciliation as the ordering principles of communal life—in other words, they must first possess the art of politics—before they could live harmoniously in each other's presence and enjoy the security and amenities of a city.[27]

Protagoras appears to have conceived the physical city as a conglomeration of houses without any overall design: houses huddle together confusedly for warmth and security just as human beings might do. A real city, however, must show some design—some evidence of centralized planning and control. Its existence presupposes the habit of collective effort under a working sociopolitical structure of large compass. In the thought of Protagoras, artisanal and material achievement is put in a separate category from the endowment and cultivation of the sociopolitical virtues. His doing so prompts one to raise the general question: How did thinkers in the classical period conceive of the relationship between material progress and progress in the intellectual, aesthetic, and moral realms? To answer this question, we need to distinguish between pure and qualified progressivists. Pure progressivists viewed culture optimistically as moving forward in stages from primitivity to civilization, and they took civilization to mean all those things that differentiated people from animals. Thus, pure progressivists probably saw material and spiritual advancement as one process. By contrast, qualified progressivists did not recognize a connection between the various components of culture: one component might advance while others stayed put, and indeed advance in one component might cause the decline of another. In the fifth century, thinkers (for example, Herodotus) still commonly assumed that progress consisted in a succession of separate, unrelated inventions and that these inventions did not have a past. Progress, in other words, was the adding of new things to whatever had previously existed rather than a movement with a historical momentum that necessitated changes in culture along a broad front.[28]

Other lines of thought further complicated the idea of progress. There was the view, reported by Plato, that whereas arts such as medicine, husbandry, and gymnastics developed the powers of nature and could show progress up to the limit of nature's potential, the fine or shadowy art of politics had little in common with nature and was a matter of philosophical opinion, subject to endless disputes.[29] Such a view of politics impaired belief in moral-social progress. Against it was the opinion that politics was an art or a skill, and like other arts and skills

the new was superior to the old. Thucydides, for example, believed that in political skill "the new must always prevail over
the old." He did not, however, have moral superiority in mind.
The new was simply more effective; it could uphold the state
better than could the outworn methods of the past.[30]

In the fifth century, the material standard of living in
Greece was probably no higher than it was a century earlier.
Greek citizens did not feel that it had to be better; and although
they appreciated economic power and advances in political and
military technology they did not aspire to greater control over
their physical environment. Progress meant greater knowledge
of the eclipses, better sculpture, more serene music rather than
larger houses and greater volume of commercial exchange and
industrial production. The Greeks did not necessarily couple
material and technical progress with enlightenment in the social
and moral-aesthetic sphere; or, if they did wonder about the
effect of the one upon the other they thought that it was ambivalent. Skill in political art could lead to greater efficiency but
also to more tyrannical control, and improvements in military
art were as likely to encourage more wars of greater violence as
to impose peace. Thinkers might belong to different philosophical schools and yet agree that the rise of civilization did not
entail moral progress for either the individual or society. Sophists, by subscribing to the view that "might is right," ruled out
any possibility of moral improvement. Thucydides seems to
have thought that material abundance provided the ground for
the rise of political power, but political power unfortunately lent
itself to corruption.[31] Sophocles, for all his enthusiasm for man's
dominion over nature in *Antigone*—man conquering all but
death itself—concluded that man's ingenious engines were as
likely to lead in haste to evil as to good. Democritus was a pro-
gressivist who yet declared that human existence was immersed
in difficulty and pain, which could be palliated not so much by
material abundance as by limiting one's needs.[32]

In the fifth century, the idea of progress probably attracted
more adherents than the older idea of a Golden Age. Nevertheless, the Golden Age continued to have a strong appeal. From
experience the Greeks learned that civilized life could mean economic competition and social unrest, as well as aggressive policies that made wars frequent and, with the help of technology,
more devastating. Whereas a Protagoras was able to make fun
of the "noble savage," and announce that if his partisans were

compelled to live with him they would soon long to "revisit the rascality of this world," the fact remains that there were such partisans who liked to depict better times in the distant past or in distant lands, and who even had praise for animals whose lives were imagined to be much more carefree than those of human beings.[33]

As the fifth century drew to a close, frequent political turmoil, the decline in power of independent city-states, and the apparent dissolution of inherited forms of social life made the idea of progressive culture seem vain. New philosophical schools produced thinkers who emphasized self-sufficiency— the virtue and dignity of a self-contained existence. Moderates among them, such as Antisthenes and Aristippus—followers of Socrates—were not opposed to all acquisitions of knowledge; indeed, to Aristippus, cultivating the mind was essential to being human. But if they believed in education they stressed ethics to the neglect of other branches of learning. Both thinkers concerned themselves primarily with the goodness and happiness of the individual, and these qualities were more likely to be acquired at a distance from the demands and distractions of society.[34] A trend discernible in the fifth century became far more evident in the fourth century, when the oppressive complexities of urban life made the simplicities of rural living, idealized in bucolic poetry, attractive even to cosmopolites. The Cynics who appeared at this time went the extra step and condemned civilization altogether. Diogenes considered it a positive impediment to virtue. All the improvements of civilization, rather than promote courage and justice, merely fueled the appetite for endless pleasure. As against the accretions of culture which fostered a softening of body and spirit, Diogenes had praise for animals and "the first men," who were able to live without fire, houses, and clothes, without any nourishment other than those provided by the earth itself, and without the conventions and laws of social existence.[35]

Built Worlds II   5

In the last chapter, we have noted that the creation of a material world has aroused unease among cultivators of simple means as well as among people in technically advanced societies such as China and Europe.[1] In this chapter, we shall look more closely at one complex society and culture—the European in order to see how certain key ideas concerning the good and the appropriate have emerged and developed; and we will do so in one broad context, namely, the transformation of nature. In Europe, this transformation has ranged in scale and intensity from clearings in the forest to broad sweeps of cleanly tilled fields, from modest vegetable gardens to grandly designed landscapes and architecture, from work unselfconsciously performed in answer to the needs of livelihood to work done with much forethought in conscious awareness of creating art.

Rural Landscape

Historically, people have tended to view the countryside more as nature than as art, more as a timeless triad of forest, pasture, and field than as a humanly constructed landscape.[2] In archaic Greece, Hesiod conceived of an earth that during the Golden Age was able to produce abundant fruit.

He did not, however, have wild nature in mind; rather he, like Homer—that other great teacher of the Greeks—envisaged an orderly countryside of fields and groves that could only have been made by human beings and maintained with effort.[3] Awareness of human world-making was thus suppressed. Such suppression occurred not only in a remote and primitive past but also subsequently in history, and it helps to explain a curious fact, namely, the prolonged dominance of environmentalism—the idea that climate and topography governed human life—in Western thought. Whereas to us it is obvious that the inhabitants of the Mediterranean basin have not merely submitted to nature but have artfully and conspicuously altered it, to the Greeks and Romans their densely textured landscape of vineyards and irrigation ditches, villages and villas, and hills denuded by goats, has always been (more or less) that way, and was as natural as "the winds for which there were so many names, the deep blueness of the sea, and the bright Mediterranean skies."[4]

We see, then, that in the Western world one major achievement of culture—agriculture—was taken to be "almost nature" rather than a willful transformation or distortion of it. Images of the good and the moral could therefore draw upon the rural scene and its presumed ways of life. Hesiod significantly used an image of ripening fields to stand for the prelapsarian age of gold. Farmers and farm life, and the farm itself, represented the good. Greek writers of the classical period, notably Aristotle, were generous in praise. Aristotle characterized farmers as "the first and best kind of populace" and believed that "there is no difficulty in constructing democracy where the bulk of the people live by arable or pastoral farming." Roman writers could rise to even greater enthusiasm. Cicero wrote that, among human occupations, "none is better than agriculture, none more profitable, none more delightful, none more becoming in a free man."[5]

One of the fullest praises of farm life in antiquity is Xenophon's (ca. 430–355 B.C.). He drew attention first to the material advantages, the "food and nourishments that afford the greatest pleasures, the flowers that can be used to decorate temples and give the most fragrant odors." He then noted that farm work made the laborers healthy and strong, and their supervisors alert and manly, for "they must exercise themselves with walking." The farm encouraged hospitality: there was no better place to shelter strangers in winter and entertain friends in summer. On the farm people became brave and resourceful for they needed these qualities to protect the earth's produce against wild beasts. Husbandmen were loyal. When enemies threatened their country they rose to defend it, whereas the artisans would "choose to sit still in the way they have been brought up than put themselves into the least danger."[6]

Praising agriculture has become, since the eighteenth century, a commonplace rhetoric of the Western world. In the eighteenth century, Italian poets celebrated the growing of rice and hemp in verse. In France, the Marquis de Saint-Lambert addressed poetic eulogies to the turnip. In England, pastoralism, as a literary genre, was revived by Alexander Pope and Ambrose Philips. But of the multitude of encomiums directed at farm life and the farmer, perhaps the most influential is Thomas Jefferson's ringing declaration: "Those who labour in the earth are the chosen people of God . . . whose breasts he has made his peculiar deposit for substantial and genuine virtue."[7] These were not mere words, for the sentiment expressed by them has been translated into political programs that have deeply affected every major area of American life. In the last two hundred years, the virtues attributed to country folk are much the same as those given by Xenophon and writers of the classical period. If a new emphasis has been added, it is (especially in the United States) the farmer's political integrity and the idea of a wholesome family cooperatively engaged in humankind's most basic task. A common weakness in the poetic and political literature of praise is its sentimentality: the picture that emerges is far too sunny and immaculate to be real. Yet a principal reason for admiring farm life, noted in both ancient and modern times, is its direct bruising encounters with the real, its stoical character, its familiarity with injury, disease, and death.[8]

Farm life, being close to nature, is praised. For the same reason, it is deemed—contradictorily—crude and ignoble, at least the part that stretches beyond the well-managed farms of the prosperous and the estates of the rich. Members of the governing class have traditionally shown contempt for laborers and especially for laborers in the field. Even when they give approval they seem to do so condescendingly. The phrase "children of the earth" is suggestive. To praise is to liken the peasants to children; to condemn is to liken them to animals. Either way laborers, bound to their biological nature and to the soil, lack the ingenuity and the power to create a material world.

Of course, this is quite untrue. Peasant-cultivators *have* created a large and intricate material world. But it is not recognized as such by society's elite who are blinded to the fact by their keen awareness of the fundamental impotence of people who depend on the land for sustenance. Peasants are not only socially and politically impotent, they are also physically powerless to ensure an adequate yield of food no matter how hard they try. It has been a common belief in premodern Europe that labor does not guarantee fruit. In the traditional Christian view, labor is a form of punishment for the original Fall from grace, and its value for sinful men lies largely in its power to redeem. Fruitfulness, whether of land or of other living things, is a matter for divine Providence, which cannot be constrained. Given the uncertainty of harvest in Europe throughout the premodern period this dictum must seem a self-evident truth. John Calvin (1509–1564) admonished: "Nor do we believe, according as man will be vigilant and skillful, according as they have done their duty well, that they can make their land fertile; it is the benediction of God which governs all things." And the prelate Jacques Bossuet (1628–1704) said: "At each moment, the hope of the harvest and the unique fruit of all our labors may escape us; we are at the mercy of the inconstant heavens that bring rain upon the tender ears."[9]

Changes in the landscape, as a result of human effort, might be vast but if they occurred over a long period of time they could seem slow and almost natural. As Francis Bacon put it, "The improvement of the ground is the most natural obtaining of riches; for it is our great mother's blessing, the earth's; but it is slow."[10] If anywhere we can point to the countryside and say, "an obvious artifact," they are surely the reclaimed marshes of the Low Countries, which by the seventeenth century had already acquired their artificial geometric appearance of neat polders intersected by canals and supervised by windmills. But the changes were not the result of dramatic fiats laid down from above; rather they took place slowly over the centuries—indeed millennia—through the effort of countless millions of forgotten individuals, many of whom were peasants and petty farmers. From the late Middle Ages onward, however, changes did occur at a faster pace: productivity rose strikingly with innovations in techniques of farming and in the control of water. The standard of living in the Low Countries noticeably improved, and yet even in the seventeenth century it showed a great deal of variation from farm to farm, and even prosperous farmers continued to live in a state of uncertainty, their well-being still dependent on the vagaries of weather.[11]

England's "agricultural revolution" of the eighteenth century drew heavily on the technical innovations of the Low Countries. Although the changes that had taken place were neither so original nor so fast and widespread as to warrant the word "revolution," nevertheless the word is appropriate if we think of a shift in consciousness: more than ever English landowners and farmers were conscious of their ability to control nature—to have mastery over the processes of food production and to see the farm estate as a humanly created landscape. Englishmen, armed with capital and scientific knowledge, believed that God's providence could indeed be constrained. Not only fertility but beauty was something that human beings could create and own. Agricultural societies for the dissemination of ideas were established. Visitors from France and Germany came to admire not only the productivity but the comeliness of the English countryside. In this respect, Gainsborough's famous painting "Mr. & Mrs. Andrewes" is revealing. The background for the squire and his wife was not a great garden but a rural scene of rich harvest and livestock.[12] Indeed, the landscape garden sought inspiration from the farm, and both were evidently the works of men.

Consciousness raised issues other than productivity and comeliness. What was the moral standing of the rural landscapes that emerged in the course of the eighteenth century? Up till this time, "moral" was essentially mores or custom: human obligations to each other and to nature were dictated by immemorial ways. Certainly, socioeconomic inequality was not seriously questioned anywhere. In the countryside, it was assumed that the landowner had broad legal rights as well as customary privileges over his peasants, tenants, and hired hands, that the one enjoyed the abundant fruits of proprietorship, the other the much smaller rewards of their tenant rights and labor. A new moral sensitivity surfaced, however, in the eighteenth century, which in Europe was a time of not only scientific but social revolution. Reform-minded observers, while they appreciated the productivity of the rapidly changing country scene, could not rest content with it: they were driven to raise questions of an explicitly social and moral nature. Arthur Young (1741–1820), for example, recognized the need to modernize agriculture with large infusions of capital, yet he believed that such a step necessarily enhanced the predominance of the landed interest. Enclosing land to create large compact units, more amenable to scientific experimentation and to the making of profit, destroyed the livelihood of small tenant farmers and farm laborers who depended on the resources of the commons, and it disrupted the social institutions of village community that supported, however inadequately, the poor, the old, the sick, and the disabled, all of whom came to be seen as unwanted burdens. To morally sensitive eyes, rich land could take on a dark meaning. Both George Crabbe (1754–1832) and William Cobbett (1763–1835) noted an inverse relationship between the richness of the soil and the condition of the laborers. Where one found a rich corn country, the laborers in it, deprived of the resources of the commons, were likely to be miserable, but where the land was too poor to have tempted capitalist farming and remained heavily wooded, the laboring people could feed their pigs in the woods, trap wild game, and do, as Cobbett put it, "pretty well."[13]

A different kind of question with moral overtones emerged in the argument between those who would push scientific agriculture very far and those who saw it, when pushed too far, as commercial greed and at the same time a war against organic life—and ultimately human life. Consider the transformation of European and, later, American agriculture in the period between 1750 and 1900. In the eighteenth century, enclosure proceeded apace in England (followed by France and parts of Germany) together with the introduction of new agricultural techniques. One consequence was a certain simplification of the social scene. The complex quasi-feudal order of the centuries unraveled sufficiently to become two distinctive realities: on the one side were profit-conscious landowners and smaller farmers who have benefited from the consolidation of their fields, and, on the other, tenant farmers with holdings too small to be economical after enclosure and landless laborers. As for the use of the land, agricultural practice became at first *more* rather than less intricate: witness, the adoption of a rotational system that added root crops and nitrogen-fixating legumes to the traditional succession of grains. But as agricultural technology continued to advance in our period, farming did become simpler, more labor efficient, more profitable, and it culminated in the monoculture of large commercial estates. Soil productivity no longer depended on a complex rotational system when, beginning with the works of chemists such as Sir John Benet Lawes

(1814–1900) in England and Justus von Liebig (1803–1873) in Germany, fertilizers made up of simple chemical elements or compounds gained acceptance. As powerful machines came into use toward the end of the nineteenth century, agriculture was pushed further toward simplification. Vast fields of corn or wheat serve as a vivid image of boundless wealth—they *are* wealth and an extraordinary example of technological success— but to ecologically minded critics such as the geographer Carl Sauer (1889–1975) they evoke paradoxically images of poverty: genetic poverty in the diminished gene pool and, more generally, in the diversity of life; and human poverty in the simple-minded exercise of power over nature, and the single-minded quest for profit at the expense of other human values.[14]

Critics may feel that large-scale commercial farmers are indulging in technological fantasy. Against monocultural estates, they evoke an attractive picture of villages and farms that "grew" gradually and wisely over time. No doubt such villages and farms existed. They were a way of life, redolent of human warmth and happiness in good times, but full of suffering when harvests—too frequently—failed. It gives us a certain perspective to remember not only the suffering but also the fact that often no clear line can be drawn between "natural" landscapes of traditional agriculture and willed landscapes of commercial enterprise. They are better seen as a range of types that differ from each other in degree of economic motivation, complexity, and the need for overall planning. Moreover, agricultural change in modern times has not always been, straightforwardly, toward simplification. A planned landscape, originally simple, can in time become complex through the unplanned additions of nature and of human beings. The landscape of East Anglia, for example, has its roots in the ambitious enclosure movements of the eighteenth century, which were an exercise of will aimed at agricultural improvements and greater profit. By law the arable land was divided into semirectangular fields, and these were often laid out in disregard of the topographical contours. There was an air of defiant artificiality in the drainage ditches, the straight hawthorn hedges, and the regular rows of trees. Local farmers and nature lovers commented adversely on the starkness. Yet in a few generations this landscape "has evolved into a pleasing and highly diversified ecosystem; its ditches and hedges harbor an immense variety of plants, insects, song birds, rodents, and larger mammals."[15]

The word "ecosystem" in the above sentence is a new technical term favored by modern naturalists. Since the environmental movement of the 1960s, however, words such as ecosystem, ecology, and their cognates have also gained a broad, diffuse, moral meaning. Nowadays, to label a landscape "ecologically sound" is to give it high praise rather like saying of someone that he is morally sound, or of food that it is good and wholesome. Implicit in all these terms is the idea of the natural whole, of things working together providentially in complex harmony, and of the human obligation to maintain it. Carl Sauer, when he uses the word ecology, eschews its narrow technical meaning; he uses it, rather, as a metaphor for human responsibility toward nature, not only because it provides the ultimate support for all human needs and aspirations but also on account of its own inherent beauty. Aldo Leopold, perhaps more than any other single individual in our time, has taught Americans to pay closer attention to the integrity of land and wild life: it is he who has successfully introduced moral terms such as "land ethics" and "ecological conscience" into the public discourse.[16]

Garden

If the farm has a warm moral appeal, so has the garden. The distinction between them was not, in fact, always sharp. If to the hired laborer the farm always meant toil, to the wealthy owner it was often viewed as a garden retreat to which he could repair in the hot season. The garden, for its part, was at one time also a miniature farm; that is, it did not become a purely aesthetic place until the fifteenth century on mainland Europe and a little later in England. Planting fruits and vegetables alongside decorative flowers was a common practice during the reign of Elizabeth I. Thus, John Gerard, well-known author of *Herball* (1597), mixed flowers with turnips and lettuces in his garden; he even tried to raise potatoes and sugar cane, though without success. Gerard and others like him were horticulturists and amateur botanists, who had extensive book knowledge of plants but who also worked with their hands in the spirit of scientific experimentation.[17]

Work with one's hands has aroused contradictory attitudes in the West. The Greco-Roman tradition judges it suitable only for slaves. The Bible teaches, however, that though hard work is a curse, light work can be a blessing. Even in the Garden of Eden, Adam and Eve did not stay idle but tended the garden and exercised dominion over the animals. As Augustine put it, the agriculture of our first parents was not labor but *exhilaratio voluntatis*, the will's joyful participation in divine creativity; and where, he asked, "can reason speak more intimately with nature than when setting out seeds, planting slips, or trimming shrubs?"[18] In a monastic garden, monks tended the herbs, thus reenacting a role before the Fall. In Elizabethan England, authors of garden manuals could rarely resist the chance to moralize. If Augustine evoked the image of "joyful participation in divine creativity," more mundane moralists stressed the virtue of being profitably occupied. A manual might make the point that one advantage to having a garden is that "there will be something to do." The garden, an oasis of bliss in comparison with arable fields where toil must rule, nevertheless contains weeds that have to be rooted out, and its trees must be "reformed" by "good government."[19]

The garden then is a place of wholesome work and it is a place close to God. In Genesis, God himself strolls in the garden in the cool of the evening. These are Biblical images. Adding to them and enhancing the symbolic resonance of the garden in the Western world are other images that have their roots in Greek and Oriental thought. They portray the garden as haunted by the Muses who inspire its visitor to poetry, philosophy, or love, all of which elevate the individual to feelings of cosmic harmony. Poetry and philosophy link the self to the great panoply of nature, as does the beloved who becomes the cosmos; and to the lover (mystic or troubadour) everything in nature is changed and, in their language, "the whole earth becomes like a single garden of love."[20]

Human beings yearn for bliss, and bliss is identified with a place—Island of the Blest, Taoist paradise, or Eden. In the imagination, this place is the antithesis of the turmoil and ruthless use of power in society. But what if, instead of looking for a paradisiac place somewhere on earth, one were to try to build it? All grand efforts at gardenmaking run into deep contradiction, for one then boldly applies power, technological ingenuity, and artifice to create a natural world of innocence. Potentates have seldom shown any awareness of the paradox. In China, emperors ordered the erection of the most extravagant parks and gardens in the name of a life close to nature and even Taoist simplicity. One imperial park of the Han dynasty, built to the west of the capital city of Ch'ang-an, boasted thirty-six palaces as well as exotic animals from the most distant parts of empire. In this huge park, natural land forms mingled with artificial lakes and islands designed to evoke the legendary Isles of the Blest of the Eastern Sea.[21]

In Europe, the ideal of the garden was powerfully articulated by monks, poets, philosophers, and architects. But whereas poets and philosophers used mere words, architects used costly materials. In the Renaissance and early modern period, architects with the resources of their wealthy patrons at their disposal could build on a monumental scale. But there was confusion—indeed, contradiction—in the idealized images. On the one hand, the garden stood for organic nature, on the other, the cosmos. The latter ideal triumphed, and with it the justification for monumentality and artifice (cosmetics). The pleasure garden was far more architecture than organic nature. Medieval gardeners spoke of building rather than planting their gardens, thus admitting the artifice. In the Renaissance period, landscaping leaped to another level of ambition and ingenuity. Gardener-architects sought to dominate nature, totally transforming it by human and technological power. When a site lacked water for fountains or had an unsuitable topography, the builder took the lack and the unsuitability as challenges to be overcome. His mentality was quasi-militaristic, which is understandable because the skills needed to move earth, build retaining walls, terraces, pools and avenues were also those needed for military construction. Outstanding Renaissance architects such as Giuliano da Sangallo and Bramante built both military fortifications and gardens.[22]

Great gardens of the seventeenth and eighteenth centuries were even more megalomaniac in conception and execution. Whether of the earlier formal style or of the later "natural" (English) fashion, they were equally artificial—conjoint feats of engineering and aesthetics. In the formal garden, plant life was strictly disciplined in the interest of arabesque patterns of the kind found in richly embroidered cloths of gold; and in the English natural garden, plant life was arranged together with topographical elements to simulate the picturesque perspectives of art. Using power for display was nowhere more prominent than in the manipulation of water. Bubbling water has always been a part of the Edenic and bucolic image; it is nature and nature's sweet sound. However, in the sixteenth and seventeenth centuries, the new science of hydraulics was able to discipline water and transform it into sky-shooting monstrosities and thundering musical "organs." Building great fountains demanded not only engineering skills, but also human toil and sacrifice, as the construction of Versailles grimly illustrates. To bring water to its hundreds of fountains, architect-engineers sought to lay some forty miles of canals and aqueducts. Thirty thousand soldiers labored day and night on the enormous project, which was abandoned after three years as cost continued to soar and thousands of soldiers had died of injury and malaria.[23]

An economic landscape must defer to economic necessity and to conditions of soil and climate. Imagination cannot be fanciful if it is to produce prosperous farms. The aesthetic landscape or garden, by contrast, is free play. There the imagination recognizes no constraint. Backed by sufficient power, nature can be made to perform in any way that suits human fancy. In the dream world of *Alice in Wonderland*, gardeners are obliged to paint white roses red before the ill-tempered queen arrives. In the life of an absolute monarch, such a curious event can indeed happen. Absolute power tends toward immorality because it erases the idea of limit and obscures the distinction between the real and the stuff of dreams. At Trianon, the entire color scheme of the garden was on one occasion changed while Louis XIV ate his lunch.[24] At Marly, green chambers made of trees and trimmed hedges were repeatedly taken down and put up, woodlands were quickly converted into lakes and as quickly returned to dense woodlands, all to accommodate the fancy of an easily bored, aging monarch and his courtiers.[25]

The garden is not only a product of play but also an arena *for* play. Pictures of the Tudor garden show men and women playing cards, paddling in a stream, rolling on the ground, teasing monkeys, fishing in the ponds, splashing each other with water, wandering about in a maze, chasing each other, making love.[26] In addition to these impromptu lighthearted activities, the garden has traditionally provided a setting for musicals and drama, many of which, particularly in the princely courts of the sixteenth and seventeenth centuries, feature gods and goddesses frolicking in an elaborate stage of cloud-bedecked heaven and pastoral earth. The serious world of work is left far behind in a pleasure garden. Yet it can be introduced and mocked as a dress-up game for those who have never had to labor. In both China and Europe, the ruling elite have been known to play at the simple life. In China, a beautiful pavilion on an artificial island may carry a plaque that exhorts incongruously, "Farm with diligence." At the Summer Palace near Beijing, a row of farm houses stand on Longevity Hill; there the Empress dowager Tzu Hsi (1834–1908) used to watch her ladies struggling to feed the chickens. Still, in China, agriculture is a critical component of an ancient imperial rite that has been maintained through the centuries. Feeding the chicken has a residual element of seriousness in it—a reminder of the dependence of the whole edifice of civilization on farm work. Europe lacks such a tradition. The image of Marie Antoinette playing the dairy maid on the grounds of the Petit Trianon signifies only an awareness of a literary pastoralism. With the rise of social consciousness and turmoil, such theatrical make-believe is quickly turned into a symbol of aristocratic frivolity and arrogance.[27]

The princely gardens of Europe were arenas for display rather than play. Their principal reason for being was to exalt their owners and provide an appropriate setting for ostentation. Embodiments of power and prestige, they were instruments for acquiring even more power and prestige. Supreme artwork and beauty no doubt existed in abundance, but one might well wonder what effects of elevation or serenity they could have had on owners so bent in converting everything into the coin of power and status. Louis XIV knew that Versailles was uncomfortable. He did not enjoy strolling in its gardens, but he gloried in it as stage and symbol. One account of why it was built illustrates well the childishness and veniality of the great. Nicolas Fouquet, a man of enormous wealth, sought to impress his royal master by entertaining him at his magnificent estate Vaux-le-Vicomte. Louis *was* impressed but also angered that a minister of his should presume to live in greater splendor than he. The king's envy resulted in Fouquet's downfall. The disgraced minister's talented artists and artisans were drafted to build Versailles—a place grand enough to defy all competition.

In the seventeenth century, a garden could be designed to flatter in the same way that a letter addressed to a noble patron began and ended in fulsome homage. One of the most ambitious conceptions of the garden in Queen Anne's England belonged to the Duke of Beaufort. Plans showed twenty radial avenues stretching far into the countryside. A contemporary observer noted how certain gentlemen sought to flatter the duke by planting trees on their own estates so that their alignment extended the duke's vistas.[28]

The garden of power and caprice differs radically from the gardens of contemplation and of innocence. The one overwhelms nature and enters the colorful pages of political-architectural history; the other two reflect, respectively, the value of transcendence and the value of innocence in the midst of nature, and they find exemplars in the courtyards of religious houses or on the lovingly tended grounds of unpretentious homes everywhere. What have all these three types in common other than exposure to the sky? Gardens of contemplation and of innocence may well promote serenity and virtue, but the other garden, for all its particular aesthetic excellences created by the foremost artists of its time, is steeped in and stained by the pomp and vanity of this world.

Architecture and the City

Gardens, their artifice notwithstanding, can still evoke nature and its moral authority. By contrast, buildings and cities are indisputably manmade. What then gives them authority? The question is all the more urgent because historically monuments and cities appeared rather suddenly on the human scene, without prior, long and gradually accretional stages of growth as hamlet, village, and market town. According to Paul Wheatley, great cities in antiquity began as centers of religious and political power capable of commanding the material and human resources of a broad region.[29] These ceremonial centers boasted monuments from the start. At first few people lived there permanently, but as more and more of them moved in to serve the elite, and as the total population rose, the centers were able to add manufacturing and commercial enterprises to their original functions. In short time, a ceremonial center could be transformed into a full-fledged royal city, with shrines and palaces at the core, commercial and residential quarters at the periphery, and the whole area circumscribed (in many instances) by a wall. An imposing architectural complex might thus stand starkly above a primitive countryside of scattered hamlets and villages.

To the question, What gave architecture its legitimacy? the answer is the cosmos. Shrines, palaces, the city, the status and power of the elite all drew their authority and moral sanction from nature—not terrestrial nature with its irregular and unpredictable moods, but the grand orderly nature of the heavens. If there was domination it was the natural domination of the superior over the inferior, of heaven over earth. The austere geometry of the walls and the vertical thrust of the shrines were natural symbols of a supraterrestrial reality. Sacred monuments in proto-urban and urban cultures found their justification there. The urge to build could be seen as obedience and homage rather than as inordinate human willfulness and ambition. The palaces of the great could also be justified by an appeal to the cosmos, for in ancient thought "sacred" and "secular" were often fused. Kings were also priests, or they assumed a mantle of sacredness about their persons. To a lesser degree, the higher servants of a semidivine ruler, by claiming some of the reflected glory, could vindicate their own opulent style of living, which was made to appear seemly, mirroring the hierarchy of nature.

The physical city did not seem an obtrusive act of will for another reason. In the West, a strain of thought rooted in classical antiquity regarded the city far more as people striving to live well together than as a material environment. To the extent that attention was turned to the physical character of the city, it focused on hygienic and utilitarian matters. Thus Aristotle (*Politics* 1331a) advised that the site of the city should be chosen with an eye to health; important were such considerations as whether it was exposed to cleansing winds and accessible to spring water. Vitruvius, writing as an architect-engineer, also emphasized the importance of a healthy site. For Aristotle, and even for Vitruvius, the physical city was not so much a proud human construction as a practical human adaptation: it was a world erected by people to mediate between nature and themselves. When these writers turned to houses and streets, they again stressed security and other practical needs. Thus Aristotle argued that while he could see the convenience of having houses laid out in the regular Hippodamian fashion, the new plan failed to provide for security at the time of war during which "the antiquated mode of building" would have enjoyed the advantage of confusing the enemy.[30] Vitruvius argued at greater length for the practical city. Public buildings, he wrote, should be located "with a view to general convenience and utility." If the city were on the sea, the forum was to be built close to the harbor; if inland, in the middle of the town. The temples of those gods that protected the state should be built on the highest points within the city. As to the temple of Mars, Vitruvius' recommendation was guided by both practical and magical concerns. The temple should be erected outside the walls on an open space where the soldiers could train; moreover, "when that divinity is enshrined outside the walls, the citizens will never take up arms against each other, and Mars will defend the city from its enemies and save it from danger in war."[31] Whether the emphasis was on religion, on health in relation to topography and climate, or on the requirements of socioeconomic life, the willful thrust of construction—of creating an artificial world on top of the natural one—was masked.

An architectural treatise of the fifteenth century that has had a sustained impact throughout the Renaissance and later is Leone Battista Alberti's *Ten Books on Architecture*. Like Vitruvius, Alberti gave much thought to site and location, to health, and to the way streets and houses might be arranged to best serve the city's practical needs. Again the physical city was considered more a shelter that mediated between nature and people than a large and powerful source of influence in its own right. However, Alberti did present one line of argument, new in architectural writing and mirroring the proud humanism of his time, that vaunted rather than underplayed human achievement. The basic idea was that the house should reflect the status of the occupant: the higher the status the more splendid the house. In part, this idea was an extension to the secular realm of the ancient belief that architecture appropriately strove to be monumental because it housed the gods. In part, it reflected a belief, common to Renaissance humanists, that architecture projected a rhetoric of meaning—ornate or plain—that paralleled verbal rhetorical devices; and one would therefore expect the house of a prince to be grandiloquent—to be copious in stone—as one would expect that of a humble cleric or artisan to be plain.

People took for granted that princes lived in palaces, commoners in modest houses, and peasants in hovels. Alberti sought to translate this belief in natural hierarchy into finely graded architectural expression. When a given state of affairs was deemed natural, any departure from it would have been wrong—morally wrong. To speak in a manner unsuitable to one's social station was wrong. Likewise, to be dressed or domiciled either above or below one's station. Alberti's treatise was, in a sense, a work of architectural etiquette. He showed how princes and noblemen could be housed in a fitting manner, and perhaps also unwittingly justified architectural display by freeing it from the accusation of personal vanity and willfulness.[32]

Clothes and the house both protect and adorn, and to the extent that they adorn they are bound to social roles and behavior, which themselves manifest deeply held, unarticulated moral beliefs and values. Let us attempt a moral reading of clothes and buildings. We will begin with clothes, which are the simpler text. Clothes, propriety, and morality are so intimately linked that, as Quentin Bell has pointed out, in praising clothes it is difficult not to use adjectives such as "right," "good," "correct," "unimpeachable," or "faultless," all of which are taken from the language of conduct. On the other hand, in discussing people's moral shortcomings, it is natural to lapse into sartorial language and speak of a person's behavior as "shabby," "shoddy," "threadbare," "down at heel," "botched," and "slipshod."[33] Clothes and the moral stance intersect in other ways as well. High fashion in clothes is subject to the lure of extravagance; and extravagance is a moral term, its literal meaning being the waywardness of a vagabond—departures from the right path. Moreover, in aiming at a conspicuous or elevated image high fashion is tempted to deny our biological nature; it forgoes its protective purpose to become almost solely a device for projecting fantasies of self.

Extravagance in clothes has clear limits. The length of a train may be long but there must be a length beyond which it will seem ridiculous to all eyes. By contrast, buildings have no clear limit tied to the measure of the human body. They can be as large and fanciful as imagination is able to reach and technology allows. Indeed, should the building be a house of God, the human imagination is obligated to overreach itself. Consider the great abbey churches and cathedrals of the period 1050 to 1350. The inspiration behind them was an image of the majesty of God and of the City of God, an image drawn not from the Gospels with their homely accounts of common life but from the Book of Revelations with its projections of bright, bejeweled splendor. Art in all its forms was pressed into service to create a microcosm so beautiful that as worshipers stepped into the church they might feel that they had already entered the New Jerusalem.[34]

In erecting churches, the imagination was easily diverted from their primary religious purpose to the subsidiary ends of making images and objects of beauty. By drawing attention to themselves, artworks of the late medieval period threatened to become barriers rather than portals to the other world. Houses raised to honor God turned by subtle, unacknowledged steps into houses of human pride—the pride, at first, of princes and, later, of prosperous burghers. It was easy for people to shift their attention from the ineffable God to tangible art, but since great art itself did not yield its beauty to the casual eye, they readily lowered their sights still further, from art to the glittering metals and gems of which art might be made, and to quantitative indices of greatness. In late medieval France, collective pride took the form of building the tallest vault or spire on the house of God. The cathedrals of Paris, Chartres, Rheims, Amiens, and Beauvais competed with each other in foolish disregard for the laws of engineering. The vault of Beauvais C the-dral soared to 157 feet and three inches only to collapse.[35] 1 ide is the deadliest sin. In raising religious edifices, the archi ct-engineers and their patrons demonstrated how easy it wa to mask pride under the claim of glorifying God.

Greed and vainglory, common as they were, did not al gether bury the moral sense. Pious men, including some in p sitions of power, were shocked by the extravagance of adori ment in the churches and the passion for construction. Bernar of Clairvaux disdained the richly colored Cluniac churches. "C vanity of vanities, but more folly than vanity! Every part of the church shines, but the poor man is hungry. The church walls are clothed in gold, while the children of the church remain naked." He wondered why the richer the churches were the more willingly men gave.[36] One cause of the building mania of the late twelfth century was the Church's decision to grant indulgences not only to Crusaders—their movement was then on the wane—but also to those who helped to erect the houses of God. Pierre le Chantre, a highly placed cathedral dignitary in Paris, complained in 1180 of the constructions of his time which, in his view, were a sickness of epidemic proportions. Much of the money, he noted, came from the tainted sources of usury, avarice, cunning, lies, and the deception of preachers.

As the popularity of architecture continued to rise in the thirteenth century, so did the prestige of the master builder and of the mechanical arts generally. It was a common practice to speak of God himself as Architect or Artisan. The human master builder, for his part, no longer worked with his hands and sought to distance himself from those who did. By carrying gloves and a stick, he hoped to project an air of authority. Equipped with authority, he was prone to order others about their business. Architects and master masons began to act like proud creators. Their prestige was such that busts of themselves were placed in the churches they had designed.[37]

Houses of God easily served as houses that accommodated the swelled egos of men. By late medieval times, it was no longer necessary to indulge the ego under the pretense of honoring God, for by then the purely secular buildings—the municipal and guild halls—were well able to match the architectural opulence of churches and cathedrals. During the Renaissance and Baroque periods, potentates would not have felt any need to justify the magnificence of their private estates. If they had wanted to, they could always appeal to natural hierarchy—the divine order of things. Architectural monuments, both private and public, suited the temper of Renaissance princes who took seriously their role as co-creators with God and who presumed that the creations themselves were able to embellish and elevate the tenor of both private and public life.

In the modern age, arguments in favor of architectural magnificence on grounds of religion or natural hierarchy have lost almost all their relevance. Capitalist magnates created sumptuous houses for themselves simply because they had the means to do so and because architecture visibly confirmed their wealth and power. They did not, however, build only for themselves; they also built for each other and for, and with the help of, the rising ranks of the middle class; that is, they invested in the construction of palatial banks, department stores and shopping arcades, libraries and galleries, opera houses and theaters, railway stations and bridges—all proud landmarks of the late nineteenth-century metropolis. The bold use of new materials such as iron and of the new principles for spanning vast space has produced some truly magnificent specimens of architecture, inspiring in their sheer size and technical verve. However, the desire for social status in a rising class that is not yet sure of its standing has also led its architects to find significance and beauty in conventional symbolism and mere ornateness. Late Victorian architecture demonstrates how easily the imagination can work against itself, as, for example, by allowing the facile route of decoration to overcome the originality that has its source in engineering technology.[38]

Buildings that pretend to be great need not, of course, be

---

so. They can be merely gross. Buildings that are in fact great, proven as such through surviving the passing fashions of taste, must *do* something for their occupants beyond the obvious rewards of practicality and prestige. But what can they do? How can architecture enhance the self, making it in some moral-spiritual sense better? Assuming that architecture has a measure of power to do good, that power depends very much on the attitude—the state of being—of the beholder. Without doubt a princely palace can boast of magnificence and often an abundance of individual artworks of subtle beauty. Their owner is fortunate. Yet, one wonders about the owner's ability to derive full aesthetic-moral benefit from such a superfluity of excellence, for to see anything justly requires a receptive, patient way of looking, a self-denying posture of attention, that is at odds with the pride and self-regard of people of great power and wealth. Great wealth is often ill-gotten. There is poetic justice in the thought that artworks, as art, may withhold their life-giving magic from their owners, or yield it only in those moments when their owners renounce their pride of possession.

What one owns one may not be able to enjoy. Per contra, it is obviously possible to enjoy something one does not legally own. A basic condition for enjoyment and benefit is not ownership but access, which can create an illusion of possession. Access, however, is not a sufficient condition. We have access to great public buildings and spaces, and yet the benefit we derive from them may be severely curtailed by the feebleness or wrong-headedness of our response. It is all too easy to be swayed by the sheer size and glitter of buildings, or by their projection of status. Possessiveness and inattention, traits that are not confined to any socioeconomic class, rather than ownership, are barriers to true enjoyment.

Dreams of grandeur can be fulfilled in private houses and gardens. Even more so they find consummation in the raising of ideal cities. In ancient times, such cities were undergirded by cosmic-religious beliefs and rites. As these beliefs weakened the architectural vocabulary might nevertheless be retained, adapted to serve the presumption of, first, princes, then, in a bourgeois and democratic age, the collective ego of nation-states. For sheer visual magnificence, few designs could match those of the Baroque period. Its pattern of avenues radiating outward like sunbeams from palace or monument was well suited to the divine pretension of kings. Even democratic governments have found use for it, as in the capital cities of the United States and Australia, for even in a democracy citizens need handsome settings for ceremonial display.

Cities (with a few exceptions in antiquity) have not been created just to be monumental art or political stage. They must also function as shelters for communal living. A tension exists between these purposes. "Living" is "messy," inchoate, intimate, and micro-scale; at its most basic level, it has to do with the fact that human beings have bodies that must be fed. By contrast, "art" (the fine arts as well as political art) rises above necessity; its practice calls for the use of a simplifying and clarifying imagination. In the twentieth century, not only art and the simplifying imagination but living itself seems to have lost touch with its roots in nature.

Consider, first, the need of the body for food and the dependence of the city on agriculture. Is it actually possible to forget this dependency? It would seem so, for the tangible evidences of the tie with food production have progressively faded. Even in cities of the nineteenth century the tie was close and readily observed. "No English city," wrote H. J. Dyos and Michael Wolff, "had severed itself from its rural connections. The largest of them still conducted extensive backyard agriculture, not merely half-a-dozen hens in a coop of soapboxes, but cow-stalls, sheep-folds, pig-sties above and below ground, in and out of dwellings, on and off the streets, wherever this rudimentary factory-farming could be made to work."[39] As late as 1866, in London alone, "cowkeepers still had over 9,000 milking cows in stalls at the rear of their town dairies."[40] Cities have tried to retain some sort of direct link with agriculture—with the source of life. Providing allotment gardens for workers is one well-known example. In modern cities, the need to grow food seems, however, more psychological than economic. There persists the desire to see something edible come out of the ground rather than in cellophane packages on the shiny counters of the supermarket: hence the myriad tiny vegetable plots that city people of diverse social classes and incomes have maintained in their backyards, or even on skyscrapers, as in Manhattan, to as late as the 1950s.[41]

If city living seems a little unreal for lack of direct contact with the biological sources of life, it can also seem a little unreal for lack of close contact with other human beings. The moral texture of life feels thin in the absence of intimacy. All direct human exchanges have, it is true, moral import, even those that occur in a modern department store, for when we buy or sell in such a store we are after all engaged in calculations of self-interest, and we show by word and gesture interest or boredom, deference or rudeness. Nevertheless, it is not in a modern mall but in an old neighborhood that one finds intercourses of the greatest intricacy and emotional depth. Borrowing sugar from a neighbor, smiling at a baby, quarreling with a merchant over skipped delivery, or with a man over a woman are the kinds of acts that acquire in time an emotional-moral tone and weight that the cooler exchanges in modern shopping centers lack. Understandably, residents of an old neighborhood become angry when their world is forced to make way for a new thoroughfare or business complex, or even a new housing estate to which they can eventually move. The planner can point to economic advantages for the city and perhaps better housing elsewhere, if not there, for the residents themselves. It may be that the residents can see the public gain in urban renewal and the advantage for themselves of a new place and a new start, and yet discern the arrogance of architect-planners who presume that the webs of human reciprocity, knitted over time and supported by a physical environment that has been humanized by innumerable subtle adjustments, can be replaced as it were overnight.

Nevertheless, it is irresponsible romanticism to accept uncritically the old and the inchoate as warmly human and good. Old quarters can, of course, be unhealthy slums—dark, dirty, socially disintegrating within and isolated from the greater city without. Since the end of the eighteenth century, in part under the inspiration of neo-Classicial ideals, attempts have been made to open up the cluttered old cities of Europe in the interest of light and hygiene.[42] An outstanding example is Baron Haussmann's surgery on nineteenth-century Paris. His efforts have been attacked as a political move to destroy the refuges (actual and potential) of rebels. True, the great boulevards made it easy to transport soldiers to centers of conflict, but they were built for sound social and aesthetic reasons as well, based no doubt partly on Haussmann's own frustrating experience in the warrenlike Paris of his youth.[43] Haussmann's new tree-lined boulevards brought air, light, visual clarity, and beauty to Paris; in addition, they permitted movements of people and goods over the metropolis and thereby create a greater community of citizens.

Whatever criticisms have been directed at Haussmann during the turmoil of construction and soon after, the Paris that he has created is now universally admired. A vast imaginative effort, so vulnerable to attack as crudely simplifying on the aesthetic level and darkly motivated on the political plane, has turned out extraordinarily well. We cannot help but wonder about the urban renewal projects of our own time, especially those that have taken place since the end of the second world war, both in Europe and in America. Have they all proven to be life-negating disasters of the power-driven reductive imagination, as critics were inclined to think in the angry mood of the early seventies, or have some demonstrated unsuspected viability?

The city everywhere reflects the mind at work. Every slab in the sidewalk, every lamp post, is of course the result of calculation and imagination. Where the individual constructions are limited in scale and uncoordinated with each other, the urban fabric that results is likely to show the complexity, verging on chaos, of a natural growth. Such a place, at its best, has human warmth and diversity, but it is deficient in large-scale visual inspiration and in a sense of the whole; it may also be unhealthy for lack of hygienic measures applied city-wide. At the other extreme is the crystalline form of a totally planned city. Such a city, at its best, has visual splendor, but it may well lack true neighborhoods. The one, we might say, is good—that is, rich in neighboring activities—but it is not beautiful and perhaps not even sanitary; the other is beautiful and sanitary but it is not in a cozy human sense good.

Between these two poles lie all possible intermediate types, graded according to the degree that a city has been subjected to planning, that is, to the imagination of a relatively few powerful individuals. Most cities in the Western world have assumed a certain internal pattern that is the result not of master plans, but of the plans and designs of many individuals and groups, working with varying degrees of coordination—though unsupervised by central authority—in response to social and economic forces at large. Over the course of the last two centuries, the product of such efforts is the modern, spatially segmented metropolis. Its configuration represents a cleaning up and a thinning out of the older order of dense, inchoate living. Economic activities have come to be concentrated in certain parts of the city, residential quarters elsewhere, and these quarters are themselves segregated by income and class. Industries and the poor, with the bad odor imputed to them, are confined to areas far removed from the affluent. Medical authorities of the nineteenth century still believed that not only dirt but bad odor itself was a threat to health. In the late Victorian era, the removal and segregation of foul fumes were a major hygienic enterprise, carried out at the same time as the more positive steps of installing bathrooms, improving the operations of the water-closets, and extending the sewage network.[44]

Together with the cult of hygiene and of health was the denial of almost all visible signs of physical suffering and death. The abandonment of urban graveyards in favor of parklike suburban cemeteries, and, in the twentieth century, the increasing use of hospitals by not only the indigent but also the affluent sick and dying, and the increasing efficiency of ambulances and sanitary trucks to remove maimed human beings, animals, and even trees have all contributed to the creation of a physical environment which for all its obvious merits can seem a little unreal, as distant from the ineluctable ills of mortals as the brightly rational ethical systems—the credos of humanist faith—that have bloomed in the same period.

The city means both people and buildings. Until the eighteenth century, however, thinkers and reformers have given far less attention to the characteristics of the physical setting than to the human relationships and institutions it sustains. "What is the Citie, but the People? True, the People are the Citie" (Shakespeare, *Coriolanus*, act 3, scene 1). Having considered a few of the moral issues raised by architecture, we now turn to human relationships—to questions that we all recognize as at the heart of morality, namely, how people see each other, treat each other, and envisage the nature of exchange.

6 Social World and Exchange

In the presence of others, we inevitably convey shades of coolness and warmth, hints of friendship or hostility. Most of the time, however, we are unaware of the fact that our body posture and facial expression reveal an evaluative-judgmental stance. Even if in privacy we have a theoretical understanding of body language, that understanding is inoperative when we are actually talking and listening to others. Speech does express intention, but it has a subtext that escapes our conscious awareness: how we say something may contradict what we say.

Of course human exchanges are also conducted deliberatively. We smile to impart friendliness, pay and receive compliments because we wish to reveal how we feel, and exchange gifts with the aim of cementing a profitable relationship. Yet, although such acts are consciously performed, we are little aware of their moral significance and import. Is it right to show warmth to someone because we want a favor from him? Society takes such behavior for granted. Almost everyone acts thus. But not all. Some individuals may vigorously question it. Moralists have lived who, straining at necessity and accepted practice, envisage a more open and generous world. What will such a world be like? What moral axioms will it rest on?

Great moralists past and present and in different cultures show a certain family resemblance in the exalted reach of their imagination, but the moral worlds they envisage differ importantly in detail because they rest on different axioms or principles. The principles upheld in Western culture have been strongly influenced by its Hebraic-Christian tradition. They were not, of course, laid down once and for all but took time to develop and win allegiance.

Three such principles are outstanding. First, every human individual is credited with transcendent importance. Exchange between persons may outwardly emulate the natural order— say, the reciprocation of protection and deference in a baboon troop—but it is in essence a false parallel because, in the Christian view, the worth of a human being rises far superior to his social status. Second, the web of beneficent exchange should be as large as possible. Limitation of membership is necessary in practice; ideally, however, the moral community cannot exclude anyone who sincerely seeks admittance. Third, although in public affairs people must be responsibly calculative, in personal contacts they should remain warmly spontaneous. Ours is a time when more than ever people are aware that acts in the public sphere, such as the allocation of scarce resources, have large aggregate consequences that demand calculation because they cannot be grasped intuitively. On the other hand, it remains true that in personal encounters the outcome of an act can have ramifications so subtly detailed and specific as to be unpredictable. Under such circumstance, one should trust one's generous impulse.[1] A further dilemma arises out of our awareness that public and private spheres cannot always be kept separate; nor is it even desirable always to do so. Clearly what is considered good in one sphere affects how one acts in the other. Calculations in public life will degenerate into mere exercises of power and expediency unless they are informed by an imagination that keenly recognizes the worth of the individual and the supraeconomic meanings of exchange.

"Worth" and "supraeconomic" are elastic terms, capable of being construed in exalted ways. The question we now need to ask is this. At what point does the attribution of value to people and their acts move from imagination to fantasy? That is, at what point do we lose touch with reality in our enthusiasm? Earlier we have noted that a moral edifice, like a material one, can be a beautiful work of art and yet fit ill with the capabilities and desires of the people who live there. What is being considered now, however, is not imagination applied to an external sheath in either the material or nonmaterial sense but imagination applied directly to human individuals and to the kinds of relationship they can have. We are asking what constitutes a just perception of human individuals and how they might relate ideally, yet realistically, with each other. The answer is elusive and provisionary because the ability to see is progressive and tends to be self-fulfilling: the more we see in a person the more she will exhibit these qualities, and the more we appreciate and cultivate a relationship the more likely it is to grow into something worthy of our love. There are, naturally, limits beyond which the imagination loses all touch with reality. To the degree that our emotions are engaged, our imagination may well work to excess and we see perfection or evil where only a muddle exists. On the other hand, much of the time our emotion is not engaged and we relate to others coolly in enlightened self-interest. These abstract ideas call for concrete illustration. Let us consider, first, types of human exchange based on necessity; then, those that draw on the more imaginative and generous impulses of the mind.

Exchange and Necessity

Viewed from a certain distance, a traditional European village is an image of cooperation as finely meshed and intimate as the physical proximity of the houses. Peasants work in teams at harvest time and during the vintage; in winter evenings and again in feast and market days they meet to talk and amuse themselves. But a closer look shows that the cooperative spirit is largely an illusion. Other than on special days the families live quite separately. "Nobody considers anything but himself or his own kin," Maurice Halbwachs observes of French peasants. "Just as a village sometimes ignores, envies and detests a neighboring village, so it happens too often that families envy each other from one house to the next, without ever a thought of helping each other."[2]
Necessity demands thrift in all areas of life. Charity and friendship are luxuries that the hard-pressed peasants of traditional Europe cannot afford. About the villagers of Montegrano in south Italy (1955), Edward Banfield writes: "Any advantage

that may be given to another is necessarily at the expense of one's own family. Therefore, one cannot afford the luxury of charity. . . . The world being what it is, all those who stand outside of the small circle are at least potential competitors and therefore also potential enemies." Personal friendship is not useful because all that it gains is the help of one individual. Friendship is therefore not cultivated; instead, peasants recognize the need to "get along with everybody," especially one's neighbors, whose help may be a matter of life and death during emergencies.[3]

Of course peasants exchange labor or make each other small loans of food or cash, but they keep a careful record of what is given and expect quick return. The unsentimental character of exchange is plainly indicated in the following statement, which comes out of early seventeenth-century England. "It is enough for us to give a Cake for a Pudding, and a pinte of wine for a Pottle of beere: and when we kill hogs to send our children to our neighbours with these messages: My Father and my mother have sent you a Pudding and a Chine, and desires you when you kill your Hogges, you will send him as good again."[4]

In the upper layers of a hierarchical society, bare survival is not in question. Nevertheless, gift exchanges remain as important and are even more calculating—more finely graded—than they are in peasant communities. Survival is social but it is no less exigent for that reason: the all-consuming question is how one can maintain one's social status and gain a margin of advantage over rivals. Giving appropriately and with desired effect is a fine art and a powerful political tool. In Tudor England (to look at one hierarchical society) we see how extensive, varied, and imaginative the gifts of a nobleman had to be in order to hold on to and, if possible, extend his influence. Consider Lord Lisle and his household. As Lord Deputy of Calais (1533–1540), Lord Lisle enjoyed easy access to a wide range of commodities. What were they and who were the recipients? French wines for everyone, a marlin and a porpoise for Cromwell, a live seal for the Lord Admiral, storks for the Prior of Christ Church, barrels of sturgeon for the Lord Privy Seal, dotterels for Henry VIII. Fortunately for the Lisles, Henry VIII and his new queen Jane Seymour developed a passion for the fat quails which Lisle could supply. The quails apparently tipped the scale in getting Lady Lisle's daughter introduced into the queen's household. The Lisles themselves naturally also received gifts. The records show, for example, that Lady Lisle was presented with a dozen puffins, marmosets, and (from a French diplomat) a long-tailed Brazilian monkey.[5]

Among members of the upper class as among peasants, animals were prominent in the exchanges. To the upper class, animals were desirable as delicacies for the discerning palate, although many were valued simply as curiosities and exotic toys: thus the long-tailed Brazilian monkey for Lady Lisle, and thus the seal for the Lord Admiral, which Lisle's agent John Husee had to keep at Wapping for several weeks at mounting expense and inconvenience. The greater the lord the greater the number of people who received tokens of his largesse, but also the greater the obligation on the part of the recipients to return the favor. At the highest social level, this practice no longer held. The king and his powerful ministers received in abundance, but their favors, like those of the gods, could be withheld or dispensed as they pleased.

From what we know of gift exchange in premodern society, it appears that affection and generosity often played only a minor role. Giving was practical and amoral; it might even be considered immoral in two related senses: first, the artful calculation that is required to obtain some advantage to self, and second, the need for hypocrisy—that is, for a display of warm affection and generosity when none exists. But human affairs are never quite this simple. Although the deep motivation might be self-serving, the transactions themselves, because they are conducted face-to-face, can in time generate genuine feelings of affection. In the area of feeling the line between pretense and reality is not sharp. Pretend to like someone over a period of time and one may grow to like him in fact.

The larger the web of exchange the more secure its members feel.[6] In premodern societies the web may reach beyond human circles to the spirits of ancestors and of nature. What is the psychological and moral character of the linkages in the web? Between equals, exchanges are prompted by need tempered with affection. Between persons of unequal power, a relationship of propitiation and patronage is the norm. The weak with his gift propitiates the strong. The strong on his part dispenses favor to the weak, paternally or patronizingly. When the strong is an ancestor or a nature deity, the gift to him is called an offering and the act is deemed pious. Society commends it as showing gratitude to powers who have provided the supplicant with life and the means of sustenance. Filial piety is the model for ancestral or nature piety: parents love and nurture their child who in turn respects his parents and renders them service. Between parents and child such exchange may indeed occur: it is natural. Nevertheless, parents have been known to abuse their power and children can be ungrateful. Society must then exert pressure so that at least the outward forms of piety are observed. Between ancestors and nature spirits on the one hand and villagers on the other, reciprocations are seldom genuinely fond or pious. Villagers are driven by necessity to propitiate the powers, and the powers are expected to provide protection and blessing. They might even be coerced to perform. Villagers can, for instance, bribe them with increased offering or threaten to withhold it altogether. In China, villagers can even threaten to appeal to a higher authority—the emperor himself, who as the Son of Heaven ranks above the local spirits of mountain and water.[7]

Although self-interest lies at the basis of mutual help, it is not wholly acceptable. People choose to mask the self-interest with a display of generosity and affection that can deceive even the deceivers. To show generosity, one gives a little more than one receives. In small-town America, neighbors try to do just that: a little more sugar is returned than was borrowed, and borrowed tools are given back shining, cleaner than they were. Generosity of this kind is ironic for it is inescapably calculating: neighbors have to keep in mind that one cup of sugar was received and hence one-and-a-half cups must be returned. However, certain kinds of gift have a natural tendency to increase so that their value is beyond strict accounting. Live animals are one example, and we have noted that in the past potentates liked to offer each other rare animals as tokens of esteem, and in our time heads of states may still do so: witness, the exchange of the American musk ox for the Chinese panda to seal the restoration of diplomatic relations between the United States and China. Another example of a gift that has the power to multiply is knowledge. One reason why the elites of society maintain vast social networks is the value of the information passed along them, formally and informally; and information may well be the most important gift of all, for it empowers the recipient and is able to build on itself. The traditional prestige of the teacher lies in his ability to pass on useful and even possibly life-enhancing knowledge; and in our time the imparting of technical knowledge from one country to another is regarded as a true gesture of friendship.

I have thus far emphasized the ulterior motives of the gift. But of course it can also be a natural impulsion of fondness that complements or supplements the somatic gesture of throwing an arm around another's shoulder and the exchange of affectionate words. When the gift is a supplemental expression of fondness, its value is symbolic and does not depend on costliness or rarity. The focus of attraction is each other. As a Nzema man of southern Ghana will say of his friend, "I love him because he is beautiful," or more specifically, "because he has beautiful hands," or "speaks well."[8] Two individuals, in love, form a small closed system: their exchange of looks, gestures, and gifts shuts out the world. From one point of view, it has the appeal of unworldliness, from another, it is binary egotism. In contrast to the mutual absorption of lovers, friends share their worlds with each other: they stand side by side rather than face-to-face, and although they may start with a nucleus of two the circle of exchange is capable of expanding to include others.[9]

Friendship can be a subtle and deeply rewarding human bond, but it can also be taken in a lighter, more superficial vein as that which transpires when individuals derive mutual benefit from an association. The benefit, though principally tangible and material, may also include the simple pleasure of being in each other's company. Trading partners often see themselves as friends. Even in the modern commercial world the idea persists that traders are not solely after material advantage, that underlying it is genuine good will expressed by a warm handshake, enquiries after the "wife and kids," and the exchange of small gifts and Christmas cards. The traditional marketplace is a bustling social center where people seek the excitement and pleasure of meeting relatives, friends, acquaintances, and strangers. In Dogon (west Africa), for example, the market is protected by a shrine of the Dogon twins, who represent the idea of partnership in mirth and commerce. Once a year the village priest offers a sacrifice at the shrine, asking God to send more strangers. The Dogon clearly recognize the multiple advantages of broadening the web of exchange.[10]

Traditional markets are so full of effervescent life, verging at times on chaos, that they can be considered a temptation. Rulers in the past welcomed them for the wealth they brought in, but were also suspicious of them for the disruptions they could inflict on the orderly procedures of society. In ninth-century Europe, Charlemagne wondered whether "this continual running around markets" would lead to the decline of agriculture. In China, Confucian officials raised the same question. They were worried because they thought that the merchant's way of life had enough appeal to draw people away from the land. To forestall disorderly conduct and crime, officials tried to confine markets to specific locations and to designate the times when they could open, but with little success. The dynamism of markets resisted rigorous control.[11]

As we have seen, neighborly exchanges within the village are practical in nature and rather joyless. By contrast, trips away from home for the purpose of trade are happy occasions. One source of happiness is freedom from toil on the land and from the tight social bonds of village life. The journey to the market is itself a liberating experience. Villagers who go to market, after all, do not live from hand-to-mouth but have a surplus to sell. At the market, which is largely a world of acquaintances and strangers, they can afford to be more open and generous, dispensing friendly touches, shouts of greeting, even token pieces of merchandise, without incurring onerous social debts and obligations.

A lively marketplace resembles, in some ways, a pilgrimage center. The one is often deemed profane, the other sacred. Yet in England the place of buying and selling may occur in the shadow of the market-cross, and in Africa, next to a sacred tree or shrine. The pilgrimage center, for its part, is rarely a place given over to dedicated worshipers only. Very often it makes room for both religious rituals and secular entertainments, and it bustles with the buying and selling of religious mementos and other goods. The anthropologist Victor Turner, after making a tour of such Mexican pilgrimage centers as the Villa de Guadalupe, Chalma, Acámbaro, and Naucálpan, has this to say: "At all [of them] there was dancing by brightly feathered troupes of traditional performers. Often there were rodeos, bullfights, and fairs with Ferris wheels and roundabouts; and always there were innumerable stalls and marquees where almost everything could be had, from religious pictures and objects to confectionary, food, clothing, and domestic utensils. Communion, marketing, the fair, all went together in a place set apart."[12]

Both the marketplace and the pilgrimage center are packed with strangers; both offer liberation from bondage to local mores and the temporary experience of a larger community, with its different ideals. Pilgrims enjoy prestige. Their moral standing is higher for having had contact with a higher order of reality at the shrine, even though behavior there may transgress the customs of home. By contrast, farmers who have returned from the market, though they may be envied for business success, are likely to be viewed with suspicion by those who have stayed at home. "Opening up" at the pilgrimage center connotes contact with a superior world; at the marketplace it connotes immorality.

Let us review the moral standing of reciprocity. In all societies helping each other lies at the core of moral behavior. If what is exchanged between two individuals is guided by love, of which gifts and service are merely the outward expression, we seem to have a type of human relationship that approaches the ideal. Yet, if the exchange is limited to two individuals, the long-range effect will be psychologically enervating and sterile, that is, without effect on the world. To mitigate the sterility of mutual regard, to remove the temptation toward self-seeking even in a relationship of love, a certain amount of time is encouraged to lapse between each act of giving. One reason why the parent-child relationship serves so well as a model of morality is that the time lapse there is imposed by nature. The parent gives the child material sustenance and selfless love; only many years later will the child be capable of returning in kind. Between friends, a delay may be deliberately imposed. This is indeed the case among the Trobrianders of the south Pacific, a people who place high value on friendship. An armband is handed over but a man must wait until his friend makes a return visit before he receives a necklace, and of course the value of the gift is never subject to bargaining.[13] Among the villagers of northern Papua New Guinea, the etiquette of exchange appears to follow a cycle. When a stranger visits a village he is likely to be greeted effusively and receive gifts apparently out of a pure, generous impulse. If his stay is short he may depart with the impression of having visited Eden. If his stay is longer than two days, he will find the villagers aggressively insisting on quick reciprocity. If his stay is even longer he will find that his friends fall into two categories: those in one want something in return for every gift, those in the other offer gifts as gestures of pure affection, but after a lapse of time will make a request of the recipient who is then expected to respond spontaneously.[14]

Bargaining and calculating for self-advantage are, in most societies, taken for granted. They are considered a neutral mechanism that produces mutual benefit, or a game, enjoyable in itself, with happy results for all parties concerned. Because the outcome is mutual benefit, exchange does not call for further justification. And yet, as we have seen, it is not always taken for granted: a nagging feeling remains (for example) among the Trobrianders and Papuans that a higher morality exists which requires giving without thought of return. Under the pressure of this higher demand, people feel obliged to go through a show of pure affection and generosity.

Awareness of "what is in it for me?" is reduced if instead of a narrow reciprocity, people engage in what Lewis Hyde calls "circular" giving. A gives to B who gives to C who gives to D who gives to A. Generosity is eventually recompensed but only after a long delay and it will not come from the individual to whom one has given. The larger and more complex the society the more likely its people are to engage in circular giving that involves not only friends and acquaintances but total strangers.[15] In a modern society the circle of giving may be so large that it cannot be encompassed by direct experience. What is envisaged seems linear—a long line that extends into a distant future inhabited by strangers. Modern parents, for example, care for their children with little expectation of material return; their children will in time care for their own offspring, and so on down the line. Other human relationships may show a similar linearity. A social worker helps someone who, perhaps out of gratitude, helps someone else. The favor one does is not returned. One's action does not necessarily gain a friend or an ally because he may not be seen again. In a large modern society, we often help strangers and are helped by them, though not usually by the same ones. True we pay and are paid for all kinds of services, but the relation between the amount of pay and the service rendered, say, a student or a welfare client is seldom clear. Moreover, the amount we pay (a measure of the time and energy taken out of our life) is necessarily very little compared with the goods and services received. What we receive at a department store, an art museum, or a hospital is the cumulated labor, skill, and knowledge of a host of total strangers, most of whom are dead.

Images of Person and Community

How people see and behave toward each other is strongly influenced by the socioeconomic system under which they live. We have seen at one extreme the tight net of exchange among neighbors in a traditional village, and at the other the open circular transactions of modern society. But the socioeconomic system is not totally controlling. The quality of a human relationship depends on other contingencies and circumstances as well: the contingency, for instance, of individual temperament—the fact that some people are naturally withdrawn whereas others are naturally outgoing—and the circumstance of culture. By culture I mean the ideal images or concepts that a human group has been able to construct. Individuals may themselves create the image: thus two friends, not content with their relationship as defined by custom, seek to develop it in accordance with their own picture of perfection. But friends are more likely to draw upon ideals that already exist in the culture. What are these ideals?

Consider, first, those that have grown around the human person, then, those around community and exchange. Moralists in the West have argued that the person is of great value in himself—he is an end in himself—and hence is not to be treated as the mere means to ends defined by others. In the Christian tradition, an individual is considered to be of such importance that under certain circumstances his welfare may not cede even to that of his group. Why does a mere individual have this degree of importance? The degree—it is true—varies in different cultures, as are the reasons given. The Greeks, for example, value man for his divine reason, his capacity to conceive the good. Confucians value him for his "evaluating mind" and for his capacity to exercise *jen*. Upanishad thinkers value him for his soul, *atman*, his inner essence which is the same as Brahma, the inner essence of the universe. These are a few of the idealized, abstract reasons for granting respect. In actuality, respect is given a person not so much for what he is (e.g., creature of God or possessor of *atman*) as for what he is capable of being— that is, for his ability to fulfill society's ideals. A society may have a hierarchy of ideals. Confucians, for instance, have envisaged the sage kings, whose achievements are so lofty as to be almost beyond emulation. The less exalted categories of "superior man" (*chün-tzu*) and "gentleman" (*shih*) are within the grasp of ordinary mortals.[16] The existence of these more realistic standards makes it possible for degrees of respect to be earned by all members of society who aspire to virtue and success.

Models of man can be inconsistent. Consider Taoism. In sharp distinction to Confucianism, Taoism holds that man has no special status in nature. The Taoist sage does not elevate himself above other animals; and indeed he may well see himself now as a horse, now as an ox, and so forth. A human being may possess unique excellences but these are temporal and have no lasting significance. What is of real value in a person is his *te*, the localized manifestation of the *tao*. But everything in nature possesses its own internal principle, and there is no clear sense that the human principle is greatly superior, or that human beings have more of it. If human beings do not differ essentially from other manifestations of nature, they can hardly be conceived as differing much among themselves. Taoism logically takes the view that human beings are equal, not only at birth but as adults. Yet Taoism also speaks of the sage—by definition a superior being. Clearly not everyone is a sage. How does an individual attain sagehood if not by having and cultivating a superior *te*, or by diligently purifying himself so as to allow the *te* to emerge?[17]

Buddhism, too, is inconsistent in its appraisal of the human individual. We have noted earlier (chapter 3) that Buddhism is an extremely austere world view that denies man almost all consolation. Thus not only is his body a bag of filth, worse, there is no soul: at death, man disintegrates without residue. Nevertheless, certain doctrines ensure the importance of human beings as a species and individually. One doctrine teaches that it is not necessarily best to be born a deity because deities are still subject to the taking of action and its inevitable consequence, and they will fall to a lower state once their merits have been exhausted. By contrast, human beings are potentially able to escape the cycles of rebirth altogether and attain the everlasting bliss of Buddhahood. As for the human individual, his exalted and rather lonely position is guaranteed by the doctrine that only he can save himself from the relentless operation of karma through devotion to Buddha's teaching and good works.[18]

If human beings are regarded as worthless, clearly community is impossible. If they are seen as possessing a value that varies with their social status—that is, with their power, their

---

usefulness to the group or the elite—some kind of community will emerge but one that is likely to be exploitative. If they are viewed as worthy of love and respect for themselves and for their contributions to the group, community will follow naturally. And yet there is a paradox. Emphasize the individual beyond a certain point and community is at risk. This is obvious when the individual is encouraged to be selfish in grossly materialistic ways. But community is also at risk when the individual aspires to sagehood—to a pure state of enlightenment insofar as this is attainable. The Upanishads teach that the individual self is the same as the universal self, and that as soon as a man realizes this he is liberated. The self, to Upanishad thinkers, is dearer than everything, dearer than wealth or even a son. "He who reverences the self alone as dear is not perishable." Such belief does not encourage community. In contrast to this extraordinary stress on the worth of the self, Buddhists hold that the self is the most deceitful of delusions. Yet they also hold that action is initiated by a self, and action produces consequences that can lead to ultimate enlightenment. Early Buddhism offers as model the passionless ascetic arhat, who through self-discipline and the accumulation of merits is able to end his own ceaseless incarnations and suffering. The arhat is worthy of respect but he is not an entirely sympathetic figure; he cannot be emulated by too many people without endangering community. In reaction against the passionless arhat, Mahāyāna Buddhism has conceived of the loving and compassionate bodhisattva. The bodhisattva, although he has already attained enlightenment, delays his entry into Nirvana until he has saved all others from this world of misery. Mahāyāna Buddhism places greater emphasis on compassion and altruism than on an individual's desire for his own ultimate salvation. Compared with early (Hinayāna) Buddhism, it promotes the idea and ideal of mutuality and community.[19]

Greek thinkers, like those in India, have been more inclined to stress individual enlightenment than the realization of a communal ideal. Altruism itself tends to be advanced as good on the basis of levels of self-interest—from the crude "if I help another person, I will put him in my debt and increase the chances that he may help me some day," to the lofty "I should help another person because a life of sympathetic concern for others is the most rewarding and fulfilling kind of life."[20] Even at the most elevated level, the point of departure remains the self.

Given the view that an enlightened individual is largely independent of society—a view to which Plato and his followers subscribe—how can it be otherwise? A just life, for such thinkers, rests on the attainment of harmony within the self and between the self and the cosmos; it can be lived in any society or in none. Nevertheless Plato's philosopher, having seen the light, is under obligation to return to the cave—the world of flickering shadows; he has some responsibility for others and will agree to carry the burden of government for the good of the community as a whole.[21]

In sharp distinction to world views that stress the individual attainment of sagehood or salvation is Confucianism, which from the start gives primary consideration to the family—the exemplary kernel of community. The principal virtues of Confucianism are *jen* and *hsiao*. *Jen* builds on a natural affection for one's kin and *hsiao* is filial piety, that reciprocal relationship ordained by nature which with cultivation can reach beyond the family to the world. Confucianism has its own sages, but the most admired ones are the kings of antiquity, esteemed more for their public virtue than for their heroics of self-discipline and the attainment of other-worldly states of being. Understandably, Confucian officials find certain basic tenets of the imported religion of Buddhism unsympathetic, in particular, the monastic vocation which removes men from the family and the world. In response, Chinese Buddhists argue that, far from being unfilial (as Confucians have accused them of being), they practice the *ta-hsiao*, or great filial piety. By abandoning household life and becoming monks, their piety extends beyond their own parents to the parents of others, and indeed to all living things. As Ch'i-sung, an apologist for Buddhism during the Sung dynasty, has pointed out, in the endless cycles of transmigration it is conceivable that one's parents are reborn as animals. The killing of an animal therefore incurs the risk of killing an ancestor. Rather than take such a risk the Buddhist seeks to protect the life of even the humblest organisms.[22]

A characteristic of the ideal community, in the view of some thinkers, is that its membership is limited: the Chinese extended family is one model of the ideal and another is the Greek polis of no more than a few thousand citizens. When China became an empire, the Confucian model was enlarged unconscionably to cover the empire, with the emperor as the paternal figure for all his people, and with lesser paternal figures for smaller groups in a nested, hierarchical structure. The point of radiation remained the small group—the family. *Jen* was still the natural affection that resonated primarily among kinsfolk, although from there it could reach out in diminishing degrees to neighbors and strangers. The assumption of universality here is unconvincing because it so greatly distorts the original ideal of limited membership. If, however, a people's interest should turn from the quality of communal ties to the challenge of individual salvation, a possible unforeseen consequence is an expansion of the idea of community so that it does become truly universal. We can put the notion in general terms this way: if the stress is on the communal "we," an outside "they" group is implied, and the result is the well-known "we-they" distinction that negates universality. But if the stress is on "I," a universe of other "I"s is implied; together they constitute a universal community, provided, of course, that each "I" in its search for sagehood is by the nature of the vocation also compassionate.

If we see Confucianism and Buddhism as representing opposite extremes in their attitude toward the relative importance of self versus group, Christianity may be seen as occupying a middle position. In its historical development, Christianity has tried to give supreme value to the individual and yet at the same time elevate the meaning of community to the height of membership in the mystical body of Christ or in the Kingdom of God. Consider, first, the individual. No other religion or ethical system puts quite such great weight on the importance of every human person. Even in the post-Christian era, this exalted view is retained. How we ought to treat another—and especially how we ought to act toward a stranger—is influenced by this inherited, largely unexamined value and belief. The doctrine of God as the sole creator responsible for every thing that exists and the doctrine that among creatures human beings rank only a little below the angels have certainly contributed to the lofty image of the human person; but far more important, because it comes to us not as an abstract doctrine but as a deeply moving story, are the detailed incidents in Christianity's central event— the incarnation. Christians are taught to see God incarnate in an infant, in a boy apprenticed to his carpenter father, in a humiliated and crucified man. People in all walks of life absorb the lesson with ease because they are able to identify with the life story of Christ, so human in its common touches and particularity and yet a cosmic event concerning someone described in the Nicene Creed as "God of God, very God of very God, begotten not made." This drama of salvation for humankind as well as for every member, requiring God to be crucified on the cross, imparts infinite worth to every individual. Every individual counts—a theme made extraordinarily vivid in the parable of the Good Shepherd who puts the entire flock at risk in his search for the one lost sheep. And this sense of the worth of a particular self extends not only to that intangible entity called soul but to the body as well, since God himself was once incarnate in the flesh.

By placing a higher value on the individual than on the group, Christianity could seek to include among its members all conditions of man, slave and free, and from all nations, Jew and Greek. Christ himself made light of kinship bonds, and a major reason why the patricians of Rome considered the new religion subversive was that it failed to show respect for familial piety and the local gods.[23] Balancing this exalted view of the human person (despite his sinfulness) is an equally elevated view of the new community. In this new community, how will people see each other, how will they feel and act? Whereas the Christian view of the individual is made vivid by the drama of Christ's life and death, its view of the community lacks comparable sharpness of detail. Nevertheless, a few vivid images do exist, preeminently that of the Eucharistic supper, at which Christ shares bread and wine, that is, his body and blood, with his disciples. Ritually enacted, the supper reminds Christians that they are members of the body of Christ and that the ties between them are stronger than even those between the closest kin. Community in Christian thought has expanded from this nucleus, based on ties other than blood or propinquity, to include (potentially) the whole of humankind; it is also to include the dead (the saints) and beyond them the angels and the archangels. Included at the lower end of the hierarchy are animals, who enter the Kingdom by the grace of their human caretakers, or as a part of a generally redeemed nature at the end of time. Excluded from the Kingdom are the unrepentant destined for hell and those who are already in hell. But Christianity has envisaged another category of beings—the denizens of purgatory—who although they suffer horribly from the sins they have committed on earth are still in communion with God and his saints, and will one day join the company of heaven.

In conceiving purgatory, Christianity has introduced a

unique kind of bond between the living and the dead. As one scholar puts it, whereas "Pagans prayed to the dead, Christians prayed *for* the dead."[24] To many people in the world, the dead are a source of power; hence it is expedient to pray to them and offer them sacrifices. Christians pray in this spirit when they ask for the blessing or intercession of the saints. But few individuals, after death, are immediately translated into heaven; most have to submit to prolonged periods of punishment in purgatory. This idea of an intermediary realm of punishment emerged in the early centuries of Christianity. Official endorsement, however, came only in 1274; thereafter, for the next five hundred years, it continued to stimulate the imagination of the Latin Church in its attempts to order the cosmos.

A number of factors accounted for the popularity of purgatory. To the hierarchy, it meant an extension of their power beyond the living to the dead, whose punishment could be reduced by prayers and, above all, by celebrations of the mass. Living members were reminded that they could not escape the arm of the Church even after they had left this world. The rise of individualism had an effect on the acceptance of purgatory. From the twelfth century onward people showed more and more tremulous concern for what would happen to them the moment after death. Would they plunge into hell and suffer eternal damnation, or into purgatory which, for all its torments, was an antechamber to heaven? To an increasing number of communicants, life seemed good, and they were eager to see its blessings continued. A greatly enlarged conception of space and time, and a corresponding gain in the size of the membership in communion made the idea of purgatory seem reasonable. An inspiring image of community was to emerge, which showed besides living communicants a long line of one's forebears, at varying stages of salvation, aided in their progress by the prayers of the Church, the intercession of the saints, and occasionally, the dramatic intervention of angels as they dived to the edge of hell to snatch souls from the permanent embrace of the demons. During the late Middle Ages, a growing sensitivity to and desire for the finer discriminations of justice in this life made the existence of a realm of graded punishments in an afterlife welcome. People were less willing to accept the idea that the commitment of merely venial sins could end in everlasting torment.[25]

Not least among the reasons for the wide acceptance of an

intermediate purgatorial realm was the bond of affection itself. The fond heart yearned to believe that even beyond death the suffering beloved could be helped. One of the earliest adumbrations of the idea of purgatory and—more important—one of the tenderest expressions of love is recorded in an early third-century text called *The Passion of Perpetua and Felicitas*. Perpetua was imprisoned during the persecution of Christians in 203. While in prison she dreamed of her dead young brother Dinocratus.

> "I saw Dinocratus coming out of a place of darkness, all burning and parched with thirst, filthy and clad in rags, bearing on his face the sore that he had when he died. Dinocratus died of illness at age seven, his face eaten away by a malignant canker, and his death repulsed everyone. In the place where he stood there was a basin full of water, whose lip was too high for a small child. And Dinocratus stood on the tip of his toes, as though he wanted to drink. It caused me pain to see that there was water in the basin but that he could not drink because the lip was too high. I woke up with the knowledge that my brother was being tried. But I had no doubt that I could relieve him in his trial. I prayed for him every day."

A few days later, Perpetua had another vision:

> "The day we were put in irons, this is what I saw: I saw the place that I had seen before, and Dinocratus, his body clean, well dressed, refreshed, and where the sore had been I saw a scar; and the lip of the basin that I had seen had been lowered to the height of the child's navel, and water flowed out of it continuously. And above the lip there was a golden cup filled with water. Dinocratus drew near and began to drink from it, and the cup never emptied. Then, his thirst quenched, he began playing happily with the water, as children do. I awoke and I understood that his penalty had been lifted."[26]

Perpetua's intercession was totally selfless. She dreamed of her dead brother and prayed for him when she herself suffered torture and was about to be put to death. Whatever our own belief, as we read this account it is difficult not to feel the power of a love that sought to reach beyond earthly life. At a minimum we were made more fully aware of the possibility for extraordinary tenderness between sister and brother. Perpetua must have been endowed with a great capacity for love, but Christianity surely nurtured this natural capacity with its own powerful images of tenderness and *caritas*, and with its doctrine of intercessory prayer that enabled a Perpetua to hope for and envisage forgiveness and bliss for the dead.

Perpetua prayed for the dead. In most accounts of purgatory this was the direction of concern and of benefit. From the fourteenth century onward, however, the relation between men and women on earth and suffering souls in purgatory underwent a change toward reciprocal benefaction. The living through their prayers were able to transfer merit to the souls in purgatory. At some point, these souls began "to acquire not only merit but also the power to transfer their merit to the living, to return service for service, to give assistance to men and women on earth."[27] The communion of saints was enlarged to embrace redeemable souls at the very mouth of hell.

Christianity, as a vital religion, continued to use its imagination to deepen and expand the concept of community. In our time, one of the most eloquent expositions of the Christian "way of exchange" is that of Charles Williams, and I shall end this chapter with a sketch of his ideas. Exchange, we have noted earlier, can be: a method of survival, a skill for climbing the social ladder, a system that maintains the hierarchy in which the superior dispenses patronage and the inferior offers deference, goods, and services. Proud individuals have always despised the very idea of exchange. For Aristotle, the great-souled person "is disposed to confer benefits, but is ashamed to accept them, because the one is the act of a superior, and the other the act of an inferior."[28] Christianity no doubt has its share of great-souled princes who are also proud, but "proud saint" is a contradiction of terms. Pride is the distinctive sin of Satan. In the fifteenth century, he is defined as one who "desires to be the only source of good to those dependent on him" (*Malleus Maleficarum*, 1484). Christianity, in sharp distinction to Greco-Roman morality, regards humility as a cardinal virtue: whereas every good person is generous in giving, the Christian should also have the humility to receive, as a small child receives.

Charles Williams sees the way of exchange exhibited everywhere in the universe. Its myriad elements exist in interdependence whether they are aware of it or not. Even physical laws and concepts of order may be restated in the vocabulary of the way of exchange.[29] However, the kind of interdependence that is closest to us is that which holds among living organisms, especially human beings. The broad facts of human interdependence are readily seen. Awareness of them enables people to formulate explicit rules of behavior, but how one person's actions can affect another, intentionally or unintentionally, in the short or long run, and what such dependencies and effects mean morally are seldom pursued beyond the practical needs of society. Mary Shedeler, interpreting Williams' view, writes:

> A forest fire started by carelessness can very well leave its originator not only unharmed, but ignorant that he has caused it. . . . But deathly effects are not thereby annulled; they are borne by others, that is, by the innocent [who] may deliberately take upon themselves the impact of an evil energy. Firemen do this, safeguarding the forest or the city by placing themselves in jeopardy, substituting their skills, equipment, and lives for the inadequacies of other citizens.[30]

We do not have to set fire deliberately or through carelessness to affect the fate of others. The simple fact of our existence can cause others great harm. The birth of Christ himself had as consequence the slaughter of the infants of Bethlehem. As obviously, our existence can be a cause of incalculable good, whether we will it or not. The Holy Innocents could not save themselves, but they saved the infant Christ, and Christ could save others, though himself (as the accusation went) he could not save. In such a moral universe, sacrifices of self in things large and small are an obligation, while forcing another to sacrifice himself is an outrage.[31]

The way of exchange operates at different levels. Whatever form it takes in the Kingdom of God, in natural communities its most common form is the division of labor. "One sows and another reaps; one tends the farm or the shop while others attend to transportation or justice or the home. They bear each other's burdens; they give and receive in substitution."[32] Exchange in small communities is direct: people barter their goods and services. Large complex societies require a more flexible medium, which is money. Bartering suggests self-seeking, getting the best of a deal, and money is laden with meanings of greed and the lust for power. Yet, to Williams, they need not do so; that they do is a stigma of our Fall. Furthermore, the exchanges that enrich us all go far beyond goods and services. We differ in temperament and are differently endowed in talent. These too might be exchanged to the degree that through an imagination enlivened by love we can live in one another. Rigor and relaxation, for example, are both desirable; the one is proper to sanctity, the other to sanity. It is rare for people greatly gifted in one virtue to be equally well endowed in the other, but, Williams says, "the exchanges of Christendom are very deep; if we thrive by the force of saints, they too may feed on our felicities."[33] Because no individual can have all the wealth, "this man's patience shall adorn that man, and that man's celerity this; and magnificence and thrift exchanged; and chastity and generosity; and tenderness and truth, and so on through the kingdom."[34]

"Bear ye one another's burdens" (Galatians 6:2). This injunction is usually taken to mean helping another person materially and trying to console him with comforting gestures and words. In Williams' conception of the kingdom, human exchanges are expanded to include the bearing of each other's psychological afflictions—grief, fear, anxiety, sleeplessness, and pain. These burdens can be taken over as simply as the taking over of a parcel. "A man can cease to worry about x because his friend has agreed to be worried about x. No doubt the first man may still have to deal directly with x; the point is that his friend may well relieve him of the extra burden." The man "who gives has to remember that he has parted with his burden, that it is being carried by another, that his part is to believe that and be at peace. The one who takes has to set himself—mind and emotion and sensation—to the burden, to know it, imagine it, receive it—and sometimes not to be taken aback by the swiftness of the divine grace and the lightness of the burden." People do not want to admit their own inadequacy; when they feel fear or anxiety they are reluctant to give it to someone else to carry. In this sense too it is harder and more blessed to give than to receive. "It has a greater tendency toward humility and the intellectual denial of self."[35]

The way of exchange, as Williams conceives it, goes so far beyond what we normally think of as exchange, with its undertone of the calculative and the mechanical, its presupposition of separate individuals superficially engaged with one another, that he sometimes uses another term "co-inherence." The way of exchange or co-inherence lies at the core of community, and it proceeds not only among living human beings but between the living and the dead, and indeed Williams sees co-inherence as the operating principle for the whole of God's creation. This grand and yet somehow also intimate and warm spectacle, sketched by Williams with his unique syntax and vocabulary, is Christian in inspiration and important to him for that reason— for the fact that it is not merely the inflamed product of an idiosyncratic mind. He would have found further assurance in the fact that non-Christian cultures also clearly recognize the way of exchange. The Roman cult of piety is an instance of it, and of course piety and reciprocal affection lie at the heart of the Chinese moral-ethical tradition. In our time, the concept "web of life" expresses a belief in the interrelatedness and interdependence of things, and the modern science of ecology, at least in its popular guise, is strongly colored by moral sentiment.

The way of exchange seems plausible. It is grounded on common human experience and its traces are discernible in the world of nature wherever one looks. Exchange in the human world, as described by Williams, depends uniquely on the imagination. It is not only that we as individuals have special talents and resources which can contribute directly and tangibly to the wealth of community, but that we as individuals can *imaginatively* appropriate the talents and endowments of our fellow human beings. Thus, possessing the virtue of prudence myself I can admire and in my imagination live the audacity of another, and he in turn can participate in my quieter gift through an act of selfless attention. Both of us are thereby enriched.[36] This mutual dependence is radically different from the unrelenting aspiration for self-sufficiency—from the belief that, if possible, in oneself should be concentrated all talents, all experiences.

Community and the way of exchange, as I have just presented them, are appealing works of the human imagination. Even as we admire them the question arises as to the extent they verge on fantasy, that is, have become ideals beyond the human moral capacity to, not only attain, but progressively approach. Yet, unless ideals of being and of behavior are envisioned and constantly held before our eyes as goals, we can never know what we are capable of becoming: we shall lack the motivation to take the next step and our narrow lives, real and satisfying in their own terms, may well be judged unreal in the shadow of that large, unrealized potential.

7 Individuals
Good-Simple vs. Good-Wise

The idea that our grasp of the good and the real may be corrupted by wayward or excessive imagination is illustrated in the history of two common models of the good person, one of which couples "good" with innocence and simplicity, and the other with knowledge and wisdom. Although these models appear to be incompatible, one still yearns for the possibility that they are, after all, in accord and can be embodied in one person. Such a person would be *mirabile dictu* good, unworldly, and yet also learned and wise. To help us envisage such an individual and how he or she might differ from ordinary folk, we may resort once more to the three levels of morality, distinguishable from each other on grounds of awareness, that I have broached earlier. Let me restate them. At the first level, the moral person is simply a dependable fellow who follows the customs of his group. At the next level, he esteems the established values and practices of his group but he also questions them from time to time for their inconsistencies and perhaps in the hope of finding ethical principles of a higher and more general order. At the third level, he is in addition driven by a vision of the ineffable good.

Moral persons of the first type must be in the great majority for any society to function. They therefore do not stand out and do not serve as models of conduct in any publicly recognized way.

One notable exception, however, comes to mind—the farmers. In China as well as in the Western world, farmers have been singled out from people in other humble occupations. Esteemed in the first place for the essential nature of their work, they are also valued for such qualities as simplicity, directness, and wholesomeness. In distinction to moral persons of the first type are individuals who question the established rules. They are moral and responsible in their doubts and in heeding the dictates of their conscience. They can be admirably courageous and intelligent, but on the other hand they can also be offensive egotists and fanatics. As for individuals inspired by a vision of the good, they may be the supreme type of the good person, but on the other hand they may be the most deluded of human beings, their vision of the good a chimera and a personal obsession.

Simplicity and Goodness

Rulers of society have shown ambivalence toward the farmer. In China, this ambivalence is suggested by the contrasting meaning of two words *chih* (solid virtues) and *wen* (refinement). Country people no doubt possess the solid virtues but they are crude. City people may be refined but they are likely to lack the solid virtues. Hence, to Confucius and Confucians, the truly good person must combine *chih* with *wen*.[1] Yet life on the land, close to nature, had genuine appeal for the Chinese people generally, at least those not bound to ceaseless toil. Taoists favored it on account of its simple and pleasurable tasks, its absence of vain striving and idle curiosity. Confucians regarded farming as an occupation suitable even for the scholar. The student who aspired to official life might honorably support himself during the long period of preparation by working on the land and even as a pig breeder, although menial jobs would normally have disqualified him from rising up the official hierarchy.[2]

In the Western world, the status of the farmer has fluctuated widely from one extreme to the next. We have noted Aristotle's and Cicero's high praise. More generally, we can take the prominence of peasants in ancient Latin literature as a sign of respect; and indeed Latin was a language of peasants. Humble workers on the land figure importantly in the farming treatises of the Republican period (Varro's *De re rustica* and Cato's *De agricultura*) and, in an idealized guise, they occupy the center stage of bucolic poetry. Nevertheless, through long periods of Western history, those who till the earth and care for its flocks have been, when noted at all, caricatured as lowly creatures of the earth and relegated to the foot of the body politic. Even in Rome's Imperial era, agricultural workers have begun to fade in treatises on rural economy and they quite disappeared from the meager literary records of the early Middle Ages.[3] A long period of neglect and contempt was followed by dramatic resurrection during the eighteenth century. The cultivator—now no longer a peasant but a free farmer—becomes again (but more fully and with far greater political effectiveness) a model for the good and virtuous life. "Independent" and "democratic," rather than the ambivalent "simple" or "childlike," are the more common words of praise. The farmer's identification with nature, however, persists and along with it the image of someone without guile and artifice, at the opposite pole from the theatrical posturing—the fantasy life—of the urban sophisticate.

In the Christianized West, the idea that a good person is childlike rests on the authority of Jesus himself who said: "Let the little ones come to me; do not try to stop them; for the Kingdom of God belongs to such as these. I tell you that whoever does not accept the Kingdom of God like a child will never enter it" (Luke 18:16–17). Accessible to children, the Kingdom of God may be closed to the learned Pharisees. Is learning itself a handicap? The church's answer has been ambivalent. Knowledge of worldly ways is no doubt a handicap, and perhaps even knowledge of the world, but what of scripture and the doctrines? The monks are ideally trustful and obedient, childlike denizens of a secluded "paradise" on earth. Yet they are also learned and they demonstrate that it is possible to be both learned and good. However, the single human being who best exemplifies Christian perfection is Francis of Assisi, and he comes to us across the pages of history as the archetypal child, impatient of learning, but open and joyous, in love with God's creation, and in his utterances full of the green-fuse of poetry.[4]

Simplicity and wisdom are closely linked in Western thought, as they are in the religious thought of other traditions such as Taoism and Zen Buddhism. In the West the link is so widely accepted that we tend to overlook the paradox. Oxymoronic expressions such as "wise fool" and "God's fool" are taken in stride. Francis of Assisi is God's fool, someone foolishly detached from the world's lures and entanglements and hence able to see and live the truth. Literature has eloquently strengthened this belief. In Shakespeare's plays, the fool may blurt out a truth. He speaks out of simplicity and from the vantage point of his marginal social position.[5] In the real world, Renaissance princes kept fools as pets and entertainers, treating them condescendingly if not cruelly. But affection and even respect could also develop. In 1619, Philip Cradelius preached a lengthy sermon at the funeral of Hans Miesko, who for many years was the official fool at various courts of Stettin-Pomerania. Cradelius exhorted his congregation to use fools as mirrors for their own weaknesses, and at the same time to discern in them that paradoxical combination of natural folly with spiritual wisdom. The preacher did not doubt that Miesko, for all his weak-wittedness, was a good Christian and would go straight to Heaven.[6] Such belief was not exceptional in premodern society. In Eastern Europe, for instance, idiots were regarded as living shrines, repositories of sacredness entitled to food and clothing from everyone. More generally, Victor Turner notes that folk literature abounds in symbolic figures such as "holy beggars," "third sons," "little tailors," and "simpletons," who have a knack for exposing the pretensions of holders of high office and returning them to the sane ground of common humanity.[7]

Literature in the nineteenth century continues the tradition of coupling simplicity with goodness, condescendingly at times but perhaps as often with unmixed admiration. Steerforth in *David Copperfield* exemplifies the former attitude. David has invited his sophisticated friend to visit him at Mr. Piggotty's humble home at Yarmouth. Steerforth shows interest because he thinks it not without fun to see "that sort of people." What sort of people and how do they differ from us? "Why," opines Steerforth, "they are wonderfully virtuous, I dare say—some people contend for that, at least; and I am sure I don't want to contradict them—but they have not very fine natures, and they may be thankful that, like their coarse rough skins, they are not easily wounded."[8]

Literature also provides evidence of high regard. Herman Melville's handsome sailor, Billy Budd, and the peasant heroes in Tolstoy's cosmos come to mind. Billy is distinguished by inarticulate charm, natural ease, and a childlike confidence that the world wishes him well which in turn enables him to wish well of the world. His rough sailor mates can discern the goodness in him and respond. To the evil Master-at-Arms Claggart, however, Billy's innocence seems a deliberate provocation. And in Captain Vere, we have the figure of a good and wise man, but not good or wise enough to save Billy Budd from death by hanging. Tolstoy has created several portraits of simple goodness. One of them is Platon, a peasant soldier who beguiles Pierre, the idealist landowner, at their first meeting. Platon displays not only the comeliness of youth but such childlike qualities as his loving but inconsequential talk, his warmly affectionate but noncommittal relationship with people. Long after his death, he remains for Pierre "all that is Russian, good and sound." The meeting with Platon transforms Pierre's life. All his projects for Russia, as Natasha discovers after her marriage to him, must undergo the test of whether Platon—this blessed simpleton—would have approved.[9] In real life, Tolstoy showed deep admiration for the unspoilt talent of the peasant boy Fed'ka, who contributed a story to the school journal *Yasnaya Polyana*. Observing Fed'ka at work gave Tolstoy ecstatic pleasure but also guilt feelings, as though he had in some way "profaned the [peasant boy's] pure primal innocence." Tolstoy, strongly influenced by Rousseau, believed that man was born perfect, and that at birth he embodied the harmonious union of truth, beauty, and goodness. To that ideal state the peasant boy stood much closer than his far better educated school mentors.[10]

The peasant hero or blessed simpleton has largely disappeared from serious twentieth-century literature. The priest in Georges Bernanos' novel *The Diary of a Country Priest* (1936) has some of the traits of the simple good man of country background and roots, but he is hardly uneducated and is not, psychologically, simple. Yet the image recurs, in journalism if not in works of fiction. Simone Weil and George Orwell both served the cause of the anarchists during the Spanish civil war. Both were intellectuals, enamored of the good, who have been indelibly impressed by encounters with humble people of natural courage and virtue. Weil recalled the capture of a fifteen-year-old boy, a member of the Falange.

> "As soon as he was captured, and still trembling from the sight of his comrades being killed alongside him, he said he had been enrolled compulsorily. . . . He was sent to Durruti, the leader of a column [of militiamen

composed of volunteers from various countries], who lectured him for an hour on the beauties of the anarchist ideal and gave him the choice between death and enrolling immediately in the ranks of his captors, against his comrades of yesterday. Durruti gave this child twenty-four hours to think it over, and when the time was up he said no and was shot."[11]

Orwell met an Italian volunteer in a Barcelona barrack.

"He was standing in profile to me, his chin on his breast, gazing with a puzzled frown at a map which one of the officers had upon the table. Something in his face deeply moved me. It was the face of a man who would commit murder and throw away his life for a friend. . . . There was both candour and ferocity in it; also the pathetic reverence that illiterate people have for their supposed superiors. Obviously he could not make head or tail of the map; obviously he regarded map-reading as a stupendous intellectual feat."

The encounter between Orwell and the Italian volunteer lasted only a moment. They never met again; yet several years later, Orwell could say that this strange image of selfless courage and generosity was his most vivid memory of the whole war.[12]

Wisdom and Goodness

Coupling goodness with innocency of knowledge seems paradoxical; coupling goodness with wisdom is tautological, for the ability to discern right from wrong, the true from the false, is good—is indeed one of its principal meanings. A good person may not be wise, but a wise person is good. Knowledge of a certain kind enables an individual to be good, or moral in the two higher senses of that word. From this perspective, innocence is a temporary condition that one grows out of and ignorance is a fault and a severe handicap. Yet the word "wise" carries a certain ambivalence. It means judicious: judiciousness, however, can suggest shrewdness, a trait not fully compatible with being good. Moreover, knowledge is power, and power is rightly suspect: a wise man is uncomfortably close to being a wizard whose magical powers may not always be used for virtuous ends. A third difficulty is this. It does not seem right that a good person should know that he is good. The idea of the holy fool is readily acceptable because he is presumed ignorant of his own virtue. A wise individual does not enjoy this advantage. When he is aware of his own goodness it is somehow diminished or becomes suspect. Socrates, Christ, and Confucius have all renounced for themselves the label of "wise and good."

Ambivalence toward wisdom was less evident in the past. A wise man was a very knowledgeable person, a prophet, long before he became a wizard with its decayed sense of trickery and magic. It is also easy to believe in the existence of a truly good, wise, and powerful man if he were a vague, distant historical figure rather than a near historical individual for whom documentary material is available, or a contemporary exposed to critical view. In both the East and the West, wise rulers were postulated for a legendary past. Chinese scholars have diligently promoted the idea of a political golden age in which rulers were not only wise and benign but powerful and effective. However, rulers of the well-documented historical period could seldom lay claim to wisdom and goodness unless they, like Wen Ti of the Former Han dynasty, affected a pose of passivity. By the Late Chou period, the honorific labels of wise and good could be appropriately applied only to teachers who did not exercise direct political power.[13]

In ancient Greece, the king had the necessary military-political power to maintain peace between organized villagers and warriors of aristocratic caste. As the power of the palace waned, the two antagonistic parties periodically clashed. Attempts to resolve the conflict by peaceful means at the dawn of the seventh century B.C. made wisdom seem a possession of great practical value. The Greeks came to revere sages whose knowledge of human nature and of the world enabled them to devise laws that unified the different parts of the city and gave its people a sense of harmony. Who were the sages and what were they like? Those mentioned by Aristotle were an odd lot: they included Thales, who was a speculative philosopher and a statesman; Solon, who besides being a poet and an arbiter of Athenian political conflicts renounced the opportunity to be a tyrant; Periander, who though he did become a tyrant nevertheless raised his city of Corinth to enviable prosperity; and Epimenides, who was an inspired shaman.

A sage, in other words, could be many things. A basic source of his confused image and—later, the split image of the philosopher—lies in the fact that historically he had one root in the public debates of the agora and another in the mysteries, one root in worldly knowledge and power and another in gnosis.[14] In time the sage was regarded as primarily a holy man who possessed a type of knowledge superior to ordinary life and not wholly of this world. As a result, his position in society became more marginal. To those in power he could seem irrelevant or subversive, and yet a potential source of salvation and renewal in periods of bafflement and stress.

By ca. 400 B.C., neither Greek nor Chinese thinkers could seriously believe in the existence of philosopher-kings in whom political power and wisdom were harmoniously conjoined. In the West, skepticism eventually reached a point when it was possible to ask whether being wise was fully compatible with being good. Significantly, words that bear the Greek root for wisdom sophistication, sophistry, sophistical, to sophisti cate—all retain an equivocal or even predominantly negative meaning. In modern times, the word "sage" (as in "Victorian Sage") can be used only ironically; and while one may still speak of a "good person" without irony, the person thus evoked tends to be the simple brave soul. A highly educated man or woman may also be a good person but the link between education and moral elevation seems, at best, tenuous. The claim that goodness and knowledge are necessary to each other and can dwell naturally in the same individual is convincing if we are able to offer incontrovertible examples. Are there such examples? Let us consider four persons: two from ancient times—Socrates and Confucius, and two from our modern secular age—Ludwig Wittgenstein and Simone Weil.

Socrates

Socrates, judged a corrupter of youth and put to death on a charge of impiety, never exercised political power. He was an independent thinker, guided by his own daemon, who enjoyed the company and admiration of the young. The wider public tended to see him as a figure of fun—a pedantic paradox-monger and free thinker. His wit, which he used as an implement in the search for truth, was sometimes turned against him as merely the clever trick of a debater.

Socrates was content at first to move in small select groups. He did not see himself as having any larger mission until he faced a crisis in his late thirties. The crisis occurred when the oracle of Apollo declared that he was the wisest of men. Socrates sought to challenge the oracle by finding men wiser than he, and failed. In time he learned the declaration's true meaning, namely, that he was wise because he at least knew the depth of his ignorance concerning the sort of knowledge that really mattered, which was the proper conduct of life. He was one-eyed in a kingdom of the blind. Recognition of this fact obliged him to persist in seeking true knowledge which he believed essential to being a good person. Furthermore, through his unique method of interrogation he tried to induce others to seek this knowledge with him. Henceforth, as Plato noted in the *Apology*, the "wit" Socrates became the "founder of a moral philosophy."

Socrates combined in himself courage and patience, simplicity and self-control. Anger and hatred played no part in his life. One day, someone who was arguing with him ran out of arguments and gave Socrates a slap in the face. Socrates replied quietly, "It is very annoying not to know when one ought to put on a helmet before going out." In his search for truth, he was never dogmatic. Significantly, his daemon, rather than command him to act, always forbade him from making an act that could be unjust or untrue.[15] Committed to exalted notions of truth and of being and utterly indifferent to bodily comfort, Socrates was nevertheless a relaxed figure, at ease with himself and the world. He seemed to enjoy banquets, at which he drank convivially as much as his companions without ever, like them, sinking into drunkenness. Out of his sense of duty to the state he accepted the death verdict for sedition even though he denied the charge and even though he could have easily escaped the penalty with the connivance of his friends. The wisdom that Socrates disclaimed for himself was recognized as his by his contemporaries. When the governor of the prison bade Socrates farewell he called him the "bravest, gentlest, best" man who had ever been under his charge; and Plato ended his account of the death scene with the words: "Hereupon Crito closed his eyes and mouth, and so ended our friend, the man we hold the best, wisest, and most upright of his age" (*Phaedo*).

The serenity of Socrates' last days and hours lends conviction to posterity's belief in his goodness. Not needing consolation himself he yet sought to console his young friends with the argument that the soul survived the body to share in the eternity of Truth and Goodness which it knew. Even more convincing as evidence of his deep humanity were the common touches of thoughtfulness for others. Socrates washed his own body so that others would not have to perform the office upon a corpse. His last words were the plain, "Crito, we owe a cock to Asclepius; do not forget to pay the debt."[16]

Confucius

Confucius was a man of remarkable originality and courage, and not at all the staid figure painted by tradition. He showed, for example, a streak of radicalism when he put forward the idea that the wise man should rule even though he had no hereditary claims to authority. Confucius was also somewhat naïve. Because he believed that goodness and knowledge were by their nature social and should be manifest in the government of both private and public spheres, he seemed unaware of their almost certain conflict in the exercise of political power. He could see that the hereditary rulers of his time were deficient in wisdom, and he would gladly have dispensed with them. Since the removal of venial rulers was out of the question, he sought to provide them with able and virtuous advisers, including himself. In this effort he met with only modest success.

Confucius possessed deep learning as well as a strong personality that impressed not only the young but people in power. However, he was far too committed to his moral principles—to his vision of the good—to submit to the compromises necessary to gain leverage with the hierarchy. Confucius, who taught all his adult life, would have been more persuasive and influential if he had allowed himself long speeches of compelling eloquence. But he did not because they conflicted with his belief in sincerity. A polished man of the world, he was nevertheless suspicious of all forms of ostentatious display.

At age fifty, Confucius knew that if he were to put his principles to practice he could not afford to defer governmental service much longer. When his own ruler offered him a position on the Council of State he accepted. But the position was essentially a sinecure. Confucius, rather than adapt to a life of ineffectual ease, boldly set off in search of another ruler who would listen to him. He wandered over the face of China at an age—

nearly sixty—that was old for a man of those times. He met with hardships on the road and courteous but insincere treatment from the princes he sought to serve. There was a touch of the ridiculous in the travels of an old man still driven by his ideals, but, as H. G. Creel put it, it was a "magnificent kind of ridiculousness, found only in the great."

Self-confidence and perseverance are indicators of greatness, but the truly great and good must be able to see his own limitations. Confucius, though driven by a vision of the good, was also the sort of fellow who could relax, take time for music and play the lute. He appreciated modesty. Unlike such noted teachers as Mo-tzu and Hsün-tzu, he was quick to admit his own ignorance to his students. Modesty showed also in his conversations which frequently revealed a sense of humor that gave bad moments to pious commentators of a later age. His dislike of pretension was demonstrated during a near fatal illness. The disciples of Confucius, believing that their master was on the threshold of death, dressed up as though they were ministers in attendance upon a high dignitary. Confucius asked: "By making this pretence of having ministers when I have none, whom do you think I am going to deceive? Is it not better that I should die in the hands of you, my friends, than in the hands of ministers?"[17]

Wittgenstein

The idea of a philosopher-king cannot be taken seriously in modern times. Lincoln may flicker in our minds as a possible example, and perhaps Dag Hammarskjöld if we think of a contemporary. But the moral stature of these good persons is compromised, not so much by the need to act boldly in ambivalent situations as by the need to assert the self regularly throughout one's political career. The politician, in other words, must have a large ego and enjoy the limelight, traits that conflict with the high conceptions of what it is to be good. Moreover, worldly power depends on possessing worldly knowledge, which includes knowing the weaknesses and strengths, fears and vanity, fatuous needs and desires of human beings. The kinds of knowledge typically possessed by a man of the world or a politician seem somehow contaminating; and the same is true of the knowledge of human nature possessed by a novelist or a playwright. "One can imagine a saint painting a picture (Fra Angelico) or composing music. Can one imagine a saint writing a novel?" asks the novelist Julien Green, a life-long seeker of the good.[18] Wittgenstein notes that while one easily speaks of "Beethoven's great heart," nobody can speak of "Shakespeare's great heart."[19] The heart is corroded not so much by having a generalized knowledge of good and evil as by having to attend closely to the foibles and failings of human character, which is the lot of a politician who must know how to exert influence and which is also the lot of a novelist or playwright in the practice of his art.

By comparison with literature, the kind of knowledge necessary to high achievement in painting, sculpture, dance, and music is innocent. Innocent also are the abstract areas of knowledge, above all, philosophy, which still carries a trace of its old meaning of wisdom. "On 29 April 1951 there died in Cambridge, England, one of the greatest and most influential philosophers of our time, Ludwig Wittgenstein."[20] From the numerous writings about him since his death, it is clear that he was a charismatic figure, regarded by his admirers as not only a great thinker but a good man. Something of the character and extraordinary talent of the man can be glimpsed from his accomplishments and jobs. Roughly in chronological order, he was: a student of aeronautical engineering who contributed to the design of an improved type of jet propeller, a musician of professional caliber, an experimental psychologist, a logician and mathematician, a soldier in the Austrian army during the first world war, an elementary school teacher in a village, an assistant gardener in a monastery, an architect and sculptor, a professor of philosophy at Cambridge University who, during the second world war, worked first as a porter at a London hospital and then as a medical technician in a laboratory in Newcastle. Wittgenstein was driven by an insatiable longing for the good, which for him as for all mystics lay beyond language and thought. Logic and truth, music and aesthetics, submission to the discipline of building a complex machine or a house, but above all behaving decently were all exploratory thrusts toward the good, which gave Wittgenstein's life a thematic unity despite the range and disparate nature of his activities and achievements.

In our doubting age, wisdom sounds pretentious and inauthentic if it is presented as a large body of works, a shining possession, a total commitment to a set of doctrines or a rounded, coherent way of life. We of a skeptical bent are more likely to acknowledge true wisdom in an individual if it appears as something hesitant, and positive only in the clear recognition of a lack, which provokes a thirst for the supernal good. Wittgenstein fits this model. His achievements—even his philosophical works—lack a monumental character. He criticized civilization for its passion to construct. "It is occupied with building an ever more complicated structure. And even clarity is sought only as a means to this end, not as an end in itself."[21] For Wittgenstein, on the contrary, clarity is valuable in itself. He wished to see rather than to make, and if he made things it was in order to see and to submit himself to reality.

Wittgenstein's reluctance to impose on the world is reflected in his personal habits. He has always wanted to do without: as a young man he gave up a large fortune, and throughout his life he was conspicuously spartan in his needs. An intellectual and a philosopher of the greatest distinction, he nevertheless sought to serve people in the humble capacities of village teacher, monastery gardener, and hospital porter. The following anecdotes concretely illustrate the nature of his moral sensitivity. Wittgenstein and Rush Rees were taking a vacation in a remote part of Ireland. Wittgenstein caught sight of a family making hay and quickly said: "We are going back. These people are working, and it is not right that we should be holidaying in front of them." One morning the local fishermen had landed on the pier a large catch of mackerel, some of which were still alive and displaying the usual brilliant coloring of fish just out of the sea. Wittgenstein said in a low voice: "Why don't they leave them in the sea? I know fish are caught in the most horrible way, and yet I continue to eat fish." Another time he said to Rees: "If it ever happens that you get mixed up in hand-to-hand fighting, you must just stand aside and let yourself be killed."[22]

Weil

Simone Weil, who died in 1943 at the age of thirty-four, had published little in her life and was known to few people outside her family and small circles of school friends and intellectuals. Since the end of the second world war, however, she came to be widely known in England, France, and the United States as someone who combined a questing, original mind with super-human charity—a "Saint in an age of alienation, our kind of saint," as Leslie Fiedler put it.[23] Those who admired her (including such luminaries as André Gide, T. S. Eliot, and R. H. Tawney) found in her life and thought an antidote to the tawdry materialism and secularism of modern times. Simone Weil was a mystic and a visionary who yet rejected any effort to reenchant the world by means of religion and nostalgic voyages into the past. Indeed, she admired secularism and embraced it because it had the courage and honesty to refuse easy consolation in ungrounded sentiment and the supernatural. When at the beginning of her career she taught philosophy in various provincial schools, her conception of social reality was Marxian and wholly secular. She might be described as a typical intellectual of the early thirties but for the unusual vigor and clarity with which she expressed her beliefs, and her need to put them into practice—that is, to be active politically, such as organizing workers so that they were better able to influence their employers, and to know through direct experience how it felt to be a laborer in the vineyard and a worker in a Renault factory. Even as a child Simone Weil showed, besides intelligence of a high order, an extraordinary capacity to feel for those less fortunate than she. One example: at the age of eleven she disappeared from home for a long time (thus making her parents worry) in order to attend a meeting for unemployed workers.[24]

Simone Weil seemed born with a hunger for good, a trait she came to see, with perhaps more charity than accuracy, as innate in all human beings. She was, however, deeply suspicious of moralism of both the religious and the secular variety. "Doing good," other than in the area of strict obligation which it is our duty to extend, is suspect because it so often has its source in a desire to be admired and in an assumption of superiority that can humiliate and diminish the recipient. Simone Weil yearned for the transcendent. Despite her impatient activist temperament, she sought to wait: an attitude of waiting attentiveness was itself a petitionary prayer as well as an ascetic practice that guarded one against the assault of fantasy. When God finally touched her, it was unexpected and overwhelming. Still, despite her great love for Christ and for certain rituals of the Catholic Church she resisted baptism. She did not join the Church because she felt more strongly the vocation to be an outsider; she did not want to be "in," when so many non-Catholics and non-Christians were "out." Called a mystic by her admirers as well as detractors, Simone Weil herself would have abhorred the name if it signified a tendency to turn inward at the expense of paying attention to the beauty and horror of the world.[25]

Simone Weil was in love with reality. Joy is the feeling of reality, beauty its manifest presence.[26] The criterion of the real is necessity—that which imposes itself on us. Opposed to the real is the imaginary, which Simone Weil viewed harshly as a source of evil. Human beings, she seemed to think, live in terror of the void—a feeling of emptiness at the heart of being.[27] When we are not engaged in specific tasks, we can feel the void, but it looms large especially when we are in pain, suffer from frustration or humiliation. Confronted by the void, the imagination springs to life to fill it up with pleasing dreams and thus regain for the individual a specious sense of balance and contentment. Emma Bovary is in all of us. We are all in varying degree fantasists, able to conjure scenarios of revenge in the void of humiliation; love and fame in the void of neglect; wealth in the void of poverty; immortality on the threshold of death. The filling of the void with imaginary consolations makes true contact with reality impossible. "That is why," Simone Weil wrote, "average human beings can become prisoners, slaves, prostitutes, and pass through no matter what suffering without being purified."[28]

We are not quite real and the things we make, particularly artworks that do not answer to practical exigencies, also tend to have a weightless arbitrary character. Nevertheless, for Simone Weil, carefully constructed objects merit esteem, and this is not only because a truly human existence requires them but also because the true nature of created things is that they are "intermediaries, leading from one to the other without end, and ultimately to God."[29] The mediating character of great art is transparent, but it is there in humble objects as well, which, properly viewed, are graded means to superior ends. The city itself (for all its defects) is a supreme human creation—and, for Simone Weil, an intermediary, that is, a point of departure for the Heavenly City, and deserves our love for this reason. To force people out of their home and city is evil not only because it deprives them of a particular livelihood, shelter, and fount of warm human sentiments, but also because it deprives them of the opportunity to freely give up what they have—to uproot themselves.[30]

In presenting sketches of these four figures of "wise and good" I have emphasized what they have in common. One marked trait is worth noting once more because it is shared also among "the simple good." This is a certain indifference to hardship. Socrates is famed for his ability to transcend fatigue and the onslaughts of nature. Confucius sings in the rain. Wittgenstein and Weil both despise the soft life. For our four exemplary figures, this indifference arises primarily out of their absorption in things of far greater importance, but there may well be another reason—one which has been made explicit in the case of Simone Weil—namely, hardship signifies contact with reality. The "wise and good" who do not work with their hands to earn a living must guard against the wayward flights of the free mind. One way to do so is to submit their body to the rude impacts of nature.

More than two thousand years separate our ancient from our modern exemplars of virtue. How do they differ? One striking difference is a sense of ease in the former and of strain in the latter. Socrates and Confucius, for all the quarrels they have with their own society, are fundamentally at home in their culture and world. This is not so with Wittgenstein and Weil. True, they have their light moments. Wittgenstein, for instance, plays practical jokes on his American student Norman Malcolm while they are on their country walks.[31] Simone Weil has her moments of levity and serenity, especially when she is surrounded by the beauty of nature. Her close friend and biographer, Simone Pétrement, notes that Weil can be charming, as a young woman is charming, and on occasion even playfully flirtatious.[32] Yet the prevalent tone of their lives is a forbidding seriousness, grounded in the feeling that the society they know is deeply flawed. The tragedies of their time (outstandingly, the two world wars) no doubt have had an effect, but even more is a general dissatisfaction with society, including much of its proud intellectual achievements. For Wittgenstein, the intellectual life as he knows it at Cambridge is too often frivolous and stained by snobbery. Philosophy seems to be largely clever conversation, a way of being smart and sophisticated, or a game that does not touch the major concerns of life. For Weil, there exists an intolerable gap between the pain in the world—a pain that she sees everywhere and feels in her body—and a delusory, escapist sense of well-being based on a technological prowess that has generated great material wealth. In contrast to Socrates and Confucius, both Wittgenstein and Weil have periodically felt an insistent personal need to serve society as a manual worker or laborer, as though their lives in the world of the upper bourgeoisie are a little unreal.

Fantasy and Imagination 8

Good people have always existed if only as sports of nature and happy circumstance. But they are not so common as we could wish. The wish for them is there, kept alive in a separate compartment of the mind even in the teeth of contrary evidence. When Tolstoy writes such works as "The Power of Darkness" (1886) and "Hadji Murat" (1896–1904), he recognizes violence and cruelty in people close to the soil. Elsewhere, however, he gives redeeming roles to children of nature that can strain our credulity. Ironically, to the extent that Tolstoy wishes to be most simple and direct he may be moving beyond reality into a world of romance. This tendency in the individual or group to fantasize, whether the effort takes the form of stories or tangible creations, is the theme of this chapter.

Individual Fantasies

As visualizing, thinking, and dreaming animals, the distinction for us between imagination and fantasy is almost always fuzzy. In the course of the day, as our energy and ability to attend fluctuate, we slip easily from one mode to the other. Nevertheless, a difference between them exists and can be recognized. If we take imagination to be an attentive mode of inquiry, a vigorous engagement with the real, then fantasy, by contrast, is rudderless delusory imagination, an easy way to fulfill desires. Richard Wollheim provides us with an illustration of the difference when he compares John Stuart Mill's imaginative venture with that of Emma Bovary, a character drawn by Flaubert to exemplify a common type of provincial morality. One day, Mill asked himself whether he would be happy if all the socioeconomic reforms he and other Benthamites had envisaged were to come true. In performing the exercise, he was careful to include all that he knew of himself and of the world. The answer he arrived at, which was "no," surprised him and triggered the great mental crisis of his life. Consider, now, Emma Bovary. In the weeks following the great ball at Vaubyessard, she simply allowed her mind to fill up with such ego-pleasing images as her return to the chateau in the capacity of the vicomte's favorite guest, her travel to the glamorous capital, and her chatting on a plane of equality with ambassadors and duchesses. Mill used his mind to inquire. The image he conjured had sufficient integrity and force to administer a shock. His imagination gained for him new self-knowledge. By contrast, Emma produced fantasies the effect of which was to sink her deeper into self-delusion.[1]

The widespread human tendency to daydream is curtailed when external nature makes heavy demands. Thus in harsh winters, our mind, to the degree that it is forced to cope with nature's threats, must accept nature as it is and not as projections of our wishes. On the other hand, when balmy days arrive, we can sit in a rocking chair on the porch and dream unopposed by intransigent reality. The same is true of the social world. Confronted by a demanding job or in the midst of an active exchange with a fellow human being we cannot easily fantasize, but later in the privacy of our own room we can: we are free then to improve on reality. Although these remarks have the ring of common sense, they can be challenged. Their reverse would seem to be equally plausible. It may be that precisely in the harshness of winter our imagination seeks release in fantasy, and that precisely in the calm days of summer we can best attend to nature as it is.

The questions raised here are concretely illustrated in the story of Carolina Maria de Jesus, a woman of the slums of São Paulo in Brazil. Carolina kept a diary which a journalist discovered in the late 1950s. The publication of this work transformed her overnight into a celebrity first in her native Brazil and then in North America. In the diary, Carolina tells of her filthy home and the equally squalid homes of her neighbors. She notes matter-of-factly the hunger that invades every shack, that drives her to hunt for reusable paper and scraps of metal which will bring just enough to keep her and her children alive. The book is packed with harsh details. A reader may feel that this ability to look at life straight is a characteristic virtue of the poor, for unlike members of the middle class, they cannot easily turn their eyes from the painful and humbling necessities of the human condition. Yet, is it true that the poor are better at facing the real? They may be least able to do so precisely because they are bent under its burden. As Marxists have come to know, the poor are not the natural revolutionary leaders of the world. They may prefer diversionary illusion to understanding, escapism to political struggle, since neither probing into the sources of social and personal dis-ease nor strenuous action promises immediate rewards. Carolina, in her diary, was an exception. Note, however, that at first she herself thought little of her work. When the journalist who discovered her asked for samples of her writing, she proudly offered her fictional romances built around the glittering lives of the rich. Writing plays and novels, she explained, was a way to escape. "When I was writing I was in a golden palace, with crystal windows and silver chandeliers. My dress was finest satin and diamonds sat shining in my black hair. Then I put away my book and the smells came through the rotting walls and rats ran over my feet. My satin turned to rag and the only things shining in my hair were lice."[2]

If the burden of survival disables the poor from facing certain facts of their condition, what about the well educated and well-to-do? Secure in a background of love and in material things, they have the confidence and time to probe the world around them. To a degree, this is true. Detailed and penetrating observations of social life have come from members of the professional middle class: the writings of reformers such as Friedrich Engels and Charles Booth, and of novelists (Zola and Balzac, for example) come to mind. Yet, just as Carolina is exceptional in her world, so are Booth and Zola in theirs. Economic security is as likely to imprison as free the imagination. Money, because it is both abstract and able to command goods and services as though by magic, strongly encourages daydreaming. For this reason alone the affluent fantasize as much, if not more, than do the poor. Money, after all, has the power to make many dreams come true.

But no matter how sheltered one is materially, death remains inevitable. An event that none has personally experienced is one of the most powerful stimulants to daydreaming. Flaubert's characterization of this proclivity, activated at the prospect of death, is classic. Emma Bovary believed herself to be nearing her end and grasped at the chance for one more self-aggrandizing drama. She asked for the sacrament. While attendants prepared her room, she

"felt a powerful influence sweep over her, relieving her of all pain, all perception, all feeling. Her flesh found rest from thought: a new life had begun; it was as if her soul, ascending to God, were about to be swallowed up in His love like burning incense vanishing in smoke. The sheets were sprinkled with holy water, the priest took a white wafer from the sacred pyx, and as she parted her lips to receive the Body of the Savior, she swooned in a celestial bliss. The curtains swelled softly around the bed like clouds, and the rays of the two tapers burning on the night table seemed to shine like dazzling halos. Then she let her head fall back, fancying she heard in space the music of seraphic harps, and perceived in an azure sky, on a golden throne in the midst of saints holding green palms, God the Father, resplendent in majesty, who with a sign sent to earth angels with wings of fire to carry her away in their arms."[3]

For most human beings, decay that prognosticates death and death itself are either veiled in fantasy, or denied. Jean-Paul Sartre, one of the most clear-sighted and courageous individuals of our time, denied that his eyes were failing when they were. As he lay dying, Simone de Beauvoir—another brave individual proud of her and Sartre's ability to face facts—burst into tears and flung herself into the arms of Dr. Housset. "Promise me that he won't know he's dying," she pleaded, "that he won't go through any mental anguish, that he won't have any pain!" For a philosopher who throughout his professional life had argued for authenticity and the need to rise above false consciousness, his own cozened end, staged by his life-long colleague in the search for truth, was ironic.[4]

Fantasy permeates human relationships. This is particularly true of love, which is grounded on dependency and need. Frustrated love is among the most powerful generators of illusion. When the beloved is absent or fails to act in a desired manner, images of compensations grow unrestrained. The images are unreal, yet the events they depict can seem to have actually occurred so that at the next meeting, if the behavior of the beloved fails to conform to expectation, a lacerating sense of betrayal takes hold; and in the effort to overcome the feeling of disappointment and pain love can turn into hatred. The more emotional the personal bond the more likely it is to breed fantasy. The lover has unreal expectations of the beloved, the ambitious parent of his child, and the young child of his powerful parent. Friendship, by contrast, is built on a shared interest in the external world rather than on unyielding need. When friends turn their attention on each other, they can do so free from the distorting lens of emotional dependency.

Group Fantasies

Fantasies are easily shared, despite their freewheeling thrust, which suggests that outside madness the seemingly wild, individualistic images of a particular mind are in fact constrained by culture and the group. Myths and moral edifices, of the kind sketched in chapters 2 and 3, may be regarded as group fantasies. In common with the tall stories of secular culture, myths pile detail upon detail, improbability upon improbability, and yet far from arousing suspicion and antagonism in their listeners they are warmly received. Modern scholars treat myths with respect, for beneath the enchanting flow of implausible events they discern codes and charters for society. A serious purpose is there, but I think we should also see myths as the mind at play. In playfulness, they soar beyond details taken from ordinary life to touch the edges of the impossible.[5] Many myths indeed move into the realm of the fantastic and the grotesque, where they take on the surrealism of nightmares and dreams. Such accounts, when read in a book, can seem childish or absurd. However, in context, in the extraordinary settings in which they are told—they have the power to entrance—that is, suppress all doubt and appear utterly convincing. At a level beyond common sense, they make sense. Their comprehensibility is transposed to nature and society. The world itself, for all its disjunctions and shocks, seems comprehensible, which it must if people are to live in it.

Consider a cosmological story of the Bushmen (!Kung San) of the Kalahari Desert.

> "At night when the sun sets, the people with no knees catch it and kill it, for the sun is meat. They put it in a pot, and when it is cooked they tell their children to run off and play, and when the children are gone the no-knee adults eat it. When the children come back, the adults pick their teeth and give what they remove to the children, and then they take the shoulder blade of the sun and throw it back into the east again, where a new sun grows and rises in the morning."

But how can people without knees lie down? A Bushman informs his ethnographic enquirer, no doubt half teasingly, that he has gone west to satisfy his curiosity and found that, as he had suspected, the no-knee people do not lie down but rest by leaning against the forks of a tree.[6]

Bushmen know of human beings different from them and far more powerful than they are. In the above tale such people are distinguished by not having knees. The no-knees are able to obtain food from the sun without exhausting it; that is, they can return the sun to the sky. They eat the food and give the bits that stick in their teeth to the children. In this practice, as in anatomy and power, they differ from the Bushmen, who are fond of their young and in times of scarcity will deprive themselves so that the children may eat. Bushmen seem to find assurance in the virtue of their own behavioral code by envisaging its opposite in an alien people. This tale, like others in their repertory, is filled with extravagant imaginative flights that are at odds with their normal commonsensical ways of managing a difficult life. Yet it typically contains gratuitous details that anchor it in the familiar, such as the food that sticks in the teeth and the logic that no-knee people sleep standing up, propped against trees; and of course it draws attention to the vital role of the sun in human life.

High cultures in premodern times have created exceedingly complex cosmographies. To our critical eye, they can seem extravagances that bear little relation to observable facts. We dismiss them as science; or, if we admire them, we do so as we would free works of art. Yet, although premodern cosmographies are indeed highly imaginative constructions, they can also lay claim to being true pictures of the real. High-culture cosmographies, besides their religious function, have intimate ties with the nascent astronomies of their time, which rely on instrumental techniques of varying degrees of sophistication. Consider an Indian world-picture that can be found in the Viṣṇu Purāṇa of the fourth century A.D. Stated in barest outline, the cosmos "is composed of a flat disk marked by a series of concentric circles, with a second disk of heavenly bodies moving about it. Mount Meru constitutes the pivot that joins the disk of heaven to the disk of the earth and defines their relationships." A full account will overwhelm the uninitiated reader: details swarm and proliferate, multiple planes of existence connect in the most intricate ways, vast spaces stretch the limit of imagination and yet are numerically defined. The geometry and geography of this universe, seemingly the product of phantasmagoric minds, nevertheless derive from the measuring principles of the astrolabe. A parallel can be seen between the astrolabe's planispheric projection of disks lying one on top of the other and the planes of existence of the Purāṇa universe. Mount Meru, one notes, is located on the Tropic of Cancer, which marks the limit of the sun's northern progress. The sun does not and cannot move beyond Meru. In the Viṣṇu Purāṇa this limit is presented in the mythopoeic language of salvation.

> As far as the sun shines in front, so far he shines behind and on either hand, illuminating all places except the summit of Meru, the mountain of immortals; for when his rays reach the court of Brahma, which is there situated, they are expelled and driven back by the overpowering radiance which there prevails.[7]

Astronomy is the scaffold on which a cosmology of salvation is draped. How many people can understand the total picture? Very few, if for no other reason than that it is the accretional product of many talents working over a long period of time. Does it have an overall design? Yes, insofar as it successfully articulates the shared fundamental beliefs and values of a people; no, if by design one envisages the existence of a single originating and controlling mind that can enforce closure, or oɪ an institution that recognizes and tries to maintain the design's basic features. In the absence of closure or of institutional proctoring, a schema may in time become obscured through the steady accumulation of new adventitious elements. The inhabitants of a large and complex edifice are likely to attend only to those parts that are dramatic and gaudy, or those that directly address their hopes and fears.

Buddhist cosmology—a vigorous offspring of Hindu thought—provides an example. It embraces innumerable world systems, each of which has thirty-one planes of existence divided into three major categories: the *kama loka* of sensual forms and desires, the *rupa loka* of intellectual enjoyment, and the *arupa loka* of no perceptible bodily form and no sensation. The lowest and most corporeal of the categories is *kama loka*. In this category are six heavens and five worlds. The lowest of the five worlds contains eight major (as well as a number of subsidiary) hells, located in the interior of the earth. Few people can remember and distinguish among all these divisions and subdivisions, which proliferate as social classes and distinctions increase. Most likely to stay in the minds of illiterate and semiliterate folks are the images of heaven and hell—heaven full of sensual delight and hell full of physical torments. The imagery of hell, considered as an achievement of art, has at least the merit of vividness and power: the murals on Buddhist temples in Thailand and Ceylon are gruesome enough to arouse a shudder.[8] By contrast, the imagery of heaven tends to be vacuous, despite the wealth of details. Here is heaven, according to a Thai law book (Book of Indra):

> There is a celestial abode in the Dewa heavens, an aerial dwelling covered with gold and gems, with roofs shining with gold and gems, with rooms shining with gold and jewels, and roof points of crystal and pearl; and the whole gleams with wrought and unwrought gold more brilliant than all the gems. Around its eaves plays the soft sound of tinkling golden bells. There dwell a thousand lovely houris, virgins in gorgeous attire, decked with the richest ornaments, singing sweet songs in concert, with a melody whose resounding strains are never still. This celestial abode is adorned with lotus lakes, and meandering rivers full of the five kinds of lotus

whose golden petals, as they fade, fill all the air with sweet odours.[9]

From such accounts, it is obvious that if an individual's fantasy can be simple-minded and oppressively unimaginative, so can be that of a group.

Dreams Come True

Daydreams and fantasies have, however, their uses; they provide holidays from responsible life. Young children, who have little responsibility, entertain many fantasies, which are an ebullience of the mind just as their somersaults are a natural expression of the vitality of the body. Both kinds of exercise are aids to growth; they expand, respectively, the children's mental and physical worlds. Adults, too, need to "let go" from time to time, allow their minds to wander unfettered, just as periodically they may "whoop it up" or collapse in an armchair with the abandon of a teenager. A good spinner of yarn, no matter how fantastic, is often appreciated as one may appreciate any other temporary form of excess innocently and skillfully performed. Fantasizing, moreover, can be practical. It benignly relieves periods of stress that all human beings unavoidably suffer.[10] Frequent indulgence in fantasy, however, will have the effect of draining the world of substantiality. In the effort to escape life's restrictions, a man may end up in the prison of his own mind—one that is no longer nurtured by the external world.

Daydreams can be turned into good stories, but seldom into anything more tangible. Yet there are exceptions. As we have noted in chapter 5, potentates can force reality to conform to their dreams. Even heaven, as it is depicted in the Book of Indra, is reproducible on earth. Some gardens known to history are as fabulous (an inevitable epithet) as are the paradises of religious literature. The "thousand lovely houris" of the Book of Indra are matched by the numerous concubines, "all beautiful, respectful, virtuous and lovely of face," that are housed in the Sui emperor's garden, built outside of Lo-yang in A.D. 617. Decay cannot be permitted in heaven; hence, in the Sui emperor's garden, trees and bushes that have lost their leaves during the fall season are decked with simulated leaves of glistening fabrics; and in the lakes, along with real lotuses, are artificial ones that never fade.[11]

The powerful ruler can realize his fantasy another way, through the device of theater or spectacle, which in both premodern China and Europe often took place in the garden and was a part of its world of illusion. In Europe, the Royal Spectacle substituted for the pliant cosmos that Renaissance and Baroque potentates could not, for all their vaunted power, command. Only in extravagant masques and plays were they able to delude themselves into thinking that they, like the gods, could fulfill their every wish.[12] Far larger in scale than the theater and the garden palace was the royal city. The founding of a city stood for the founding of an entire world, a temptation to grandeur that few rulers, supported by their ambitious architect-engineers, were able to resist. The conversion of an architectural dream into reality not only tended to drain the state treasury but might cause the death of a large number of workers, as it did in the construction of Versailles. In building the imperial capital of St. Petersburg, nearly 150,000 workers were permanently incapacitated or lost their lives. Despite such casualties the Russian state apparatus continued to draw on a seemingly inexhaustible reservoir of labor from the interior. Versailles was a stage designed at a scale appropriate to the ego of Louis XIV; likewise St. Petersburg for Peter I. As these places rose from their ill-favored settings (a dry plain in the one case and a swamp in the other) they could only be described as fabulous.[13]

More ambitious than dreams that seek to transform stone are those that seek to mold human beings into a new ideal. Directed at small groups, the effect of such visionary zeal is the creation of different kinds of religious and utopian communities. Most of these disappear after a few years or remain small. Some are able to attract large numbers to their way of life in a short period of time and become conspicuously successful. Think of the Cistercian movement under Bernard of Clairvaux: 307 new communities were established between 1125–51, an achievement without parallel in the history of monasticism.[14] Think of the Mormons who could barely hang on to the edge of the Great Basin in 1847, and yet by 1877 (the year Brigham Young died) some 140,000 Mormons were able to sink roots in the desert wilderness.[15] Think, more generally, of the great American experiment—the dream of creating the new Adam in a New World. Despite great differences in scale and sociocultural milieus, these ventures have certain key elements in common: discontent with the old way of life; the appeal of a new vision propagated by leaders of strong personality and conviction; a willingness to move into a new and little-known environment; a willingness to submit to the discipline of communal life and the flexibility to adapt to unforeseen circumstance.

The word *vision* raises the issue of realism. What the prophet sees cannot be just a dream, but how realistic must it be? Bernard of Clairvaux can draw on an ancient tradition for his projects. As a feat of settlement, impressive to us now is more the scale of the venture than its newness. In distinction, the Pilgrim settlers of the eastern seaboard could not draw on past experience; they lacked assurance that their vision of life in the New World was sound. Nevertheless, they must act on trust. The Mormon case is similar. Mormon leaders tried to obtain the best information they could of their prospective home in Utah. The report from John Charles Frémont seemed reassuring. From its positive elements, Mormon leaders no doubt felt justified in conjuring a glowing image of the promised land that would inspire their followers to move west. When natural disasters struck in the first two years of settlement and grumbling voices were heard, Brigham Young chose not to yield. He could not, of course, simply deny the reality. In his sermon of February 4, 1849, he declared that God "will rebuke the frost and the sterility of the soil, and the land shall become fruitful." But he also asserted, in the teeth of discouraging experience, that "We have the finest climate, the best water, and the purest air that can be found on the earth."[16]

In sharp contrast to these communal ventures, which all require exit from unsatisfactory conditions at home and a new start elsewhere, are the great social revolutions of the last two hundred years. For the revolutionaries, an existing society must be demolished so that a better one can be erected in its place. The French Revolution has given birth to the slogan "liberty, equality, and fraternity"—humanitarian ideals that were a source of inspiration to the Russian and Chinese revolutions of our time. But no matter how elevated the dream of the architects of the new order, its violent imposition on existent reality can do great harm if only because revolutionaries must first lay waste a complex historical social fabric, which for all its defects and evil, also contains in its interstices much ordinary human good—the oases of mutual help created patiently by private individuals and small groups in their struggle to maintain life.

Revolutionaries and architects of a new order must be exceptionally imaginative if they are to succeed in producing a superior world. The easiest step is the first, which is to be acutely aware of the nature and extent of malfunctioning and evil in the old society; more difficult is to conceive of procedures that can effectively remove them; but most difficult of all is to see concretely the good that is to come. Liberty, equality, and fraternity are only dreams unless they can be embodied in sociopolitical institutions. What forms should these take? How are they to be established and how will they work? There is the further question, What will be the quality of day-to-day life in the new society? How can one picture it?

When the word "picture" or "image" is used, we naturally think of a world that appeals to the eye. But we live in a multisensory world, not just a visual one: the environment envisaged by most planners and designers is therefore an abstraction—a visual fantasy. If a planner can transcend this limitation and conceive a multisensory world of great beauty and subtlety, it will still only be a stage. The question remains, How will people benefit from such a world and what will their daily life be like? To grasp the human scene more firmly calls for a planner who also possesses the talent of a novelist—someone able to see in the projected world individualized moral beings engaged in the affairs and mutualities of ordinary life.

Even such brief reflections can make the task of utopian planning seem insuperable. The severe limitations of knowledge and imagination can never be overcome. Yet the world has not lacked utopian planners and social reformers of great ambition. Moreover, quite ordinary folk have dreamed of the good life in an idealized suburb, new town, or rural commune. We are all able to picture some perfected world out there or in the foreseeable future that we can eventually move into or help to create. But will we *really* like it once it becomes reality? Will we feel happy and fulfilled living there? An affirmative answer is plausible because it is easy to specify the things we don't want: that negative certainty gives us an unjustified confidence in our power to envisage the good. Take the questions just posed. John Stuart Mill, we have noted, tried to imagine a society free of the evils and imperfections of his time. He concluded that such a society, if it could be realized, would not have made him happy. William James also asked whether a society without most of the known defects could be truly fulfilling. Unlike Mill, James found his answer by visiting a real place—the famous Assembly

Grounds on the borders of Chautauqua Lake—that seemed to provide all the satisfactions and virtues human beings could reasonably want:

> The moment one treads that sacred enclosure, one feels one's self in an atmosphere of success. Sobriety and industry, intelligence and goodness, orderliness and ideality, prosperity and cheerfulness, pervade the air. It is a serious and studious picnic on a gigantic scale. Here you have a town of many thousands of inhabitants, beautifully laid out in a forest, and equipped with means for satisfying all the necessary lower and most of the superfluous wants of man. You have general religious services and special club houses for the several sects. You have perpetually running soda fountains, and daily popular lectures by distinguished men. You have the best company, and yet no effort. You have no zymotic diseases, no poverty, no drunkenness, no crime, no police. You have culture, you have kindness, you have equality, you have the best fruits of what mankind has sought and bled and striven for under the name of civilization for centuries. You have in short a foretaste of what human society might be, were it all in the light, with no suffering and no dark corners.[17]

Yet James was pleased to have left it to return to "the dark and wicked world again." He found society at Chautauqua Lake "too tame," its culture "too second-rate," its goodness "too uninspiring." It lacked, for James, strength, intensity, and danger, or what he called "the element of precipitousness." This discontent with and suspicion of any order of goodness that a human mind can conceive and human will make real is forcefully stated in a novel by the Czech author Milan Kundera. He begins with the idea of "kitsch," a mid-nineteenth-century German word which other European tongues were quick to adopt. Through repeated use this word, he says, "has obliterated its original metaphysical meaning: kitsch is the absolute denial of shit, in both the literal and the figurative senses of the word; kitsch excludes everything from its purview that which is essentially unacceptable to human existence."

We have noted earlier that the guardians of society show a tendency to expurgate from their moral-religious world view any acknowledgment of the fact of the body, its limitations and imperious demands. Shit and the passions—the underside of human reality—are excised and what is left, for all its high moral tenor, can seem too much an indulgent flight of the mind. The Russian critic Mikhail Bakhtin sees capitalism as the force that has destroyed the boisterously comedic, reality-soaked world of the Middle Ages, and created in its place the dream-like, hypocritically good world of the bourgeoisie.[18] If so, communism has done nothing to supplant the bourgeois kitsch; to the contrary, it has embraced the chaste, sentimental vision whole. Soviet films that flooded East European countries during the Stalinist era show socialist peoples who lead lives of an incredible innocence. In such films the greatest conflict that can occur between a man and a woman is a lovers' misunderstanding, one that will be removed in the final scene as they fall into each other's arms, tears of happiness trickling down their cheeks. The usual interpretation of these films is that they show the communist ideal, not its harsh reality. But suppose the good society of the propaganda machines has been made real. Will it really be better to live in it? In his novel Kundera has Sabina (an oppressed intellectual in Czechoslovakia) imagine such a world. "She felt a shiver run down her back. She would unhesitatingly prefer life in a real communist regime with all its persecution and meat queues. Life in the real communist world was still livable. In the world of the communist ideal made real, in that world of grinning idiots, she would have nothing to say, she would die of horror within a week."[19]

Sabina would seem to be a superior person who suffers from periodic attacks of *nostalgie de la boue*, a typical upper middle-class intellectual who already lives comfortably and so can afford to look down on the clean and pretty world of kitsch. If Sabina and her creator invite this criticism, then so does William James who has shown disdain for what he considers to be the sanitized, mediocre life at Chautauqua Lake. While one can sympathize with the feeling of irritation toward the bland respectability—the self-congratulatory contentment—of the good life pictured in advertisements, and toward the appetite for human-interest stories that always end happily or in moral uplift, we should remember that such images of bliss are those of decent, hardworking folks throughout the modern and modernizing world, socialist as well as capitalist. Moreover, it is too easy to point one's finger at the mediocrity and tawdriness in other people's dreams. When the challenge is to articulate concretely, in detail, a vision of the good, can even the sharpest and most imaginative minds (Mill and James, for example) and the brightest utopian thinkers and revolutionaries do much better?

9 Imagination and Creativity

In the West, the degree of esteem accorded to imagination has had a checkered history. Plato places it in the lowest rank of mental faculties, for he sees it as an instance of mere supposing, a phantom sort of knowing, unless it is a seizure by "divine frenzy" when it becomes creative (*Phaedrus*). Aristotle gives it a middle-level status between perception and intellect, but he also says that, unlike sensing and thinking, it is "for the most part false." In the modern period, Hume asserts that "nothing is more dangerous to reason than the flights of the imagination," and yet he sees understanding itself as "the general and more established properties of the imagination." Kant, while he rejects the merely "visionary" tendencies of the mind, conceives of an "inventive" imagination which is essential to knowledge because it is the source of all intellectual synthesis. Romantics of the nineteenth century regard imagination as the highest of mental faculties, intimately tied to creativity. This high standing is retained in our own time, especially in educational literature and rhetoric.[1]

The Modern Period

Imagination is esteemed because it enables us to perceive truly—because it gives us access to the real. What is real may not be good, but what is good must be real. Connecting the good with the real, which is at the center of Plato's thought, has ever since been a key idea in Western aesthetic-moral philosophy. In this book, I have drawn attention to certain premodern attitudes toward the real, to the moral standing of imagination, and to the possibility of progress. Now I should like to turn to the modern period and explore this same set of related issues, for they remain very much alive. The real, despite the fuzziness of the idea, is still an anchor among aspirants toward the good. As for progress, an idea so powerful in the eighteenth and nineteenth centuries has suffered a precipitous decline since the first world war. Progress in the technological fields is undeniable, but progress in all other areas of human endeavor—particularly the imaginative and the moral—is easily and often challenged. Indeed, among intellectuals it is considered a sign of superficiality to see any evidence in its favor. Even Marxists, whose philosophy commits them to optimism, achieve esteem by revealing the decay and moral degeneration of capitalism rather than by presenting a glowing picture of a socialist or communist utopia. The modern temper has been inclined to identify the dark side of life with the real, confronting which demonstrates one's fundamental seriousness. By contrast, imagining the bright future is fantasy and self-indulgence.

Progress is still taken for granted as both desirable and possible in our personal life: most of us not only want but think it possible to be happier, wiser, and better. In public life, the ambitious politician must still show that he believes in it: progress must remain for him a bright and rousing image to be burnished anew each time he faces the voters. Isn't it still a fairly widespread hope that "things will somehow get better?" I believe it is, despite a discernible erosion of its force among middle-class Americans and Europeans, overcome by visions of environmental degradation, resource depletion, and social unrest. The idea of progress has not altogether lost its lure. Economists all over the world still speak of development. It is the inclusion of a moral-aesthetic component at its core that makes the idea problematical. Yet I think that even then we have reason to be tentatively optimistic. "Despairing optimist," a title that René Dubos has coined for himself, is one that I should like to appropriate. To Dubos, a measure of optimism is justified by the improvements, both in beauty and in ecological diversity, that have taken place in many parts of the earth, including (a token list) his own beloved Île-de-France, the intricately terraced landscapes of South China, Hawaiian Islands whose lushness owes so much to the introduction of exotic plants, and dry lands made green by irrigation.[2]

Nature, Dubos says, does not always "know best." It is often wasteful and indifferent to the creative possibilities of situation. Human beings, who are the most plastic and perhaps the only self-critical part of nature, can improve upon the given, enriching and harmonizing its components. The given includes our own moral nature, which we can change for the better. Opting for the path of greater understanding, advocated by both religious and humanist traditions, is possible. We can always try to see reality more adequately and justly, with decreasing servitude to the deep insecurity and constricting passions of individual and collective egos. So long as such a course lies open, optimism is not mere foolishness. Why, then, "despairing"? The horrors of the modern world apart, there is the sense that wisdom itself is problematical, if we mean by it not only an awareness of our own severely constraining "heart of darkness" but also of the fact that as our knowledge of the world and as our moral sensibility increase, more and more dilemmas and contradictions of life—hitherto hidden from view—emerge, which can overwhelm us with a sense of futility.

Aspirations toward the Real

In a moral-aesthetic sense, progress is toward the real: now we see through a glass darkly, in the future we can hope for greater transparency. But what is the real? Like Augustine's observation concerning time, we know what it is until we ask. To Plato, only the eternal forms are real; the other things are all more or less shadowy distortions. In Christian thought, influenced by Platonism, only God is real and good, and all the other things are pale, passing figurations of the one uncaused existence. In the conception of secular Renaissance humanism, the real is constant, unitary, and somehow simple, like the eternal forms, the circular motion of the stars, and the fundamental moral laws. By early modern times, natural laws derived from the measurable (primary) characteristics of things are thought to be real. People speak of searching for them and discovering them as they do of new lands beyond the seas. Natural laws have the mark of reality because unlike the phenomena they describe they appear simple and invariant. In some ultimate sense, the real are regularities and patterns invisible to the senses and manifest only as mathematical equations.

Alongside this Platonic conception of the real, a strong counterbelief flourishes, according to which *things* are the bedrock of reality: realism is "thingism."[3] Fascination for things, in European science from the seventeenth century onward, is indicated by the rising popularity for collecting natural objects from all over the world and by a growing interest in natural history. Naturalists describe objects in loving detail and set them up in elaborate taxonomies. Artists, too, show a fascination for objects (natural and artifactitious), which they depict with the utmost care and skill.[4]

Science is impartial. It casts its net wide to include not only the sublime and the permanent but also the ugly and the seemingly inconsequential. It assumes a moral tone when it claims to face facts—to help people live in the real world without the embellishments and consolation necessary to a more childish and fearful age.[5] What about art? Consider a striking difference between Chinese and European traditions in painting. Painting, in these two cultures, is a representational art. It has, until modern times, shown a natural inclination to capture what is in the external world. Chinese art is famed for its portrayals of landscape which, as Arthur de Carle Sowerby and Joseph Needham have shown, are far more realistic than uninformed viewers have assumed.[6] Whatever doubt one may continue to hold about the realism of Chinese landscape paintings, faithfulness to the real is clearly evident in pictures of the smaller, discrete units of nature. We need only be reminded of the numerous representations of horses and their bearded Central Asian grooms (a theme popular since the T'ang dynasty), and of birds and flowers, such as the Sung artist Li Han-chung's "Quail" and the Ming artist Ch'en Tao-fu's "Lotus." But respectable Chinese artists have shunned the underside of life—dirt and decay, suffering and death. Their tradition would not have considered varicose veins and dirty feet, as Caravaggio in Europe had done. And Caravaggio could do so not only because he was a genius but because his art developed out of centuries of close attention to thieves on the cross and to blood-and-sweat-stained, agonized Christs. As another striking case of this concern for the darker side, think of Rembrandt, his grim portrayals of anatomy lessons and his two pictures of the slaughtered ox—great bloody carcasses—both painted, apparently, in the same year, 1655.[7] Whereas Chinese artists traditionally portray live birds and vigorous plants, their European counterparts may also depict dead pheasants and "still lifes" (such as those of the Baroque period) in which the fruits show obvious signs of decay.[8] This absorption in the physically real, warts and all, continues in the sensibility of modern Western artists. Picasso, for example, admires the physicality of Degas's "pig-faced whores." "You can smell them," he says. Picasso himself aims at this physicality. He shows some paintings to Braque and asks: "Is this woman real? Can she go out in the street? Is she a woman or a picture?" And more aggressively, "Do her armpits smell?"[9]

Experiences of reality will either quickly fade or remain locked in the private worlds of individuals, sustained only by memory, unless they are represented in art. However, in the unremitting effort to represent, the artists are easily led to create fantasy worlds of their own, remote from direct experience. The doubt about creativity that we have noted in traditional societies and in premodern times remains alive to disturb the conscience of European artists and thinkers in modern times. Artists are aware that the nature of their product is strongly affected by the means they employ. The further the means departs from the simple pen and brush or solo voice, the more the artwork must assume a complexly planned character. The nineteenth century, which could boast of magniloquent constructions—the large symphonic orchestra, the multivolumed novel, and, egregiously, the grand opera—was also a time when certain artistic consciences rebelled against the tumid scale. Such a conscience would have considered lyric poetry superior to tragedy, for whereas lyric poetry strove toward a human cry preserved almost accidentally in language, tragedy dealt too much with events and the externalities of human relations, and, moreover, it was too dependent for its realization on stage, scenery, players, managers, and seamstresses.[10] Tolstoy in his old age wanted to disown his big novels in favor of his short stories and fables inspired by folktales; and among the nonliterary arts he thoroughly disliked the opera. Tolstoy would have agreed with his contemporary, Giuseppe Verdi, who wrote after the death of his wife: "Great grief does not demand great expression; it asks for silence, isolation, and I would even say the torture of reflection. Words dull, enervate, and destroy feeling. There is something superficial about all exteriorization . . . a profanation." These are the words of a composer who spent his life exteriorizing feelings with consummate skill.[11]

Perceiving the Particular

In contrast to fantasy, which are the more or less free-floating projections of our own mind, the real confronts us as the other "out there." An attribute of the moral person is that he recognizes not only the existence of the other but also its unique combination of qualities. This specialness, once recognized, commands respect. A poorly differentiated world such as the one we are steeped in when we have a severe cold is—to the degree that it is undifferentiated—lacking in value, including the feel of moral import. It follows that the more diversified and individualized the world appears to a person the more that world is for him imbued with the beauty and worth of actualized presences, however fleeting, and the more these presences call for some kind of response—contemplative, appreciative, or in physical action.

A striking power of the human mind is its ability to discern individuality and hence value in objects. Generally speaking, the higher up the phylogenetic scale the more likely animals are to possess the power to discriminate among objects without special training, that is, show preference for one thing rather than another by virtue of a certain conflation of properties. Insects live in a world so schematic that even mating has little of the character of action between distinctive individuals. A male wasp will attempt to copulate with a piece of paper on which a female wasp has been crushed. A hen feels for her chick and will respond to its cries but should the chick be seen behind a glass plate the soundless movements of struggle leave the mother cold.[12] Rats give no sign of being able to distinguish between individual objects and persons in their perceptual field: all cheeses and human beings are much the same. Dogs can readily tell a number of objects and persons apart, preferring one particular ball or woman to another and maintaining the preference over an extended period of time. "The chimpanzee is very selective in his behavior toward a great number of objects, and is clearly able to distinguish a large number of persons (whom he sees often) from strangers."[13]

Human beings, endowed with imagination to a high degree, are able to live in a vivid reality. But they seldom do so. The world pulsates with the energy and brightness of being only in privileged moments. A unique capability of the human mind is put to little use. A variety of reasons account for the neglect, the most common and dominant of which is the need to be efficient: efficiency requires that most of the time we ignore the rich texture of reality to attend to only one aspect of it—its use. A world of tools is highly schematic because tools, by their very nature, are perceived one-dimensionally. Routine, too, makes the world schematic; and routine is a strategy of efficiency to the degree that it enables us to get the work done by not attending fully to the things at hand. Fatigue has a similar effect. In the morning, when we feel most vital, the world is packed with noteworthy objects, but with the onset of fatigue at the end of the day they lose their singularity. Shop fronts become mere intervals of space and the people we encounter on the sidewalk dull, undifferentiated figures. Reality is reduced to landmarks and directions necessary to finding our way home.[14]

What is a vase? To the fond owner it is not only a container for holding plants but a unique object of a certain weight, color, sheen, odor, and ring when tapped. To know the vase really well requires time and imagination. When I first buy it I may be drawn only to its more superficial qualities. In time, as I use, clean, and contemplate it, it becomes for me more and more a captivating presence. Can the reality of a vase ever be exhaustively appreciated? Is there a point at which I can say, after seeing how its color alters with changing light in the room, that there is no more to be known? If a simple vase is potentially inexhaustible, what are we to say of a great work of art, an animal, or a human being?[15]

Culture affects how one sees and what one sees. In our modern literate culture, realist fiction and detailed, descriptive social surveys direct the reader's attention to things that normally escape his consciousness either because they are too painful or because they have become too familiar. But even works of fantasy, by which I mean a literary genre and not works rendered fantastic and unreal through feebleness of imagination, can help. A fairy tale, for example, is full of marvels but these often occur in the midst of the furnishings of ordinary existence.

Reading such a tale, the senses dulled by routine learn to focus appreciatively once more on a loaf of bread, a wooden bench, or the smell of rain. A fairy tale also makes it possible for the reader enmeshed in the familiar to savor imaginatively certain extreme experiences—for instance, maximum mobility, which, I believe, can be better conveyed by envisaging a ride on a flying carpet than a ride in any other mode of transportation.[16]

Other nonrealist genres of literature are likewise able to introduce or reintroduce the reader to neglected and forgotten facets of the real. Pastoral poetry is distant from workaday concerns; yet as it evokes a mood and a place that breaks the coils of habit, it makes the reader more sensorily aware—more responsive, in particular, to the nonvisual qualities of an environment. Broad comedy and farce distort, sometimes grotesquely, but by challenging those safe pieties in the ordered world they restore to their audience an enlarged and problematical understanding of human nature. Artworks in the heroic mode confront people with the reality of good and evil, waking them from the slumber into which they may have fallen through indolence or sophistry. If comedy and farce allow explosive release and encourage the acceptance of human beings as the vain and deluded creatures that they are, tales of heroism can motivate their listeners and readers to paths of selfless action that bring about change.[17]

Paradoxes of Progress

In a perfect world, nothing is permanently consigned to the shadow, mere background, or insignificance. Every object, as the eyes fall upon it, calls for an appreciative response. Even in a defective world, while evil must be recognized for what it is and given no quarter, an inclination to discern worth in all manner of things is counted a virtue. Virtue is, first of all, a matter of seeing truly. As we have noted earlier, in a world in which practicality and efficiency are stressed, use objects—including people (e.g., factory hands)—are little noticed once they are absorbed into routine. Tools, however, can regain visibility with a change of context. A hammer becomes a presence in its own right when it is taken from the workbench and mounted on a pedestal in a museum. Young children, not yet yoked to practical life and work, live in a world luminous with vital objects—a world adults look back upon wistfully. Sophisticated individuals may envy the innocent eye of whatever age that can discern the thing in itself, detached from the cobwebs of meaning that accrue to it by reason of function, money value, or social status.

To the innocent eye is credited not only aesthetic but moral grace. The child is good because she does not judge in accordance with the values of the world, and treasures the sparkle of glass in the sun no less than the glitter of gold. We appear to be returning to the idea that the good person is someone simple and unlearned. Opposed to it, however, is the idea that context can greatly enhance an object's visibility and import. The magical ambience in a fairy tale is the context for seeing anew the endearing reality of ordinary household things. The daisy that casts a shadow and thus "protects the lingering dew drop from the sun" (Wordsworth) acquires heroic stature by virtue of its position between sun and dewdrop; perceived as an isolated existence, with the innocent eye, it would have been at most only a bright flower. A hammer loses its individuality in the workaday world, and yet because it is a common tool normally submerged in its ground, it can reemerge as a powerful symbol for human labor and creativity. The human person, treated as a mere hand, fades into the woodwork, but it is by being situated in work and soaked in ordinary human realities that he or she gains a sense of substance and worth.

Thus we move to embrace the opposite position, which is as much justified by common sense and experience as the first, namely, the trained rather than the innocent eye sees, and this training is an endless venture. Any object can be looked at afresh and surprising facets will emerge as it is seen in a different or in an expanded net of relations, and as culture provides new instruments for seeing. The microscope and the telescope have opened up reality at the two ends of the universal scale, whereas the movie camera, by giving us close-up shots, forces us to be aware, perhaps for the first time in human history, of the detailed topography and shifting moods of even the stranger's face.[18] Civilization, achieved at great cost and morally suspect in so many ways, is nevertheless able to provide those spacious, varied, and often new contexts in which individual objects, including human beings, can take on fresh patinas of dignity and luster. Just as we may feel ambivalence toward the supernatural edifice of a fairy tale and yet love the details it contains and illuminates, so we may question the truth of a complex moral-religious system and yet appreciate the way it can enlarge our conception of individual worth.

The moral tales of nonliterate and early literate cultures tend to be mixed genres in which the sacred and the profane, the spiritually elevating and the earthy are indiscriminately combined. By contrast, in high literate cultures the two ends of human experience may be kept—sometimes rigidly—apart. Above ground is the shining edifice; below ground, repressed from consciousness, lies the dark and dank cellar of unmentionable urges and passions. It is easy to fault high culture for denying certain fundamentals of human experience. On the other hand, culture *is* selectivity. A culture is "progressive" if it consistently selects and develops certain areas of human experience at the expense of others. It moves by its own light toward what it conceives to be a higher level of human existence.

Imagination can be bland, and "bland" (that is, somehow one-dimensional and inconsequential) even when it is fantastic. Imagination is suspect because it can obfuscate or mislead. On the other hand, it is the faculty that gives human beings their uniquely vivid world. Religion, philosophy, and poetry at their highest levels of achievement have provided people with subtle and vigorous languages by means of which they can articulate and realize for themselves the scope and fullness of human existence. Architectural and technological imagination at its best has created physical milieus that have enabled people to experience a level of well-being and stimulation that they could not otherwise have known. I offer the following examples from the last two hundred years, and if they seem commonplace, that in itself shows how tastes are shared and also how quickly the good things in public life are taken for granted: children's playgrounds, family restaurants, tree-lined boulevards, glass-roofed arcades, central heating, air-conditioned coffee shops in steamy summers, telephone booths, the subways of Moscow and Montreal, the automobile, science museums, and the bright, friendly campuses of the newer institutions of learning.[19]

Progress has no doubt occurred in science and technology. I return to the difficult question, Has there been moral progress? In the last century or so, calamities such as imperial conquest and exploitation, racism, the two world wars, and the continuing ruthless destruction of nature have made guilt-ridden Westerners shy of entertaining, even in the privacy of their own minds, the idea of moral progress. If they admit a glimmer of light, it is the full recognition of the depth and extent of evil that their culture has perpetrated. To forfend despair, they exaggerate the state of grace of non-Western cultures and peoples, who are roped off like wildlife, protected against contrary evidence and the probing intellect.

Despair of the species is a possible posture, but surely a biased one. The human story is by no means one of unrelieved darkness and horror. Bright reaches exist, and even within those that are dark we can probably find individuals of high moral seriousness, including people who, when the occasion demands, transcend mere custom. But if this picture is correct the idea of progress is again stymied, for there is no reason to believe that more such exceptional individuals live now than have lived, proportionally, in the past. Suppose, however, we consider the level of moral sensitivity in society as a whole rather than exceptional individuals; and suppose, further, that we take moral sensitivity to be a disposition to respect the humanity of strangers, or public manners. It may be, then, that in the last two centuries we can detect signs of improvement—thrusts, however tentative and unsecured, toward greater civility.

What are some of the signs? For the Western world, I offer the following list which can easily be extended. Cruelty was not one of the seven deadly sins; now it it perhaps the single human trait that arouses the greatest revulsion. The word atrocity itself came into use only in the eighteenth century.[20] Torture of political prisoners in the depths of faceless buildings is still a common practice of totalitarian regimes, but not long ago society showed no shame at all about torturing and humiliating miscreants in public places; indeed such happenings were a sort of tourist attraction. Gallows and gibbets used to dot the premodern European landscape, the more prominent of which served as landmarks and were noted as such in road guides.[21] Today, only billboards and car dumps desecrate our crossroads and highways. In modern society, it is no longer acceptable to laugh at deformed human beings. The fat lady has been withdrawn from enlightened State Fairs; even ethnic jokes are considered in bad taste. In the eighteenth century, a nobleman could combine in easy conscience an exquisite style of living with cold harshness toward underlings. Flogging as a disciplinary measure was a common practice in the armed forces. In civil life, to horse-whip someone for acts of presumed insolence, even if it did not often occur, must have been the sort of remark that dropped casually and acceptably from the mouth of an eighteenth-century squire. A general rise in the level of wealth and hence of health in the last two centuries has made people less tolerant of pain. Something must be done to alleviate, by scientific and institutional means, the extent of physical suffering in one's community, and something was done. If today's countryside is less comely than it was in the eighteenth century, its human figures are more so; they are healthier and less likely to show deformity caused by accident or congenital defect than their forebears living in the midst of pure country streams.[22] In contemporary America, public places in their effort to be accessible to the physically handicapped have become a little more humane. By law, sidewalks and government buildings must be made easy of entry and exit to wheelchairs; the enactment of such provisions reveals a level of public conscience inconceivable in earlier times. Airports provide one more contemporary example of civility. Air travel is increasingly popular. The larger metropolitan airports swarm with people on the move. Yet, notwithstanding the pervasive air of hurry and anxiety, a ritual of care for those in need of help is routinely enacted at the boarding areas.

The changes in moral landscape are real, though not by as much as we would like. Animals continue to be ruthlessly exploited and killed, though even in this ancient domain of unequal relationship a few improvements can be seen, including less mindless cruelty and extravagance, compared with earlier times, among those who seek pleasure in hunting.[23] The very rich in Europe and North America still live in luxury, but with less ostentation—their houses hidden behind foliage rather than arrogantly exposed on swathes of lawn. The poor must still clean the drains of society, but are better clothed and housed. In the great cities of our century, the rich and the poor, beauty and squalor, no longer co-exist in the same space. Conscience has grown to the extent that it must at least pay homage to virtue in the coins of selective blindness and hypocrisy. We may wonder whether a time will come when cruelty, violence, and gross injustice are simply unacceptable, not only where one happens to live but anywhere, just as now the affluent cannot bear to live— for a variety of reasons—with poverty next door.

In the modern period, moral imagination has notably expanded in two areas. First, the sphere of moral concern is enlarged so that it now embraces the whole world. The instantaneous transmission of news through the electronic media has made neighbors of people everywhere; indeed, even the word "neighbor" does not quite do justice to the degree of intimacy, for suffering humankind is brought into our living room, behind closed doors and drawn curtains. Disasters that occur at the opposite end of the globe nevertheless call for the sending of a food parcel or check from a teacher or a Rotarian in Iowa, almost as a matter of course rather than as an instance of superogatory virtue.[24] Let us note, furthermore, that this giving of food or money to a "neighbor" a thousand miles away is not quite in the traditional mode. As we have seen in chapter 6, in the traditional mode, giving rests on the presupposition of reciprocal help. Modern individual givers, by contrast, cannot expect a return: their giving is, in this sense, unconditional. There appears to be an increase in concern (unfortunately rarely sustained) for human beings in pain, however far away and whatever the nationality or color. Even animals come into our purview. In recent years, moralists have argued for extending the legal concept of right—and hence a legal rather than a merely sentimental notion of community—to animals. Parallel with this development is an increase in sensitivity to the injustice of class bias, sexism, racism, and even "speciesism," and, as a result, a desire to forbid the denigration of any group.[25]

The second area of imaginative expansion is inward. Scholars have recognized a growth in interiority in Europe in the last two to three hundred years, indicated by the demand for private space and an increase in the use of psychological terms descriptive of self and inward states of being.[26] This shift has had varied and even contradictory social and moral consequences. One consequence is egotism—the inclination to dwell on subjective states and to value them above the reality of the external world. Another is the loss of innocence as one acquires debilitating knowledge of the dark, contradictory sources of one's mood and behavior. These effects may be viewed as of ambivalent value, or even unfortunate. On the other hand, certain consequences of interiority are without doubt beneficial. Most important, interiority makes for a steady deepening of a language of moral life. Unless such deepening can occur, moral terms bartered in the marketplace soon become thin and dull. A pleasing reward of interiority is that it makes intimate friendship, as distinct from comradeship, possible: the former calls for an exploration of worlds, both internal and external, whereas the latter, being the effect of submersion in a common task, is outward directed and unreflective.[27]

Interiority encourages a critical attitude, which can be directed at self, at society, and of course at the idea of progress. A sustained critical attitude will surely end in lacerating doubt and pessimism. Under its sway, even when improvement in standard of living in many parts of the world is recognized as a fact, the nagging question persists, but at what cost? As for growth in moral sensitivity, even if we grant its existence, we may feel that the achievements are fragile artificial edifices that will collapse whenever they come in contact with brutal reality and with our own dark passions. On the other hand, nothing prevents us from saying that these elevated works of the imagination convincingly show what human beings and human society *can* be. The fact that they are fragile is no argument that they are unreal, but rather that they call for our loyalty, vigilance, and courage.

Without doubt, enlargement of the moral imagination can cause strain. Being good is much easier if we know less about the condition of the world and the labyrinthine ways of our own mind. Let us consider one instance of such strain—the conflict between rational calculation and generous impulse in moral behavior. A consequence of the spread of heightened awareness through the layers of society is that not only moral philosophers but quite ordinary citizens must face the challenge of calculation. In our complex world, the need to think step-by-step, taking as many factors into account as possible, is widely recognized. Calculation in the exchange of gifts, which we have seen as a necessary feature of traditional economies, returns in a different guise in large technological systems. And yet the idea that the virtuous act is uncalculating remains with us and colors our moral universe. After all, the gift is by its very nature free and generous—a fact probably recognized (though often subconsciously) by all peoples, including those compelled by necessity to calculate. But societies differ in the degree to which the act of giving should *seem* unpremeditated—on the spur of the moment or in secret. In the West, there exists a tradition of impulsive and secretive giving, including the ultimate gift of one's own life. When a person does good, the left hand should not even know what the right hand is doing (Matthew 6:3–4).

Confronted by a real and pressing need, the authentic hero acts without prior consultation with a moral code or considerations of benefit and cost. On January 13, 1982, Lenny Skutnick jumped into the icy Potomac River to rescue a drowning survivor of the Air Florida crash. The woman was saved. Skutnick himself had to be rushed to the hospital and put into a tub to regain his normal temperature. Upon discharge he returned home where he was besieged by reporters keen on knowing his philosophy of life, his motivation, and what went through his head as he prepared to jump. Puzzled, Skutnick said: "She was going to drown if no one moved. I jumped in."[28] This short reply marked him as a true hero. Any kind of religious, philosophical, or rational embellishment would have diminished rather than enhanced the moral beauty of the act. Here again we are faced with the image of the simple soul.

When close relatives and friends make a claim, we respond unreflectively. Custom and affection demand that we act and at the same time tell us how to act. But what if the claim were extraordinary, or if it were to come from a stranger? Faced with such a claim, we feel at a loss unless we subscribe to some general principle that makes it possible for us to adjudicate the claim. As William James puts it, we look for something "beyond" that "rains down upon the claim from some sublime dimension of being, which the moral law inhabits." But James continues, "how can such an inorganic abstract character of imperativeness, additional to the imperativeness which is in the concrete claim itself, exist? Take any demand, however slight, which any creature, however weak, may make. Ought it not, for its own sole sake, to be satisfied?" James recognizes the strangeness of thinking that every claim imposes a duty. He nevertheless insists that we take it seriously, that "life answer to life," without further justification in some abstract universal rule.[29]

Custom or tradition enables a people to act with confidence. "We do things this way because it has always been so." Given this attitude, the contradictions and conflicts inherent in human life are suppressed, and people can get on with their businesses undistracted by the awareness of dilemmas. In distinction to unformulated custom, written codes or laws generalize and simplify the values of a group and in the process render them explicit. The rules thus articulated are subject to questioning and doubt unless they are thought to have a transcendental source—and even then they are subject to interpretation and reinterpretation. Law in the Western world has had, traditionally, the aura and sanction of the "beyond." In China, by contrast, it was seen as a mere human invention and hence without the moral weight of rites that came out of antiquity and timeless custom (chapter 3). In the modern world, a person lives under a broad, richly variegated canopy of guides to behavior which differ greatly in scope, generality, and in the degree that they are consciously recognized. The guides include: unexamined customs similar to those of traditional folk; inherited beliefs that can take the form of universal rules sanctioned by the "beyond" (e.g., natural law and the canons of the Roman Catholic Church); moral axioms known to be formulated by mortals but which nevertheless have acquired an ultrahuman aura (e.g., the United States Constitution); laws that answer the needs of the occasion and can be readily amended or discarded; and abstract principles such as "the greatest happiness of the greatest number" or "lifeboat ethics" that forces one to confront if not resolve certain dilemmas.[30]

Modern men and women have come to know that even in personal relationships, occasions that unambiguously call for the generous impulsive gesture are few. Every claim imposes a duty. Yes, unless, as James himself says, "another creature should make a demand that runs the other way." What then? A supernumerary burden of our age is the awareness of conflicting demands and the felt moral obligation to resolve them fairly even in the most commonplace circumstances, such as when a man tries to satisfy the needs of a nagging child and those of the spouse, bone-tired from work, at the same time. In the public sphere, almost all problems require the carefully deliberated response. Should a wilderness area be preserved? Some affluent citizens may say yes even if preservation should cause them some inconvenience, but what if they are told that such a landscape will deprive a workers' community of the prospect for flood control and low-cost electricity?[31] In a world of instantaneous and vivid communication, the well-being of people everywhere becomes inescapably one's own concern.[32] Should Third World nations impose harsh measures of population control in order to prevent the exhaustion of their resources valuable not only to themselves but also (in actuality or potentially) to the rest of the world? To what extent are rich countries obligated to help poor ones? When the representatives of a poor nation come to the United States to make a direct appeal for generous assistance, how should the Americans respond? Is this an instance of "life answering to life"?

The quick, generous answer is often inappropriate. Questions of this kind and scale compel one to ask: What are the figures for population and resources, and how will these change in the near future? What will be the impact of technological development on society? How will the heavy investment in social reforms and welfare programs influence a nation's future political well-being? Turning to the developed nation, we may wonder how a people's generosity in one area, often the result of arbitrary media focus, will affect their willingness or ability to be generous in another. Confronted by such large public issues, we put aside impulse and fantasy in favor of responsible imagination, which is directed to the marshaling of facts and their processing with the help of sophisticated techniques. We may take this effort to be a new way of being moral, based on the willingness and the ability to examine impersonal numbers, graphs, and equations in order to see clearly the ramifying effects of a course of action.

But problems abound. Doubts emerge in profusion. Human facts are always ambiguous. Statistical data, which overcome the problem of verbal bias and sample adequacy, have their own weaknesses and tendencies to mislead. Techniques of projection are crude and will remain so in relation to phenomena that respond to human initiative, unique events, and the unique concurrences of events. The voluminous facts we collect and the projective methods we employ are intended to guard us against fantasy. Ironically, they can actually encourage it by nurturing unjustifiable confidence in scenarios of the future. Moreover, the rationality of quasi-scientific procedures may be so compelling that it veils the rationalization of our purposes, themselves relics of unexamined beliefs. Thus Marxism, so boastfully modern and secular, must nevertheless draw on the vocabulary of the Western moral tradition, strongly dyed by Hebraic-Christian values, in its conceptualization of the good; and indeed the moral language in Marxist literature and the moral fervor of some Marxists are aptly characterized by Charles Williams as Christian heresy.[33] In the final analysis, we cannot remain moral in any recognizable sense of the word, nor can our projects and creations—including homes, cities, and land-scapes—retain any sort of moral earnestness, without some-where in the background the support of a deeply felt mytho-poeic or religious model of reality.

10 Epilogue

In this book I have pressed the viewpoint that to be moral and imaginative calls for attention to the real. One common understanding of the real is that it is particular and specific—the opposite of woolly generality. The power to attend to the real is in all of us, and in that sense it is a gift of nature. This power can be almost endlessly developed. We are all capable of *becoming* more attentive to the facts of existence—more moral and imaginative— through sustained effort. On this supposition, which can hardly be denied for human beings, rests most securely the possibility of progress. Accurate and just perception, an achievement of the individual, is as obviously an achievement of society, which is able to plant in its members the desire to be or do better and provide at the same time the resources for a measure of success. Cultural resources build up, acquiring new significance and power as they do so, and here again the possibility of progress is implied.

Attending to the details of a situation does not come to us easily. In private life, we know how difficult it is to see in the midst of familiar faces one particular individual in his pressing needs and to respond to them helpfully at the right time and place. Too often we fall back on habit and custom, which allow us the comfort of living as though half asleep. In the larger public world, we know that to plan effectively calls for a high degree of imagination, a characteristic mark of which is again this attentiveness to detail even if it appears superficially unimportant. The ideal planner-designer should not only be able to envisage a physical setting in its concrete specificity but also (like a good novelist) the numerous kinds of human events that can occur there. As for scientists, their distinctive virtue is their readiness to check theory (vision) against fact. This virtue in scientific work is not to be denied despite a fashionable disposition to do so. The preferred language of science—mathematics—is itself a guard against the metaphorical flights of ordinary language. Not only specialists in responsible positions but, in our complexly interdependent modern world, even ordinary citizens must try to be both accurate and comprehensive as to facts in their major sociopolitical decisions, for what they do in their home region can have repercussions far beyond. When the facts are so numerous and confusing, it is hard to resist the temptation to disregard the bulk of them, attend to only a few, and build on this small privileged number a simplifying world view or ideology.

I have laid stress on the particular. Yet obviously the particular cannot stand by itself. Its true nature and value become evident only when it is seen among other particulars in a web of relations that has no clear boundary. To perceive truly, which I take to mean the same as perceiving justly or morally, seems to call for the power of attending to both the particular and the universal. In our day-to-day affairs we are able to see well enough the detailed things at hand as well as their context, which is rarely large and does not have to be. If, however, we aspire to grow beyond our small world and its routines, what should we do? Is it better to attend to the things closest to us—family, friend, our own home—and move from such direct intimate experiences to the general and the universal, or is it better to start with a grasp of universal principles and values—with the distant, the grand, and the inspiring—and from that superior plane move down to concrete instances? Is it possible to give equal weight to both and entertain them more or less at the same time? These questions have been taken up earlier and are a central theme of the book. I will end with a brief recapitulation.

Confucians believe that love begins with the particular, within the family, and from there it irradiates the rest of the world. Mohists, by contrast, believe in universal love and see narrow loyalties, which gain their intensity by exclusion, as degeneration and incapable of expanding beyond their boundaries to cover the world. In the West, Plato argues eloquently for ascent from the particular to the universal: one moves from the love for the beauty of a particular person to love for all who share the character of being beautiful, to love of the beautiful wherever it appears, to love of wisdom and the Beautiful itself (*Symposium*, 210–212b). Aristotle, by contrast, begins with the idea of universal good will. For him, particular attachments like friendship depend on the prior existence of a general feeling of good will: the friend, after all, begins as a stranger (*Nicomachean Ethics*, IX, 5).[1]

To some seekers after truth, the gate to the kingdom is necessarily narrow. One enters it only after having confronted the gritty and sometimes sordid realities of the concretely human. Alyosha (in Dostoevsky's *The Brothers Karamazov*) has to accept first his revered teacher Father Zossima as not only dead but prematurely decaying before he is ready to perceive accurately, rather than in a romantic swoon, the sweep and mystery of heaven and earth.[2] One criticism of high-minded culture, we have noted, is this tendency to repress or to consider as vulgar the biology of life—its messy interweavings with decay and death, its smelly socks and drains, its muddle of love and hate—in favor of a world that is, if possible, wholly elevated, clean, orderly, and predictable. Against such disposition is the wish to attend to the particular, which is taken to be real, all the more so if it intrudes on one's consciousness and hence cannot be merely the mind's willful conjuration. The larger world, whether mental (e.g., an elaborate religious-ethical system) or material (e.g., the ideal city), seems by comparison less in touch with human experience and reality.

But this cannot be all. If some people aspire to the true and the good by way of the concrete particular, others appear to be drawn, naturally and from the start, to the true and the good as embodied in abstract theories and principles. The opposite of the concrete particular is not necessarily swooning fantasy or the reductive image of an egotistic mind; it can be something "hard" (in the sense of necessary and compelling) that combines the greatest generality with precision. Pure mathematicians and theoretical physicists are perhaps of this ken. To take a famous example, Einstein's mind and heart are engaged primarily by the beauty of an abstract physical order; his well-known kindliness and impartial justice toward individual human beings appear to flow out of the energy of this love for universal laws.

It may be that a strong attachment to the particular can have no overflow—indeed must militate against it—unless there exists also a longing for the good that transcends its individual manifestations. On the other hand, a longing for the good, unballasted by strong individual attachments and direct intimate experiences of the particular, can degenerate into large, vacuous pictures of the good, or into overly ambitious programs for the good that, if carried out, can do great harm. For fear of doing harm, the weight of moral opinion the world over has tended to favor the tangible particulars—especially those of nature (polished pebbles on the beach, redwood, and darters)—as the proper ends of attention and love. However, unreflective acceptance of this position may result in the loss of the savor of the particulars themselves through habitude and boredom, or, to put it another way, through the lack of resonance to worlds beyond.

The facts of the world can remain vivid for each new generation of human beings even if culture provides them with no new tales—no new contexts with which to view them. Culture, in other words, can be static and yet highly satisfactory to its members: after all, when a man is thirsty water offers him delight no matter how often he drinks it, and ceremonies, dulled by repetition to old people, will remain an epiphany to young initiates. Static cultures, however, no longer exist, and perhaps never did exist in the literal sense, except as the nostalgic fabrication of rapidly changing societies temporarily disillusioned with change. When a culture is characterized as dynamic and progressive, we may wonder, toward what end or ends? What is its encompassing vision? All functioning societies possess specific moralities and categories of good that make powerful emotional and legitimate claims. Each category of good, each moral concept, offers a necessary place of rest, but all of them, upon critical reflection, appear relative in value and subjective in thrust. Besides specific goods and moralities, more general conceptualizations of the good exist, applicable broadly to humankind (e.g., Williams' doctrine of exchange), which can serve as a powerful lure for the forward movement of society; their existence demonstrates the fruitfulness of the moral imagination. However, when ideas of the good become too abstract, such as Aristotle's good will or Mo-tzu's universal love, their ability to stir and motivate human beings diminishes.

Dissatisfaction with the current state of affairs inclines one to move on. People are pushed, for the ills of society and life can be directly experienced, and are often specific and horrible. But there has to be pull as well. What is the nature of this pull? With rare exceptions, visions of the good, insofar as they can be described, are either highly specific but insipid or too abstractly general such as universal love. Can an undefined ideal beckon? Is it possible to think of the good as simply a luminous receding horizon? Some people would answer yes, not as the affirmation of reason, but irresistibly, as the heliotrope turns from shade to light. The good is ineffable. Its very lack of specifiable content imparts to it the authority of the impersonal and the objective. A vision of the ineffable good, though it does not help resolve ethical dilemmas and problems of the day, provides a safeguard against intolerance and moral stasis. What we need is a powerful lure which limits the indecisiveness of freedom and yet does not enslave or blind.

Notes and Index

Notes

1 Introduction

1 Julian Green, *Diary 1928–1957* (New York: Carrol & Graf, 1985), pp. 133–34.

2 Jacques Le Goff, *Time, Work, and Culture in the Middle Ages* (Chicago: University of Chicago Press, 1982), pp. 92–93.

3 David Watkin, *Morality and Architecture* (Chicago: University of Chicago Press, 1984).

2 Moral Edifice and Life: Simple Societies

1 This section on the Pygmies draws upon the works of Colin Turnbull, in particular, *The Forest People: A Study of the Pygmies of the Congo* (Garden City, N.Y.: Doubleday Anchor, 1962).

2 Turnbull, "The Mbuti Pygmies of the Congo," in James L. Gibbs, ed., *Peoples of Africa* (New York: Holt, Rinehart & Winston, 1965), p. 282.

3 Turnbull, "The Lesson of the Pygmies," *Scientific American* (January 1963): 1–11.

4 Turnbull, *Wayward Servants* (London: Eyre and Spottiswode, 1965), p. 121.

5 Turnbull, "The Mbuti Pygmies of the Congo," pp. 308–9.

6 See the description of a Taoist paradise in *The Book of Lieh-tzu*, trans. A. C. Graham (London: John Murray, 1960), pp. 102–3.

7 Joseph Levenson and Franz Schurmann regard this T'ang poem as evidence of civilized taste rather than

of philobarbarianism. See their book *China: An Interpretive History* (Berkeley and Los Angeles: University of California Press, 1971), pp. 114–15.

8 Iskandar Carey, *Orang Asli: The Aboriginal Tribes of Peninsular Malaysia* (Kuala Lumpur, Singapore: Oxford University Press, 1976), p. 99.

9 Kevin Duffy, *Children of the Forest* (New York: Dodd, Mead & Company, 1984), pp. 161–66.

10 Turnbull, "Legends of the BaMbuti," *Transactions of the Royal Anthropological Institute* 89 (1959): 55–59.

11 Alex Shoumatoff, "The Ituri Forest," *The New Yorker*, February 6, 1984, p. 88.

12 Turnbull, *The Forest People*, pp. 108–26.

13 Duffy, *Children of the Forest*, p. 50.

14 Peter Freuchen, *Book of the Eskimos* (New York: Fawcett Crest, 1965), p. 174.

15 Asen Balikci, *The Netsilik Eskimo* (New York: Natural History Press, 1970), p. 206.

16 Freuchen, *Book of the Eskimos*, pp. 145–46.

17 Knud Rasmussen, *Intellectual Culture of the Iglulik Eskimos, Report of the Fifth Thule Expedition, 1921–1924*, The Danish Expedition to Arctic North America, vol. 7, no. 1 (1929), p. 62.

18 Ibid., pp. 74–75.

19 Balikci, *Netsilik Eskimo*, pp. 218–20.

20 See Adolf Friedrich, "Die Forschung über das frühzeitliche jagertum," *Paideuma*, vol. 2 (1941–43), pp. 21 ff.

21 Freuchen, *Book of the Eskimos*, p. 141.

22 Rasmussen, *Intellectual Culture of the Iglulik Eskimos*, p. 69.

23 Knud Rasmussen, *Intellectual Culture of the Caribou Eskimo, Report of the Fifth Thule Expedition 1921–1924*, vol. 7, nos. 2 and 3 (1930), p. 59.

24 Adolf E. Jensen, *Myth and Cult Among Primitive Peoples* (Chicago: University of Chicago Press, 1963), pp. 166–68. Jonathan Smith has criticized Jensen's interpretation of the Dema myth, while not denying the archaic and widespread nature of the motif of tubers growing out of the body of a slain deity. See Smith, "A Pearl of Great Price and a Cargo of Yam" in *Imagining Religion: From Babylon to Jonestown* (Chicago: University of Chicago Press, 1982), pp. 96–101.

25 Walter Burkert, *Homo Necans: The Anthropology of Ancient Greek Sacrificial Ritual and Myth* (Berkeley: University of California Press, 1983), p. 45.

26 Karl A. Nowotny, *Beiträge zur Geschichte des Weltbildes* (Wiener Beiträge zur Kulturgeschichte und Linguistik, vol. 17, Vienna, 1960).

27 Alfonzo Ortiz, "Ritual Drama and the Pueblo World View," in Alfonso Ortiz, ed., *New Perspectives on the Pueblos* (Albuquerque: University of New Mexico Press, 1972), p. 141.

28 Ruth Benedict, *Patterns of Culture* (New York: Mentor, 1959), p. 65.

29 Robert Bellah's term in his paper "religious systems" in Evon Z. Vogt and Ethel M. Albert, *People of Rimrock* (Cambridge: Harvard University Press, 1966), p. 229.

30 Byron Harvey, "An Overview of Pueblo Religion," in Ortiz, ed., *New Perspectives*, p. 208.

31 Richard B. Brandt, *Hopi Ethics: A Theoretical Analysis* (Chicago: University of Chicago Press, 1954), p. 94.

02 Mischa Titiev, *Old Oraibi*, Papers of the Peabody Museum of American Archaeology and Ethnography, vol. 22, no. 1 (1944), p. 67; Brandt, *Hopi Ethics*, p. 36.

33 Ibid., p. 193.

34 Ibid., p. 215.

35 Watson Smith and John M. Roberts, *Zuni Laws: A Field of Values*, Papers of the Peabody Museum of American Archaeology and Ethnology, vol. 43, no. 1 (1954), p. 42.

36 Brandt, *Hopi Ethics*, p. 34.

37 Louis A. Hieb, "Meaning and Mismeaning toward an Understanding of the Ritual Clown," in Ortiz, ed., *New Perspectives*, pp. 171–87.

38 Ibid., pp. 184–87.

39 Ortiz, *New Perspectives*, p. 151.

3 Moral Edifice and Life: Complex Societies

1 G. S. Kirk, *The Nature of Greek Myths* (Harmondsworth, Middlesex: Penguin, 1976), p. 227.

2 Walter Burkert, *Homo Necans: The Anthropology of Ancient Greek Sacrificial Ritual and Myth* (Berkeley: University of California Press, 1983), p. 4.

3 Kirk, *Nature of Greek Myths*, p. 139.

4 Hesiod, *Works and Days*, trans. Dorothea Wender (Harmondsworth, Middlesex: Penguin, 1973), pp. 80–104.

5 Eric A. Havelock, *The Greek Concept of Justice: From Its Shadow in Homer to Its Substance in Plato* (Cambridge: Harvard University Press, 1978); also, Walter J. Ong, *Interfaces of the Word: Studies in the Evolution of Consciousness and Culture* (Ithaca: Cornell University Press, 1977), pp. 178–80.

6 Havelock, *Greek Concept of Justice*, pp. 57, 89, 91, 93.

7 Ibid., p. 36.

8 Martin P. Nilsson, *Greek Piety* (New York: Norton, 1969), p. 47.

9 Hesiod, *Works and Days*, p. 65.

10 Thucydides, *History of the Peloponnesian War*, book 5:105 (London: Heinemann, 1921), p. 167. A favorite quotation of Simone Weil. See *Oppression and Liberty* (Amherst: University of Massachusetts Press, 1973), p. 165.

11 M. I. Finley, *The World of Odysseus* (Harmondsworth, Middlesex: Penguin, 1979), p. 111.

12 Simone Weil, "The 'Iliad,' Poem of Might," in *Intimations of Christianity Among the Ancient Greeks* (London: Routledge & Kegan Paul, 1957), p. 31.

13 Jean-Pierre Vernant, *The Origins of Greek Thought* (Ithaca: Cornell University Press, 1982), pp. 78–81; see also, L. Gernet, *Droit et société dans la Grèce ancienne* (Paris, 1955), pp. 29–50.

14 Vernant, *Origins of Greek Thought*, pp. 86–88.

15 Iris Murdoch, *The Fire and the Sun: Why Plato Banished the Artists* (Oxford: Clarendon Press, 1977).

16 Martha C. Nussbaum, *The Fragility of Goodness: Luck and Ethics in Greek Tragedy and Philosophy* (Cambridge: Cambridge University Press, 1986).

17 Derk Bodde, "Myths of Ancient China," in Samuel N. Kramer, ed., *Mythologies of the Ancient World* (Garden City, N.Y.: Doubleday Anchor, 1961), pp. 367–408.

18 Benjamin I. Schwartz, "Transcendence in Ancient China," *Daedalus* (Spring 1975): 57–68.

19 David N. Keightley, "The Religious Commitment: Shang Theology and the Genesis of Chinese Political Culture," *History of Religions* 17 (1978): 211–25.

20 Benjamin I. Schwartz, *The World of Thought in Ancient China* (Cambridge: Harvard University Press, 1985), p. 34.

21 Donald J. Munro, *The Concept of Man in Early China* (Stanford: Stanford University Press, 1969), pp. 114–15; Derk Bodde, "Feudalism in China," in Rushton Coulborn, ed., *Feudalism in History* (Princeton: Princeton University Press, 1956), pp. 49–92.

22 James Legge, "Confucian Analects," book 17:2 in *The Four Books* (New York: Paragon, 1966), p. 255.

23 Arthur Waley, *The Analects of Confucius* (New York: Random House, Vintage Books, 1938), book 16:9, p. 206.

24 Munro, *Concept of Man*, p. 68.

25 Waley, *The Analects*, book 17:12, p. 212; Schwartz, *The World of Thought*, p. 73.

26 Alfred Forke, *The World-Conception of the Chinese* (London: Arthur Probsthain, 1925); and Marcel Granet, *La Pensée Chinoise* (Paris: Albin Michel, 1934), especially the section "Le microsome," pp. 361–88.

27 Munro, *Concept of Man*, p. 31.

28 Derk Bodde and Clarence Morris, *Law in Imperial China* (Cambridge: Harvard University Press, 1967), pp. 44–46.

29 Sarah Allan, *The Heir and the Sage: Dynastic Legend in Early China* (San Francisco: Chinese Materials Center, 1981), pp. 3–6.

30 Arthur Waley, "Life under the Han Dynasty," *History Today* 3 (1953): 89–98.

31 Legge, "The Works of Mencius," book 1, part 2:3 in *The Four Books*, pp. 512–13; quoted in Munro, *Concept of Man*, p. 36.

32 Schwartz, *The World of Thought*, p. 148.

33 W. K. Liao, *The Complete Works of Han Fei Tzu* (London: Probsthain's Oriental Series, 1939–59), vol. 2, pp. 287–88; quoted by Derk Bodde, *Essays on Chinese Civilization* (Princeton: Princeton University Press, 1980), p. 182.

34 Charles S. Gardner, *Chinese Traditional Historiography* (Cambridge: Harvard University Press, 1961), p. 13.

35 Burton Watson, *Ssu-ma Ch'ien: Grand Historian of China* (New York: Columbia University Press, 1958), p. 86.

36 Watson, *Ssu-ma Ch'ien*, p. 139.
37 Ibid., pp. 150–51.
38 Ibid., p. 127.
39 H. G. Creel, *What Is Taoism? And Other Studies in Chinese Cultural History* (Chicago: University of Chicago Press, 1970).
40 D. C. Lau, trans., *Lao-tzu: Tao-te Ching* (London: Penguin, 1963), chap. 5, p. 61.
41 Quoted by Watson, *Ssu-ma Ch'ien*, p. 25.
42 Creel, *What Is Taoism?*, p. 3.
43 James Legge, *The Writings of Kwang-zze II* (Oxford: Sacred Books of the East), vol. 40 (1927), p. 66.
44 Burton Watson, *Chuang-tzu* (New York: Columbia University Press, 1968), p. 84.
45 Schwartz, *The World of Thought*, p. 235.
46 Medieval Christian visions of hell may well be inspired by those of Hinduism and Buddhism. See E. J. Becker, *A Contribution to the Comparative Study of the Medieval Visions of Heaven and Hell* (Baltimore: John Murphy, 1899).
47 Kenneth K. S. Ch'en, *Buddhism: The Light of Asia* (Woodbury, N.Y.: Barron's Educational Series, 1968), p. 32.
48 Stephen Toulmin and June Goodfield, *The Discovery of Time* (Chicago and London: University of Chicago Press, 1965), p. 76.
49 Edward Conze, *Buddhism: Its Essence and Development* (New York: Harper Colophon, 1975), pp. 48–52.
50 G. F. Allen, *The Buddha's Philosophy: Selections from the Pali Canon and An Introductory Essay* (New York: Macmillan, 1959), pp. 162–63.
51 "The Buddha was known as the *Anatta-vadi*, or teacher of Impersonality." *Buddhist Dictionary—Manual of Buddhist Terms and Doctrines: Nyanatiloka* (Colombo, Sri Lanka: Island Hermitage Publications 1, Frewin and Co., 1950); Edward Conze, *Buddhist Thought in India* (Ann Arbor: University of Michigan Press, 1967), pp. 122–34.
52 Melford E. Spiro, *Buddhism and Society: A Great Tradition and Its Burmese Vicissitudes* (Berkeley: University of California, 2d edition, 1982), pp. 100–101.

53 Vincent A. Smith, *Asoka: The Buddhist Emperor of India* (Delhi: S. Chand & Co., 1957).
54 N. A. Nikam and Richard McKeon, *The Edicts of Asoka* (Chicago: University of Chicago Press, 1959), p. 55.
55 Ibid., pp. 64–65.
56 Allen, *Buddha's Philosophy*, p. 113.
57 F. L. Woodward and E. M. Hare, *Gradual Sayings* (London: Oxford University Press, 1932), 1:128; Ch'en, *Buddhism*, pp. 19.
58 Allen, *Buddha's Philosophy*, pp. 138–39.
59 Conze, *Buddhism*, p. 155; Ch'en, *Buddhism*, pp. 70–71.
60 Allen, *Buddha's Philosophy*, p. 110.
61 Kenneth K. S. Ch'en, *The Chinese Transformation of Buddhism* (Princeton: Princeton University Press, 1973), p. 8.
62 Ibid., pp. 21–23.
63 Spiro, *Buddhism and Society*, p. 46.
64 Ibid., pp. 89–90.
65 Ibid., pp. 104–9.
66 Ibid., pp. 353–54.

4 Built Worlds I

1 Napoleon Chagnon, *Yanomamö: The Fierce People* (New York: Holt, Rinehart and Winston, 1968), p. 44.
2 Walter J. Ong, *Interfaces of the Word: Studies in the Evolution of Consciousness and Culture* (Ithaca: Cornell University Press, 1977), p. 114.
3 Hajime Nakamura, "Time in Japanese Thought," in J. T. Fraser, ed., *The Voices of Time* (New York: George Braziller, 1966), p. 82.
4 Barre Toelken, *The Dynamics of Folklore* (Boston: Houghton Mifflin, 1979), p. 96.
5 Arthur Waley, *The Analects of Confucius* (New York: Random House, Vintage Books, 1938), book 17, chap. 19, p. 214. Quoted by Benjamin Schwartz in "Transcendence in Ancient China," *Daedalus* (Spring 1975): 65.
6 Jonathan Swift, *Gulliver's Travels* (London: Folio Society, 1965; first published in 1726); see also Svetlana Alpers, *The Art of Describing: Dutch Art in the Seven-*

teenth Century (Chicago: University of Chicago Press, 1983).

7 Donald J. Munro, *The Concept of Man in Early China* (Stanford: Stanford University Press, 1969), p. 24.

8 Hans Aarsleff, "Language and Victorian Ideology," *American Scholar* (Summer 1983): 365–72; see also his *The Study of Language in England, 1780–1860* (Minneapolis: University of Minnesota Press, 1983).

9 Martin Heidegger, "Building, Dwelling, Thinking," in *Poetry, Language, Thought* (New York: Harper and Row, 1971); Leszek Kolakowski, *Religion* (New York: Oxford University Press, 1982), pp. 183–84.

10 G. E. Moore, *Principia Ethica* (Cambridge at the University Press, 1959; first published in 1903). Here is Stuart Hampshire's comment on Moore's way of doing philosophy. "If there were an entirely general answer to a question about what is intrinsically good and what ought to exist for its own sake, this eternal truth would surely not be found by reflection on meanings, as if our inherited vocabulary, rightly interpreted, was the ultimate oracle and the final guide to life," in "Liberator, Up to a Point," *The New York Review of Books*, March 26, 1987, p. 39.

11 Carol P. MacCormack, "Nature, Culture and Gender: A Critique," in Carol P. MacCormack and Marilyn Strathern, eds., *Nature, Culture and Gender* (Cambridge: Cambridge University Press, 1980), p. 16.

12 Gillian Gillison, "Images of Nature in Gimi Thought," in MacCormack and Strathern, eds., *Nature, Culture and Gender*, pp. 143–73; Mary Douglas, "The Lele of Kasai," in Daryll Forde, ed., *African Worlds* (London: Oxford University Press, 1963), pp. 1–26.

13 Robert Nisbet writes: "During the period 1750–1900 the idea of progress reached its zenith in the Western mind in popular as well as scholarly circles. From being *one* of the most important ideas in the West it became the dominant idea, even when one takes into account the rising importance of other ideas such as equality, social justice, and popular sovereignty— each of which was without question a beacon of light in this period." In *History of the Idea of Progress* (New York: Basic Books, 1980), p. 171.

14 Derk Bodde, *Essays on Chinese Civilization* (Princeton: Princeton University Press, 1981), pp. 69–70.

15 Benjamin Schwartz, *The World of Thought in Ancient China* (Cambridge: Harvard University Press, 1985), p. 207; D. C. Lau, trans., *Lao-tzu: Tao-te Ching* (London: Penguin, 1963), chap. 18, p. 74.

16 Waley, *Analects of Confucius*, book 6, chap. 16, p. 119.

17 Ibid., book 3, chap. 14, p. 94; quoted in Schwartz, *World of Thought*, p. 64.

18 D. C. Lau, *Mencius* (London: Penguin Classics, 1970), book 1, part A, chap. 7, p. 58.

19 Derk Bodde, "Myths of Ancient China," in Samuel N. Kramer, ed., *Mythologies of the Ancient World* (Garden City, N.Y.: Doubleday Anchor, 1961), pp. 367–408.

20 Schwartz, *World of Thought*, pp. 148–49.

21 Mencius, *The Four Books*, trans. James Legge (New York: Paragon, 1966), book 3, part 2, pp. 674–75.

22 Burton Watson, *Ssu-ma Ch'ien: Grand Historian of China* (New York: Columbia University Press, 1958), pp. 29–31.

23 One scholar, Robert Nisbet, has recently reversed his view concerning the Hesiodic myth of the Golden Age. He now sees it as embodying the idea of progress. *History*, p. 15.

24 Ludwig Edelstein, *The Idea of Progress in Classical Antiquity* (Baltimore: The Johns Hopkins University Press, 1967).

25 Ibid., pp. 11–12; Vitruvius, *The Ten Books on Architecture* (New York: Dover, 1960), pp. 288–89.

26 Edelstein, *The Idea of Progress*, p. 15.

27 Plato, *Protagoras*, 321–22; Edelstein, *The Idea of Progress*, pp. 22–23.

28 Edelstein, *The Idea of Progress*, pp. 33–34.

29 Harold F. Cherniss, "The Characteristics and Effects of Presocratic Philosophy," *Journal of the History of Ideas* 12 (1951): 343–45; Edelstein, *The Idea of Progress*, p. 27.

30 Thucydides, *History of the Peloponnesian War* (London: William Heinemann, 1921), book 1:71, 2.

31 See Thucydides, *History*, book 5:85–113, the argument between the Athenians and the Melians; Edelstein, *The Idea of Progress*, p. 52.

32 Antigone, lines 332–75, in Arnold J. Toynbee, *Greek Historical Thought* (New York: Mentor, 1952), pp. 128–29. Democritus' view given in Edelstein, *The Idea of Progress*, p. 53.

33 Arthur O. Lovejoy and George Boas, *Primitivism and Related Ideas in Antiquity: A Documentary History of Primitivism and Related Ideas* (Baltimore: Johns Hopkins University Press, 1935), vol. 1, pp. 19, 389ff.

34 Diogenes Laertus, *Lives of Eminent Philosophers* (London and New York: Loeb Classical Library, 1925), II, 70; VI, 6; Edelstein, *The Idea of Progress*, p. 59.

35 Donald R. Dudley, *A History of Cynicism* (London: 1937), p. 31; Edelstein, *The Idea of Progress*, pp. 60–61.

5 Built Worlds II

1 The Tikopia Islanders, for instance, have increased the size of their island by nearly one-half since the time they first occupied it some three thousand years ago. But they do not recognize this achievement. They choose to believe that the island has always been much the way it is. See Patrick V. Kirch and D. E. Yen, *Tikopia: The Prehistory and Ecology of a Polynesian Outlier* (Honolulu: Bishop Museum Press, 1982).

2 J. B. Jackson, "The Vernacular Landscape," in Edmund C. Penning-Rowsell and David Lowenthal, eds., *Landscape Meanings and Values* (London: Allen and Unwin, 1986), pp. 71–74.

3 Paolo Vivante, "On the Representation of Nature and Reality in Homer," *Arion* 5, no. 2 (1966): 149–90. As C. S. Lewis puts it, "Homer can enjoy a landscape, but what he means by a beautiful landscape is one that is useful—good deep soil, plenty of fresh water, pasture that will make the cows really fat, and some nice timber." In *Reflections on the Psalms* (London: Fontana, 1961), pp. 66–67.

4 Clarence J. Glacken, *Traces on the Rhodian Shore: Nature and Culture in Western Thought from Ancient Times to the End of the Eighteenth Century* (Berkeley: University of California Press, 1967), p. 119. On adverse change, see Plato, *Critias*, translated as "Denudation

in Attica," in Arnold J. Toynbee, *Greek Historical Thought* (New York: Mentor, 1952), pp. 146–47.

5 Quoted in Claude Mosse, *The Ancient World at Work* (New York: Norton, n.d.), pp. 25–26.

6 *The Whole Works of Xenophon*, transl. Ashley Cooper et al. (New York: Derby, 1861), pp. 652–54.

7 Thomas Jefferson, *Notes on the State of Virginia*, ed. William Peden (Chapel Hill: University of North Carolina Press, 1955), query 19.

8 As John Cowper Powys puts it, "Dead rabbits, dead sheep, dead crows, dead snakes, dead trees waylay your steps; and the consciousness of the terribleness of what may at any second happen to yourself tends to throw the issues and the dilemmas of life into a certain drastic perspective." In *The Meaning of Culture* (New York: Norton, 1929), p. 176.

9 Jacques Bossuet, *Elévations à Dieu sur tous les mystères de la religion Chrétienne* [VI semaine, XII élévation] (Paris: Jean Mariette, 1727). John Calvin, *The Sermons of John Calvin upon Deuteronomie*, trans. Arthur Gold ing [Forty-ninth sermon, July 30, 1555] (London: Middleton, 1583), p. 295. See Michel Foucault, *Madness and Civilization: A History of Insanity in the Age of Reason* (New York: Vintage, 1973), p. 56.

10 Francis Bacon, "Of Riches," in *The Essays* (Harmondsworth, Middlesex: Penguin, 1985), p. 166.

11 Frank E. Huggett, *The Land Question and European Society Since 1650* (New York: Harcourt Brace Jovanovich, 1975), pp. 45–48, 56.

12 Hugh Prince, "Art and Agrarian Change, 1710–1815," in Denis Cosgrove and Stephen Daniels, eds., *The Iconography of Landscape* (Cambridge: Cambridge University Press, 1988), pp. 102–5, 114–16. Prince notes that the landscape paintings of the period mostly indulge in nostalgia rather than show any desire to record the agricultural transformations that took place.

13 Raymond Williams, *The Country and the City* (New York: Oxford University Press, 1973), pp. 66, 82, 109.

14 Carl O. Sauer, "Theme of Plant and Animal Destruction in Economic History," *Journal of Farm Economics* 20 (1938): 765–75.

15 René Dubos, "Symbiosis Between the Earth and Humankind," *Science* 193, (August 6, 1976), p. 459.

16 John Leighly, "Ecology as Metaphor: Carl Sauer and Human Ecology," with commentaries by Kent Mathewson, Philip W. Porter, and B. L. Turner II, *Professional Geographer* 39, no. 4, (1987): pp. 405–16. Aldo Leopold, *A Sand County Almanac* (New York: A Sierra Club/Ballantine Book, 1970), pp. 237–51.

17 Norman G. Brett-James, *The Growth of Stuart London* (London: George Allen & Unwin, 1935), pp. 444–46.

18 Quoted by Terry Comito, *The Idea of the Garden in the Renaissance* (New Brunswick, N.J.: Rutgers University Press, 1978), p. 37.

19 Ibid., p. 20.

20 Ibid., p. 94.

21 Michael Sullivan, *The Birth of Landscape Painting in China* (Berkeley: University of California Press, 1962), pp. 29–30.

22 William Howard Adams, *The French Garden, 1500–1800* (New York: Braziller, 1979), pp. 40, 47.

23 Ibid., p. 88. The toll in human lives in the construction of Versailles is suggested by a letter of the Marquise de Sévigné, dated October 12, 1678: "The King wishes to go to Versailles on Saturday, but God, it seems wills otherwise, because of the great mortality afflicting the workmen, of whom every night wagons full of the dead are carried out as though from the Hôtel-Dieu. These melancholy processions are kept secret as far as possible, in order not to alarm other workmen." See Gilette Ziegler, *The Court of Versailles in the Reign of Louis XIV* (London: George Allen & Unwin, 1966), p. 30.

24 Adams, *The French Garden*, p. 84.

25 Lucy Norton, trans., *Saint-Simon at Versailles* (London: Hamish Hamilton, 1958), p. 265.

26 Nan Fairbrother, *Men and Gardens* (New York: Knopf, 1956), p. 94.

27 Pierre de Nolhac, *The Trianon of Marie-Antoinette* (New York: Brentano, n.d.), pp. 203–4.

28 Edward Malins, *English Landscaping and Literature, 1660–1840* (London: Oxford University Press, 1966), p. 8.

29 Paul Wheatley, *The Pivot of the Four Quarters: A Preliminary Enquiry into the Origins and Character of the Ancient Chinese City* (Chicago: Aldine, 1971).

30 Aristotle, *Politics*, book 7, chap. 11 (Chicago: Encyclopaedia Britannica, 1952), vol. 9, p. 535.

31 Vitruvius, *The Ten Books on Architecture*, trans. Morris Morgan (New York: Dover, n.d.), pp. 17–32.

32 Leone Battista Alberti, *Ten Books on Architecture*, trans. James Leoni (London: Alec Tiranti, 1955), book 1, chaps. 3–5; book 4, chap. 5, pp. 74–76.

33 Quentin Bell, *On Human Finery* (New York: Schocken Books, 1976, 2d edition), p. 20.

34 Georges Duby, *The Age of the Cathedrals: Art and Society, 980–1420*, trans. Eleanor Levieux and Barbara Thompson (Chicago: Chicago University Press, 1981), pp. 80–81.

35 Jean Gimpel, *The Medieval Machine: The Industrial Revolution of the Middle Ages* (New York: Holt, Rinehart & Winston, 1976), p. 116.

36 Quoted in Jean Gimpel, *The Cathedral Builders*, trans. Teresa Waugh (New York: Harper Colophon, 1983), p. 9.

37 Gimpel, *The Cathedral Builders*, pp. 38, 115.

38 E. J. Hobsbawm, *The Age of Capital, 1848–1875* (New York: Charles Scribner's Sons, 1975), pp. 286–87.

39 H. J. Dyos and Michael Wolff, "The Way We Live Now," in H. J. Dyos and Michael Wolff, eds., *The Victorian City: Images and Reality* (London: Routledge & Kegan Paul, 1973), vol. 2, p. 899.

40 John Burnett, *Plenty and Want* (Harmondsworth, Middlesex: Penguin, 1968), pp. 200–201.

41 Meyer Berger, "Rooftop Gardeners Bring Forth Blossoms High Above a City of Stone and Steel," *New York Times*, April 23, 1958; reprinted in Anselm L. Strauss, *The American City: A Sourcebook of Urban Imagery* (Chicago: Aldine, 1968), pp. 385–86.

42 Walter L. Creese, *The Search for Environment: The Garden City Before and After* (New Haven: Yale University Press, 1966), pp. 82–85.

43 David H. Pinkney, *Napoleon III and the Rebuilding of Paris* (Princeton: Princeton University Press, 1958), pp. 16–17.

44 Dyos and Wolff, "The Way We Live Now," pp. 893–907.

6 Social World and Exchange

1 Stuart Hampshire, *Moral Philosophy and Conflict* (Cambridge: Harvard University Press, 1985).
2 Maurice Halbwachs, *The Psychology of Social Class* (Glencoe, Ill.: The Free Press, 1958), p. 35.
3 Edward C. Banfield, *The Moral Basis of a Backward Society* (New York: The Free Press, 1958), pp. 110, 115–16; Norman Douglas, *Old Calabria* (New York: Houghton Mifflin, 1915), p. 124.
4 Mildred Campbell, *The English Yeoman* (New York: Barnes and Noble, 1960).
5 *The Lisle Letters*, ed. Muriel St. Claire Byrne (Chicago: University of Chicago Press, 1980), 6 vols.; see Christopher Hill's review in *The New York Review of Books*, June 11, 1981.
6 Mary Douglas and Baron Isherwood, *The World of Goods* (New York: Basic Books, 1979).
7 Yi-Fu Tuan, "Geopiety: A Theme in Man's Attachment to Nature and to Place," in David Lowenthal and Martyn Bowden, eds., *Geographies of the Mind* (New York: Oxford University Press, 1976), pp. 11–39.
8 Robert Brain, *Friends and Lovers* (New York: Basic Books, 1976), p. 62.
9 C. S. Lewis, *The Four Loves* (London: Fontana, 1964), pp. 62–63.
10 Brain, *Friends and Lovers*, pp. 153–54.
11 The Grand Historian Ssu-ma Ch'ien was given a hard time for having some good words to say about commerce and industry. Confucians felt that "nothing favorable should ever be said about the merchant class lest farmers be tempted to give up their labors and enter trade." Burton Watson, *Ssu-ma Ch'ien: Grand Historian of China* (New York: Columbia University Press, 1958), pp. 150–51; Etienne Balazs, *Chinese Civilization and Bureaucracy* (New Haven: Yale University Press, 1969), p. 71.
12 Victor Turner, "The Center Out There: Pilgrim's Goal," *History of Religions* 12, no. 3 (1973): 208.

13 Bronislaw Malinowski, *Argonauts of the Western Pacific: An Account of Native Enterprise and Adventure in the Archipelagoes of Melanesian New Guinea* (London: Routledge & Kegan Paul, 1922).

14 Erik Schwimmer, *Exchange in the Social Structure of the Orokaiva: Traditional and Emergent Ideologies in the Northern District of Papua* (New York: St. Martin's Press, 1973), pp. 47–49.

15 Lewis Hyde, *The Gift: Imagination and the Erotic Life of Property* (New York: Random House, Vintage Books, 1983), pp. 11–24.

16 Donald J. Munro, *The Concept of Man in Early China* (Stanford: Stanford University Press), p. 115.

17 Ibid., pp. 121–31.

18 Kenneth K. S. Ch'en, *Buddhism: The Light of Asia* (Woodbury, N.Y.: Barron's Educational Series, 1968), pp. 32–33.

19 Ibid., p. 69.

20 Richard Norman, *The Moral Philosophers: An Introduction to Ethics* (Oxford: Clarendon Press, 1983), p. 60.

21 Plato, *The Republic*, book IX:519d–520e.

22 Kenneth K. S. Ch'en, *The Chinese Transformation of Buddhism* (Princeton: Princeton University Press, 1973), pp. 45–49.

23 E. R. Dodds, *Pagan and Christian in An Age of Anxiety* (Cambridge: Cambridge University Press, 1965), p. 116.

24 Salomon Reinach, "De l'origine des prières pour les morts," *Revue des Etudes juives,* vol. 41 (1900): 164; quoted by Jacques Le Goff, *The Birth of Purgatory* (London: Scolar Press, 1984), p. 45. Before the nineteenth century, the idea that punishment should fit the crime was far better developed in the afterlife than in this life.

25 Le Goff, *Birth of Purgatory,* pp. 209–34.

26 Ibid., pp. 49–50; E. R. Dodds, *Pagan and Christian,* pp. 47–53.

27 Le Goff, *Birth of Purgatory,* pp. 356–57.

28 Aristotle, *Nicomachean Ethics,* book 4:3, 1124b (Chicago: Encyclopaedia Britannica, 1952), vol. 9, p. 371.

29 Charles Williams, "The Way of Exchange," in *The Image of the City and Other Essays* (London: Oxford University Press, 1958).

30 Mary McDermott Shideler, *The Theology of Romantic Love: A Study in the Writings of Charles Williams* (New York: Harper & Brothers, 1962), p. 64.

31 Charles Williams, *Witchcraft* (London: Faber & Faber, 1941), pp. 118, 160, 162.

32 Shideler, *Theology,* p. 179.

33 Charles Williams, *The Descent of the Dove: A Short History of the Holy Spirit in the Church* (London: Faber & Faber, 1950), pp. 139–40.

34 Charles Williams, *He Came Down from Heaven and The Forgiveness of Sins* (London: Faber & Faber, 1950), pp. 93–94.

35 Williams, *He Came Down from Heaven,* p. 89.

36 I have pursued this line of thinking in *The Good Life* (Madison: University of Wisconsin Press, 1986).

7 Individuals: Good-Simple vs. Good-Wise

1 *Analects,* book 6, chap. 16; James Legge, *The Four Books* (New York: Paragon, 1966), p. 72.

2 T'ung-tsu Ch'u, *Han Social Structure* (Seattle: University of Washington Press, 1972), pp. 105–6.

3 Jacques Le Goff, *Time, Work, and Culture in the Middle Ages* (Chicago: University of Chicago Press, 1982), p. 89.

4 Julian Green, *God's Fool: The Life and Times of Francis of Assisi* (San Francisco: Harper & Row, 1985); Edward A. Armstrong, *Saint Francis: Nature Mystic* (Berkeley: University of California Press, 1973).

5 John F. Danby, "The Fool and Handy-Dandy," in *Shakespeare's Doctrine of Nature* (London: Faber and Faber, 1948), pp. 102–13; Max Gluckman, *Politics, Law and Ritual in Tribal Society* (Chicago: Aldine, 1965), pp. 102–4.

6 Enid Welsford, *The Fool: His Social and Literary History* (London: Faber and Faber, n.d.), pp. 147, 148–49.

7 Victor Turner, *The Ritual Process: Structure and Anti-Structure* (Ithaca: Cornell University Press, 1977), pp. 49, 110.

8 Charles Dickens, *David Copperfield* (New York: Dodd, Mead and Co., 1943), chap. 20, p. 284.

9 Henry Gifford, *Tolstoy* (Oxford: Oxford University Press, 1982), pp. 25–26.

10 Ibid., pp. 19–20.

11 Simone Weil, *Seventy Letters* (London: Oxford University Press, 1965), p. 107.

12 George Orwell, *Homage to Catalonia* (London: Secker & Warburg, 1938), p. 1; Richard Rees, *A Theory of My Time: An Essay in Didactic Reminiscence* (London: Secker & Warburg, 1963), p. 28.

13 Watson, *Ssu-ma Ch'ien: Grand Historian of China* (New York: Columbia University Press), p. 29.

14 Jean-Pierre Vernant, *The Origins of Greek Thought* (Ithaca: Cornell University Press, 1982), pp. 58–60.

15 Jean Brun, *Socrates* (New York: Walker and Company, 1962), pp. 13–14, 64–65.

16 A. E. Taylor, *Socrates: The Man and His Thought* (Garden City, N.Y.: Doubleday Anchor, 1952); on the problem of Socrates, "What Kind of a Man Is He?" see Gregory Vlastos' Introduction in his edited book of essays, *The Philosophy of Socrates: A Collection of Critical Essays* (New York: Anchor, 1971), pp. 1–21.

17 II. G. Creel, *Confucius and the Chinese Way* (New York: Harper & Row, 1949).

18 Julian Green, *Diary 1928–1957* (New York: Carrol & Graf, 1985), pp. 133–34.

19 Ludwig Wittgenstein, *Culture and Value* (Chicago: University of Chicago Press, 1980), p. 84.

20 Georg H. von Wright, "A Biographical Sketch," in K. T. Fann, ed., *Ludwig Wittgenstein: The Man and His Philosophy* (New York: Dell, 1967), p. 13.

21 Wittgenstein, *Culture and Value*, p. 7.

22 Rush Rees, ed., *Recollections of Wittgenstein* (Oxford: Oxford University Press, 1984), pp. 128, 149.

23 Leslie Fiedler, in the introduction to Simone Weil, *Waiting for God* (New York: Capricorn Books, 1959), p. 3.

24 Simone Pétrement, *Simone Weil: A Life* (New York: Pantheon, 1976), p. 20.

25 Ibid.

26 Simone Weil, *Notebooks* (London: Routledge & Kegan Paul, 1956), vol. 2, p. 361.

27 Weil, *Gravity and Grace* (London: Routledge & Kegan Paul, 1963), pp. 5–11.

28 Weil, *Notebooks*, vol. 1, p. 28.

29 Weil, *Gravity and Grace*, p. 132.

30 Weil, *The Need for Roots* (Boston: Beacon Press, 1955).
31 Norman Malcolm, *Ludwig Wittgenstein: A Memoir* (London: Oxford University Press, 1962), pp. 31–32.
32 Pétrement, *Simone Weil*, pp. 415, 436, and Richard Rees, *Simone Weil: A Sketch for a Portrait* (Carbondale: Southern Illinois University Press, 1966), p. 21.

8 Fantasy and Imagination

1 Richard Wollheim, *The Thread of Life* (Cambridge: Harvard University Press, 1984), pp. 87–88; John Stuart Mill, *Autobiography* (London: Oxford University Press, 1924; first published in 1873), pp. 112–13; Gustave Flaubert, *Madame Bovary* (New York: Harper & Brothers, 1950; first published in 1856), part 1, chap. 9, pp. 63–64.
2 *Child of the Dark: The Diary of Carolina Maria de Jesus,* trans. David St. Clair (New York: Signet, 1963), p. 11.
3 Flaubert, *Madame Bovary,* part 2, chap. 14, pp. 231–32.
4 Simone de Beauvoir, *Adieux: A Farewell to Sartre* (New York: Pantheon Books, 1984), pp. 64, 123.
5 Wendy Doniger O'Flaherty, "Inside and Outside the Mouth of God: The Boundary between Myth and Reality," *Daedalus* (Spring 1980): 93–125.
6 Elizabeth Marshall Thomas, *The Harmless People* (New York: Vintage, 1965), p. 146.
7 W. Randolph Kloetzli, "Maps of Time—Mythologies of Descent: Scientific Instruments and the Puranic Cosmograph," *History of Religions* 25, no. 2 (1985): 116–47.
8 S. J. Tambiah, *Buddhism and the Spirit Cults in Northeast Thailand* (Cambridge: Cambridge at the University Press, 1970), p. 36.
9 Henry Alabaster, *The Wheel of the Law: Buddhism Illustrated from Siamese Sources* (London: Trubner and Co., 1871), p. 294.
10 An eloquent defense of daydreaming, including indulgence in Hollywood romance films, occurs in Manuel Puig's novel, *Kiss of the Spider Woman* (New York: Vintage, 1980).
11 *Sui Yang Ti Hai Shan Chi* (Sea and Mountain Records

of Sui Yang-ti), in the *T'ang Sung Ch'uan Ch'i Chi* (Collection of Fictional Works of the T'ang and Sung Dynasties), trans. Alexander Soper. See Loraine Kuck, *The World of the Japanese Garden* (New York and Tokyo: Walker/Weatherhill, 1968), pp. 19–20, and Maggie Keswick, *The Chinese Garden: History, Art and Architecture* (New York: Rizzoli, 1978), p. 49.

12 Stephen Orgel, *The Illusion of Power: Political Theater in the English Renaissance* (Berkeley: University of California Press, 1975).

13 Helen M. Fox, *André le Nôtre: Garden Architect to Kings* (New York: Crown, 1962), pp. 101–2; Marshall Berman, *All That Is Solid Melts Into Air: The Experience of Modernity* (New York: Simon & Schuster, 1982), p. 178.

14 R. A. Donkin, *The Cistercians: Studies in the Geography of Medieval England and Wales* (Toronto: Pontifical Institute of Medieval Studies, Studies and Texts 38, 1978), p. 22.

15 N. Anderson, *Desert Saints: The Mormon Frontier in Utah* (Chicago: University of Chicago Press, 1966), p. 29.

16 Leonard J. Arrington, *Great Basin Kingdom: An Economic History of the Latter-Day Saints, 1830–1900* (Cambridge: Harvard University Press, 1958), p. 61.

17 William James, "What Makes a Life Significant?" in *Essays on Faith and Morals* (New York: New American Library, 1974), pp. 288–89.

18 Mikhail Bakhtin, *Rabelais and His World* (Cambridge: MIT Press, 1968).

19 Milan Kundera, *The Unbearable Lightness of Being* (New York: Harper & Row, 1984), pp. 248, 252–53.

9 Imagination and Creativity

1 Edward S. Casey, *Imagining: A Phenomenological Study* (Bloomington: Indiana University Press, 1976), pp. 15–18, 183.

2 René Dubos, *The Wooing of Earth: New Perspectives on Man's Use of Nature* (New York: Charles Scribner's Sons, 1980), esp. chap. 6.

3 Harry Levin, *The Gates of Horn: A Study of Five French*

Realists (New York: Oxford University Press, 1966), p. 34.

4 Svetlana Alpers, *The Art of Describing: Dutch Art in the Seventeenth Century* (Chicago: University of Chicago Press, 1983).

5 Stuart Hampshire, "Commitment and Imagination" in Max Black, ed., *The Morality of Scholarship* (Ithaca: Cornell University Press, 1967), pp. 47–48.

6 Arthur de Carle Sowerby, *Nature in Chinese Art* (New York: John Day, 1940); Joseph Needham, *Science and Civilization in China* (Cambridge at the University Press, 1959), vol. 3, pp. 592–98.

7 Linda Nochlin, *Realism* (Harmondsworth, Middlesex: Penguin, 1971).

8 John Rupert Martin, *Baroque* (New York: Harper & Row, 1977), pp. 137–38.

9 John Richardson, "The Catch in the Late Picasso," *The New York Review of Books*, July 19, 1984, p. 26.

10 M. H. Abrams, *The Mirror and the Lamp: Romantic Theory and the Critical Tradition* (New York: Oxford University Press, 1953), pp. 84–88, 145–46.

11 Francis Toye, *Giuseppe Verdi: His Life and Works* (New York: Knopf, 1946), pp. 192–413; Jonas Barish, *The Antitheatrical Prejudice* (Berkeley: University of California Press, 1980), p. 349.

12 Roger Muchielli, *Introduction to Structural Psychology* (New York: Avon, 1972), pp. 58–59, 71–72; Roger Brown, *Words and Things: An Introduction to Language* (New York: The Free Press, 1968), p. 268.

13 D. O. Hebb, *The Organization of Behavior: A Neuropsychological Theory* (New York: John Wiley, 1949), p. 94.

14 Colin Wilson gives a picturesque account of how fatigue might affect attention so that we lose our sense of the particular and yet retain more or less intact our motor activity in *Origins of the Sexual Impulse* (London: Arthur Barker, 1963), p. 66.

15 "My view might be put by saying: moral terms must be treated as concrete universals. And if someone at this point were to say, well, why stop at moral concepts, why not claim that all universals are concrete, I would reply, why not indeed? Why not consider red as an ideal end-point, as a concept infinitely to be learned, as an individual object of love?" Iris Mur-

doch, *The Sovereignty of Good* (New York: Schocken Books, 1971), p. 29.

16 J. R. R. Tolkien, "On Fairy-Stories," in C. S. Lewis, ed., *Essays Presented to Charles Williams* (Grand Rapids, Mich.: William B. Eerdmans, 1966), p. 74.

17 Kathryn Hume, *Fantasy and Mimesis: Response to Reality in Western Literature* (New York and London: Methuen, 1984), p. 194; see also, Ann Swifen, *In Defence of Fantasy: A Study of the Genre in English and American Literature Since 1945* (London: Routledge & Kegan Paul, 1984).

18 "The movie camera lingers in close-up to let us savor the mobility of each face; then we see the face frozen in the last of its expressions, embalmed in a still." In Susan Sontag, *On Photography* (New York: Farrar, Straus and Giroux, 1977), p. 70.

19 Michael Ignatieff, *The Needs of Strangers: An Essay on Privacy, Solidarity, and the Politics of Being Human* (New York: Elizabeth Sifton Books–Penguin Books), pp. 139–42.

20 The seven deadly sins listed by Gregory the Great were: pride, envy, anger, dejection, avarice, gluttony and lust. In a review of Jeffrey Burton Russell's *Lucifer: The Devil in the Middle Ages* (Ithaca: Cornell University Press, 1985), Norman Cohen notes: "The sins to which the Devil of Christian tradition has tempted human beings are varied indeed: apostasy, idolatry, heresy, fornication, gluttony, vanity, using cosmetics, dressing luxuriously, going to the theater, gambling, avarice, quarreling, spiritual sloth have all, at various times, figured in the list. Only rarely—notably in the thought of Augustine—have the sufferings of children been ascribed to the Devil; and I have looked in vain for a single instance, in Russell's great panorama, of the Devil tempting a human being to cruelty." In *The New York Review of Books*, April 25, 1985, p. 14. See also Keith Thomas's discussion on cruelty in *Man and the Natural World: A History of Modern Sensibility* (New York: Pantheon, 1983), pp. 143–50. On the English word "atrocity," see John U. Nef, *Cultural Foundations of Industrial Civilization* (New York: Harper Torchbooks, 1960), p. 76.

21 I tried to draw attention to this neglected aspect of

the premodern landscape in *Landscapes of Fear* (New York: Pantheon, 1979), pp. 175–86.

22 John Wain, *Samuel Johnson: A Biography* (New York: Viking Press, 1975), p. 43.

23 "The rituals of contemporary hunters betray uninhibited delight in the capture and killing of wild animals. When James I hunted the stag he would personally cut its throat and daub the faces of his courtiers with blood, which they were not permitted to wash off; and it remained customary 'for ladies and women of quality after the hunting of deer to stand by until they are ripped up, that they might wash their hands in the blood, supposing it will make them white.'" Keith Thomas, *Man and the Natural World*, p. 29.

24 Daniel C. Dennett, "Information, Technology, and the Virtues of Ignorance," *Daedalus* 115, no. 3 (1986): 146–47.

25 Peter Singer, *The Expanding Circle* (Oxford: Oxford University Press, 1981).

26 John Lukacs, "The Bourgeois Interior," *The American Scholar*, Autumn 1970, p. 623. I discussed this theme at some length in *Segmented Worlds and Self: Group Life and Individual Consciousness* (Minneapolis: University of Minnesota Press, 1982).

27 Gilbert C. Meilaender, *Friendship: A Study in Theological Ethics* (Notre Dame: University of Notre Dame Press, 1981).

28 Reported in *The New Republic*, February 3, 1982. In Albert Camus's novel, *La Chute* (1956), the "hero" fails to jump in.

29 William James, *Essays on Faith and Morals* (New York: New American Library, 1974), pp. 195–97; Jacques Barzun, *A Stroll with William James* (New York: Harper & Row, 1983), pp. 150–51.

30 H. L. A. Hart, *The Concept of Law* (New York: Oxford University Press, 1961); E. Adamson Hoebel, *The Law of Primitive Man* (Cambridge: Harvard Univerity Press, 1961); Garrett Hardin, *Promethean Ethics* (Seattle: University of Washington Press, 1980).

31 Calvin Stillman, "This Fair Land," in Ervin H. Zube et al., *Land Assessment* (Stroudsburg, Pa.: Dowden, Hutchinson & Ross, 1975), pp. 18–30.

32 Michael Ignatieff, "Is Nothing Sacred? The Ethics of Television," *Daedalus* (Fall 1985): 57–78.

33 Charles Williams, *The Descent of the Dove: The History of the Holy Spirit in the Church* (New York: Meridian Books, 1956), pp. 226–27. This was also the viewpoint of Arnold Toynbee. See Robert Nisbet, *History of the Idea of Progress* (New York: Basic Books, 1980), p. 316.

10 Epilogue

1 Gilbert C. Meilaender, *Friendship: A Study in Theological Ethics* (Notre Dame: University of Notre Dame Press, 1981), pp. 8–32.

2 William Lynch, *Christ and Apollo: The Dimensions of the Literary Imagination* (New York: Mentor-Omega Books, 1963), pp. 34–38.

Index

Animals, treatment of: by Semang, 13; in literary Edens, 13; by Mbuti Pygmies, 13–14; by Eskimos, 17–19; by Hopi, 25; by Greeks, 29–31; by Chinese, 49; in Buddhism, 53–54, 57, 58; in modern period, 169, 170

Architecture: sources of legitimacy, 93–96; Vitruvius on, 94–95; Alberti on, 95–96; Church, 97–98; Victorian, 98; aesthetic-moral benefit, 99; of ideal cities, 99–100

Aristotle (384–322 B.C.), 37–38, 82, 94, 122, 158, 178

Asoka, Indian emperor (died ca. 232 B.C.), 53–54

Buddha (ca. 564–483 B.C.): life of, 55–56; Maitreya, 56–57

Child: innocence and goodness of, 1, 128, 166; animality of, 5–6

Christianity: and the individual, 105–6, 118–19; communal ideal of, 118, 119–25; and purgatory, 119–22; and the doctrine of exchange, 122–25; simple goodness and, 128; and Simone Weil, 139–40; and Cistercians, Mormons, 152–53; and the real, 160

City: in antiquity, 93–94; ideal, 99–100; distance from nature, 100; lack of intimacy in, 100–101; urban renewal in, 101–2; hygiene

and spatial segmentation in, 102–3; and Heavenly City (Weil), 140–41; Versailles and St. Petersburg, 152

Civilization: and excess, 6, 75, 162; Chinese ambivalence toward, 41, 72–74; as refinement and power, 71; stages of, 77; and moral progress, 79–80; and gardens, 89–93; Wittgenstein on, 138; and artistic magniloquence, 162; achievements of, 166–67

Clothes, moral meaning of, 96

Communal ideal: Confucian, 117–18; Christian, 118, 119–25

Confucians: on li, 43–44; on the person, 114–15; communal ideal of, 117–18; on labor, 127

Confucius (551–479? B.C.): on li, 41–42; and language, 66; life of, 135–36, 141

Cosmology (moral edifice): Eskimo, 21; Pueblo Indian, 23, 27; Chinese, 42–43; Buddhist, 50–51; and garden, 90; Bushmen, 148; Indian, 149–51

Dilemma (see also Paradox): Eskimo, 19–21; Hopi, 24–27; Chinese, 43–44; in modern society, 171–75

Dubos, René (1901–82), "Despairing Optimist," 159–60

Eden. See Garden; Paradise

Eskimos: guilt in regard to animals,